Handbook of
Everyday
Law

Handbook of Everyday Law

Fourth Edition

Martin J. Ross, J.D.
and
Jeffrey Steven Ross, J.D.

GRAMERCY PUBLISHING COMPANY
New York

Copyright © MCMLIX, MCMLXVII, MCMLXXV, MCMLXXXI by Martin J. Ross.
All rights reserved.

This 1986 edition is published by Gramercy Publishing Company,
distributed by Crown Publishers, Inc., by arrangement with
Harper and Row, Inc.

Printed and Bound in the United States of America

Library of Congress Cataloging-in-Publication Data

Ross, Martin J.
  Handbook of everyday law.

  Reprint. Originally published: New York: Harper and
Row, c1981.
  Includes index.
  1. Law—United States—Popular works.   I. Ross,
Jeffrey Steven.   II. Title.
[KF387.R6   1986]   349.73   86-8257
                        347.3

ISBN 0-517-61537-1

h g f e d c b a

To my wife, Diane, in gratitude
for her help and inspiration.
To Jeff and Elizabeth, in pride
and hopeful expectation.
To my mother and father, in memory
and in sincere appreciation.

All names used in case illustrations are fictitious. They are not intended to and do not represent any person living or dead.

Contents

PREFACE   xv

PREFACE TO FIRST EDITION   xvi

1. INTRODUCTION TO LAW   1

Why we should know law—What is the law? How does
it apply to our everyday living?—Some basic legal definitions—What is jurisdiction: federal, state, local?—The
courts: federal, state, local—What is the legal process?—
Preparation for trial—Selection of a jury—The trial of a
civil action—The court's charge—Appeal procedure—Enforcing the court's judgment—Administration agencies—
Arbitration.

2. THE CONTRACT   20

Why study contracts?—Some types of contracts, definitions—Elements necessary for a contract: the offer, general offers and rewards, advertisements by stores, auc-
tions, termination of the offer—What is an option?—The
acceptance—Consideration—Capacity to make a contract:
contracts of minors, necessaries, emancipation, incompetents, insane persons, drunkards, drug addicts, married
women, aliens, convicts, corporations—Assignments: legality of subject matter, expressly prohibited, gambling,
usury, Sunday laws, against good morals and public
policy—Factors affecting the making of a contract: mis-

take, fraud, misrepresentation, duress, undue influence—
Conditions in a contract—Contracts which can't be performed—Statute of Frauds, statute of limitations—Termination of contract—Relief from breach of contract.
Summation: Points to remember.

3. THE SALE OF PROPERTY   64

Sales in everyday transactions—Sales and contracts to
sell—Statute of Frauds—Conditions and warranties—Implied warranties, warranties of title, in sale by description, sale by sample—Warranty of merchantability, quality or fitness for use, fitness for human consumption—
Caveat emptor—When does title pass?—On sale or return,
on trial or approval, C. & F., C.I.F., F.O.B., F.A.S.—Sale
without authority—Voidable title—Fraudulent transfers of
property, in fraud of creditors, bulk sales—Relief in
breach of sales contract: the seller, the buyer—Breach of
warranty, buyer's remedy, measure of damages—Secured
credit sales—The chattel mortgage. Summation: Points
to remember.

4. BAILMENTS   83

Bailments in everyday transactions—Bailments for the
sole benefit of the bailor, of the bailee, mutual benefit
bailments, the pledge, the pawnbroker, the storekeeper's
liability, the restaurant's liability—A bailment for hire—
A bailment with services—A hiring of custody: the warehouseman, the agistor, the livery stable, boarding of pets,
the garage, the wharfinger, the safe-deposit company—
The hiring of transportation: the private carrier, the common carrier, his liability for freight, for delay, for passengers, for baggage—The hotel or innkeeper: his responsibility to guests, for property of guests, his lien. A contract for personal services. Summation: Points to remember.

5. INSURANCE   103

Introduction to insurance—What is it?—Additional ingredients of an insurance contract—Insurable interest

—Factors affecting the contract—Who may be an insurer, who may be insured—Fire insurance: the binder, the standard fire insurance policy, stipulations and conditions, cancellation, coinsurance—Extended coverage insurance —Life insurance: standard provisions, incontestability clause, suicide, nonpayment of premiums, options when policy lapses, double indemnity—Accident insurance— Health insurance—Automobile Insurance: liability, No Fault, collision, comprehensive coverage—Public liability insurance—Marine Insurance—Title Insurance—Burglary, robbery, theft, larceny, pilferage and flood insurance— Suretyship. Summation: Points to remember.

6. NEGOTIABLE INSTRUMENTS   134

How do they apply to everyday transactions?—Some definitions and distinctions—The check, the certified check—The promissory note, the acceleration clause—The draft or bill of exchange—The certificate of deposit—What is negotiation? How is it accomplished? Types of indorsements— The holder in due course—Liabilities of the parties: the maker, the drawer, the drawee, the acceptor, the indorser, the negotiator of bearer paper—Notice of dishonor—Protest and notice of protest—Material alteration—Forgery— Discharge of negotiable instrument. Summation: Points to remember.

7. AGENCY   151

How does agency fit into our everyday living? What is agency?—Some particular agency relationships—Who may be a principal, an agent—An agent's authority—Limitation of his authority—Ratification—Rights and obligations of the parties: the agent to third parties, the agent to his principal, the principal to the agent, the principal to third parties. Summation: Points to remember.

8. FORMS OF BUSINESS OWNERSHIP   161

Introduction—Types of ownership—Individual or sole ownership, doing business under a firm name, dissolution —Partnership: formation, rights and obligations of the partners, their power and authority, dissolution, account-

ing and termination—Limited partnerships—Corporations: definitions and distinctions, formation of a corporation, charter or certificate of incorporation, corporate
stock, proxy vote, board of directors, officers, rights of
stockholders, dissolution of a corporation. Summation:
Points to remember.

9. MARRIAGE AND FAMILY RELATIONS   180

Introduction—Marriage: capacity to marry, prohibited
marriages, common-law marriages, marriage by contract
—A woman's legal rights—Rights and responsibilities of
husband and wife—Children: illegitimate, adopted—Annulment, separation and divorce: voidable marriages, dissolution, separation by agreement, by court decree, alimony *pendente lite* (temporary), counsel fees, custody of
children—Divorce *a vinculo*—The "foreign divorce"— Enforcement of the divorce decree. Summation: Points to
remember.

10. TORTS   200

Introduction—Definitions and distinctions—Parties responsible for torts—The right of personal liberty: false
arrest, false imprisonment, malicious prosecution, malicious abuse of process—The right to personal safety: the
assault, the battery—The right to a good reputation: defamation, slander and libel, slander per se and libel per
se, defenses—The right of privacy—Torts of property: personal property, conversion, fraud and deceit—Real property: trespass and nuisance—Relief from torts: damages,
injunction, self-help—Negligence: contributary negligence, comparative negligence, last clear chance, *res ipsa
loquitur*, imputed negligence, responsibility of governmental agency, responsibility of property owner—The
Death claim action—Malpractice. Summation: Points to
remember.

11. WILLS AND ESTATES   224

Introduction—Definitions and distinctions—Types of wills
—The right of testamentation—Mental capacity—The form
and contents of a will—A sample will—Execution of a will

—Revocation—Probate proceedings—Intestacy and administration—Other transfers of property without a will. Summation: Points to remember.

12. REAL PROPERTY AND TRUSTS   242

Definitions and distinctions—Joint ownership of property—Adverse possession—A real-estate transaction: brokers, the binder, the contract of sale, remedies for breach
of contract, preparation for closing title, law day, the day
of closing—The deed, types of deeds—The bond and mortgage—The Lease—Homestead provisions, eminent domain
and condemnation—Certiorari proceedings to reduce assessed valuation—Trusts, the rule against perpetuities.
Summation: Points to remember.

13. CRIMINAL LAW AND PROCEDURE   265

Introduction—Definitions and distinctions—Constitutional
safeguards—Types of Crimes—Capacity to commit a crime
—Crimes against the person: homicide, murder, manslaughter, kidnaping, criminal assault, robbery, extortion,
blackmail, conspiracy, perjury, subornation of perjury—
Crimes against property: arson, larceny, burglary, malicious mischief, possession of burglar tools, criminally receiving stolen goods, forgery—An attempt to commit a
crime—Criminal Court procedure: bail, misdemeanors,
the information, the grand jury, the indictment, the
youthful offender, the indeterminate sentence, parole and
probation. Summation: Points to remember.

14. CIVIL RIGHTS AND LIMITATIONS   284

Religious freedom—Limitations on religious freedom—
Sunday closing laws—Private religious schools—Freedom
of thought—Freedom of expression—Limitation of freedom of expression—Freedom of association and assembly—Labor unions and collective bargaining—Picketing
—Personal freedoms—Police power, limitation on personal rights—Searches and seizures—Rights of an accused
in a criminal proceeding—Women's Rights—discrimination, abortion. Summation: Points to remember.

15. FINANCIAL AID AND SECURITY LAWS   300

Public assistance—Public assistance to the aged, the blind,
the disabled—Aid to dependent children—Social Security
—Retirement insurance—Survivorship benefits—Lump sum
benefits—Disability insurance—Application procedure—
Appeal—Benefits—Vocational and rehabilitation services—Benefits to children of insured—Loss of benefits
—Medicare—Hospital insurance—Hospitalization and related services—Benefit period or spell of illness—Extended
care benefits—Home health care and services—Medical
insurance and coverage—Outpatient hospital services—
Home services—Other medical services and supplies—
State participation—Unemployment insurance—Workmen's compensation—Veteran's benefits—Private pension
funds—Employee Retirement Income Security Act: participation, funding, vesting—Summation: Points to remember.

16. CONSUMER PROTECTION   312

The Federal Consumer Product Safety Act—Uniform Con-
sumer Sales Practices Act, Consumer Protection Law of
New York City—The courts and the consumer—Consumer
Credit Protection Act—Truth in Lending Act—Right of
rescission—Credit cards—Restriction on Garnishment—
Fair Credit Reporting Act—Uniform Consumer Credit
Code—Consumer protection assistance. Summation: Points
to remember.

17. TAXES   321

Definitions—Income tax, Form 1040A, Form 1040—Estimated tax—Exemptions—Head of household—Joint return
—Life insurance—Persons over 65—Retirement income
credit—Self-employment tax—Self-employed retirement
benefits—Withholding tax—Income tax collection and enforcement—Federal tax calendar—Federal estate tax,
gross estate, community property, marital deduction, taxable estate, deductions, procedural requirements—Inheritance taxes—Federal gift tax, when tax is applicable, gift
splitting, filing of return, penalties. Summation: Points to
remember.

Contents xiii

18. THE LAW AND BUSINESS 334

Starting a business—The Small Business Administration—Terminating a Business—Products Liability—The Equal Credit Opportunity Act—The Occupational Safety and Health Act (OSHA)—The Equal Employment Opportunity Act—The Fair Labor Standards Acts—Management—Labor Relations—Debt Collection Practices—The Copyright Act of 1976—Patents and Trademarks—The Freedom of Information Act—The Privacy Act of 1974—Government "in Sunshine."

APPENDIX—A Do-it-Yourself List and Suggestions 353

GLOSSARY 356

INDEX 377

Preface

The *Handbook of Everyday Law* was conceived and published in response to an urgent need for a clear, concise and simple presentation of the principles of law which confront everyone in business and in personal transactions.

Through the years, by means of each subsequent revision, the Handbook was brought up to date to include all changes in the law which were pertinent to this need.

This is a reflection of the democratic process, by which the law is continually changed in order that it may conform to changing times.

Recently it became apparent that, once again, it was essential to bring the Handbook into the present by adding those new legal provisions which affect our daily lives so directly and so vitally.

We have therefore added, among other new material, sections on the Equal Credit Opportunity Act, the Equal Employment Opportunity Act, the Occupational Safety and Health Act, the new Copyright Act of 1976, the new Bankruptcy Act, and the Freedom of Information Act.

It is our contention that a well-informed citizen will maintain his right to freedom and preserve our democratic way of life.

Martin J. Ross
Jeffrey Steven Ross

Preface to the First Edition

Here is a practical handbook for laymen that describes your legal rights and shows how to protect them. Whether you are planning to buy or sell a house, make a will, sign a contract, take out insurance, or sue for damages, this long-needed book gives you the facts on where you stand and what action you can take.

Hundreds of illustrations reveal how the law works in specific cases. Martin Ross first explains each point of law in terms everyone can understand. Then he shows you how that law is applied to a particular case. You discover the difference between slander and libel; which type of automobile accident is covered by collision insurance and which type by comprehensive coverage; what constitutes a trespass on your property; how a partnership is formed and to what extent the partners are liable.

Handbook of Everyday Law covers just about every legal problem that the average person can expect to encounter in his life. You find complete sections on the legal aspects of contracts, business, personal rights, property and criminal procedure. Where there are variations in state laws, the author discusses fully the basic law involved and alerts you to differences you might encounter.

Not only does Mr. Ross offer specific advice to help you know your rights and privileges, but he points out legal pitfalls to avoid. He gives a clear understanding of the law as it is applied to such matters as divorce, separation, forgery, negligence, trusts, sale of merchandise, and much more.

Mr. Ross is a lawyer and court attaché, and teaches law at the College of the City of New York.

So that he who runs may read, one has at hand for speedy reference an authoritative, easy-to-understand guide to all aspects of law that touch one's daily life.

JAMES B. McNALLY, *Associate Justice,*
Appellate Division, New York Supreme
Court, First Department

Handbook of
Everyday
Law

CHAPTER 1

Introduction to Law

WHY WE SHOULD KNOW LAW

We live in a complicated world. New scientific and social developments increase the tempo of our daily living activities, make them more difficult and more involved.

To keep abreast of our economic, social and scientific competition we must constantly replenish our store of information about the world around us.

We are now more than ever vitally concerned and actively interested in all community activities. We are better informed about local, national and world affairs. We read newspapers, magazines, books. We listen to the radio; we watch television. We hear contradictory opinions and varied points of view. We think and act for ourselves.

There is but one field of knowledge that we have sadly neglected. I refer to the Law, those rules and regulations which govern our every social move and action.

For too long now we have lived in general apathy concerning everything which even vaguely reminds us of the Law.

We need to reorganize our thinking and bring up to date our store of knowledge in this vital area of our day-to-day activities.

There is nothing mysterious, nothing awesome about the Law. It consists of the rules of community living. It may be more complicated, more inclusive, but it is not different in its way from the rules of our favorite game of cards or our favorite recreational activity.

We are a well-informed nation of well-informed citizens.

Each one of us, regardless of the extent of his formal education, has an acquired, extracurricular reservoir of practical, day-to-day-living intelligence and skill. We must make a conscious effort to overcome our blind and unreasonable bias about the Law.

A knowledge of law with its basic principles and applications is a necessity. We meet it, in some form, in every one of our daily business and social experiences.

My purpose in this volume is twofold.

I want to show you that law is based on the reasonable needs of the community and I also want to show you the reasonable and simple basis for each legal principle.

This book contains law for laymen and not law for lawyers. The distinction is simple. Law for laymen is explanatory and informational. Law for lawyers is technical; it is, for the lawyer, the mechanics of his profession and the tool of his trade.

This book is not intended to produce lawyers, but merely well-informed laymen, who are aware of their legal rights and privileges. We should be able to recognize the problems which confront us. We should have the intelligence and the understanding to seek adequate legal guidance when we need it.

Laws may vary from state to state. The lawmakers in each jurisdiction have the duty to legislate according to their needs as they see them. Basically, however, the principles on which the laws are founded are the same. If we understand those principles, we can easily determine, in each situation, what the law is in our own state.

WHAT IS THE LAW? HOW DOES IT APPLY TO OUR EVERYDAY LIVING?

The law, as we know it, is a structure of rules, regulations and accumulated decisions of the courts. These have been compiled and organized into separate subjects according to their application to the needs of society.

There are, generally, four categories which we can establish. First, we have the vast subject of contracts, the basis of most of our daily activities since it relates to all of our agreements in our business and social relationships. Then we have the subject of personal rights, which includes marriage, family relations, torts, wrongful acts, and legal and civil rights. The third general topic is property rights. This includes wills, estates and real property. Finally, we come to criminal law, the principles and procedures which protect society and the community from the harmful and criminal acts of the individual. The criminal law also protects the defendant. It assures the person charged with a crime of a fair and speedy trial.

The law is based upon the recorded experiences of society and the community in their efforts to define and regulate the relationships between their members. It is intended by these rules to determine all disputes by the use of law.

The laws passed by the legislatures result from a need to correct existing conditions. The decisions of the courts, interpreting these statutes, protect the individual from injustice.

For example, when two people have conflicting claims of ownership in certain property, they come to the courts to have their rights determined in accordance with the law which applies to their particular situation.

The lawyer for each litigant "searches" the law applicable to the case. By referring to the legislative enactments and court decisions, in the state, indexed under the subject, he will find "the law of the case." He will find authority, based on statute or court decision, which may be in his favor or against him.

Each side will by means of a "brief" or a "memorandum of law" present all of the authority that is available to convince the court that it should support his contention. The court will base its decision in the case upon consideration of the proof as presented and the existing law as it is to be applied.

Illustration: Albert loaned $500 to Bart to be returned within a month. When the money was not repaid, Albert brought suit against Bart. Albert is the plaintiff and Bart is the defendant. At the trial Albert testified, under oath, about the loan. Bart, in his turn, claimed that it was a gift to him which was not to be returned. The court, after listening to the testimony of both sides and considering the law, decided that it was a loan and directed that judgment be entered in favor of Albert against Bart.

To give the proceedings of a court effect and meaning, powers are granted to the courts to enforce their decisions, by reimbursing the injured party for his loss and penalizing the party responsible.

To avoid injustice through human error, the law has established a procedure of appeal to a higher court with the opportunity for reconsideration. This gives the losing party another chance to convince a higher court, an appeals court, that due to an "error" in the lower court, the decision should be in his favor and not against him.

If he succeeds in his argument, the higher court may reverse the lower court and give him the decision. It may also recognize that an error was made and return the case to the lower court for a new trial.

If he fails to convince the appellate court, the judgment of the lower court will be affirmed and he will be compelled to comply with its decision.

SOME BASIC LEGAL DEFINITIONS

At this point in our discussion of the law, we should consider some definitions. As in any game, trade or activity, we must learn its language, its terminology, before we can properly understand it.

"Laws" are rules established by a governing power to maintain peace, secure justice for its members, define the legal rights of the individual and the community, and to punish offenders for legal wrongs.

The word "law" is used to mean many things. Generally and all-inclusively, it is used to indicate all law, all authority. It is also used to mean a single enactment of a lawmaking body, a "statute."

There are many subdivisions of the main body of "law." The basic ones are "civil law" and "criminal law."

The "civil law" is the portion of the law which defines and determines the rights of the individual in protecting his person and his property.

The "criminal law" is that body of law specifically established to maintain peace and order. Its purpose is to protect society and the community from the injurious and harmful acts of individuals.

The same act causing injury to person or property, a civil wrong, also called a "tort," may also be a breach of the peace, a "crime." The wrongdoer may then be subject to both civil and criminal proceedings.

Illustration: In the heat of an argument, Carter hits Bruce over the head with a baseball bat. A civil suit, in tort, against Carter may result in Bruce recovering money damages for the injury he sustained. A criminal proceeding may, on Carter's conviction, result in his imprisonment.

The "common law" is the accumulated and organized body of previous court decisions, divided into categories according to subject matter.

The "statutory" or "statute law" is the body of legislative enactments. This also is "cited" or referred to as authority by the courts in arriving at their subsequent decision in the case.

Both the common law and the statutory law, dealing with civil and criminal matters, are further subdivided into "substantive" and "administrative" or "adjective" law.

Substantive law is concerned with those concepts which deal with the rights and duties of the individual.

Adjective law is procedural and concerns itself with the application and enforcement of the substantive law.

Most of our law, relating to business and commercial transactions, originated with the "law merchant." This was a body of regulations established through the centuries by merchants, mariners and businessmen of the trading world to carry on commerce with confidence and security. These rules were subsequently incorporated with the other branches of the substantive law into the English common law, and now adopted by most of the states as the Uniform Commercial Code.

Another classification of the civil law is divided into "law" and "equity." The difference between the two consists basically in the relief which is sought and obtainable. An action at "law" is brought when the violation of the right for which relief is demanded can be remedied by money damages.

Illustration: The damage to an automobile resulting from a two-car collision can be adequately remedied by payment of the repair bill, by the party responsible for causing it.

An "equity" action must be brought if there is no adequate remedy at law. The mere payment of money damages is not enough to give the injured party proper relief. The courts then have the power to compel the other side to do a specific act.

Illustrations: The seller of a house refuses to go through with his deal. The buyer wants that house and no other. He may sue in equity to have the court compel the seller to go through with the deal. This is equitable relief and is called "specific performance."

When a partnership business is dissolved, an accounting may be compelled by the Court to determine the distribution of the partnership assets.

Except for the type of relief available, all other distinctions between actions at law and suits in equity have been eliminated in most states. In those where the formal separation is still retained, a suit in equity is brought in a court of equity, a court of chancery or a chancellor's court. It is more formal than an action at law and requires strict compliance with all procedural requisites.

WHAT IS JURISDICTION—FEDERAL, STATE AND LOCAL?

Jurisdiction is the legal authority of a public body to act. Thus, we have three jurisdictions of government in this country: The United States or federal, the state and the local governments.

Each of these, within its own sphere of authority, has the power to pass laws and to see that those laws are properly enforced.

Federal Jurisdiction

The law of the United States is based on the Constitution and the laws passed by Congress. This is the supreme law of our country. To enforce these laws, federal courts have been established by Congress with separate and special jurisdiction in their own field.

The United States Constitution vests judicial power in the Supreme Court and such inferior courts which Congress may establish.

State Jurisdiction

In accordance with the United States Constitution, the states have their own sovereign power in their intrastate activities. The states' constitutions and the laws passed by their legislatures are supreme within their borders, unless they are in contravention of the United States Constitution.

Each state has created its own courts in accordance with its state constitution and its legislative enactments. Each state is sovereign in its own right and territory. The legislature may pass any law necessary for the protection of its interests and the administration of its power. To overcome the effects of un-controlled legislation in the various states, such organizations as the American Law Institute and the National Conference of Commissioners on Uniform State Laws have been created. Their purpose, by means of "model acts" and uniform acts, is to suggest to the state legislatures the need for greater uniformity in legislation among the states. There is thus a constant exchange of legislative information. Noticeable advances have been made in achieving greater uniformity of laws, among the states, as in the recently adopted Uniform Commercial Code to regulate transactions between merchants. The Uniform Consumer Credit Code when adopted by a state expands consumer protection within the state jurisdiction to conform with the Federal Consumer Credit Protection Act, a portion of which is known as the Truth in Lending Act.

Local Jurisdiction

The day-to-day business of the local community is carried on by the city, town or village governments. Each, within its territorial limits, has its own equivalent of the three-branch system of government, recognized in this country: the executive, the legislative and the judicial. Each unit passes laws, called ordinances, pertaining to its own residents and its own area. These

ordinances control electrical, plumbing and other regulations
in construction of buildings; they control local zoning, traffic
and police and fire requirements. The local courts and governmental agencies enforce these regulations for the protection
of the community.

THE COURTS—FEDERAL, STATE AND LOCAL

Just as there are three jurisdictions in government, there are
three classes of jurisdiction in the courts within every locality
in the United States. Each court has its own authority to hear
and determine cases brought before it according to its inherent
powers.

The Federal Courts

The residents of each state have access to a federal district
court. The civil division handles matters involving contracts,
torts, admiralty, bankruptcy and other matters of federal law.

The practice and procedure in the federal district court are
essentially similar to those of the state court, except, of course,
that they are governed by federal law.

There also are special federal courts created to handle special types of litigation. The Federal Court of Claims hears all
cases where the United States is a party and claims are made
against it. There are also a Tax Court, a Customs Court,
Court of Customs and Patent Appeals and a Bankruptcy Court.

The United States Court of Appeals, of which there are 11
"branches," one in each circuit, entertains all appeals from the
district courts.

The Supreme Court of the United States hears appeals from
each of the circuit courts when the case involves the consti-
tutionality of a federal or a state law. A matter of wide public
interest or a point of law in conflict in the curcuit courts, requiring an authoritative decision, will also be heard by this
court.

The State Courts

Each state has courts on a state-wide basis, usually distributed in all the counties. They have the power to try civil

and criminal cases relating to state laws and the rights of its citizens.

These state courts are divided into lower courts with trial jurisdiction and higher courts with appellate authority. The trial court hears the testimony of witnesses in each case. On the basis of the proof presented at the trial, the court determines the rights of the litigating parties by a decision of the Court or by a verdict of the jury.

Here too there may be specialized courts with a specific jurisdiction. Some states have a Court of Claims, where all suits against the state are brought. Some may have courts with probate jurisdiction or with special authority to hear matrimonial actions. Each state allocates specific powers to its own courts.

The appeals courts hear all cases brought up on appeal from the lower trial courts, where an error in legal procedure is claimed to have been made.

An appeal is heard by the court on oral argument of the attorneys representing both sides, the appellant and the respondent. No witnesses are heard. No testimony under oath is taken. The transcribed record of the testimony given at the trial and all pertinent papers are submitted. Both counsel may also file briefs. These are written arguments of law in which each side quotes decisions of prior cases as authority intended to bolster his contention. The decision of the appeals court is based on consideration and study of all papers.

Local Courts

Each state also has local courts on a county and also on a town or village level. These courts are limited in their authority and in their jurisdiction. Their legal process cannot extend beyond the limit of their geographical borders. A summons from such a court cannot be served upon a person residing outside of its area. It may be served upon him and is effective if he is within the actual physical boundary of the court's jurisdiction. The civil courts are only authorized to try cases where the amount of relief demanded is below a stated maximum. Claims for a larger amount must be brought in a state court.

The criminal jurisdiction of these local courts is limited to the trial of minor offenses.

WHAT IS THE LEGAL PROCESS?

The legal process can be defined as the procedure through which a person with a claim can institute an action in a court of law. If he proves that he is entitled to it, he will have the facilities of the court's authority to obtain satisfaction.

A civil action is usually begun by the issuance of a summons or citation from the court in which it is to be heard. This is a direction to the defendant named in it to appear and answer the claim of the plaintiff.

A complaint may contain several "causes of action," independent claims for relief. They may each claim the same amount of money on different legal grounds, or they may be several separate claims.

> Illustration: John loaned $100 to Robert, and received a promissory note as evidence of the debt. When John did not get his money back, he sued Robert on two causes of action, on the loan and on the note. The complaint, however, demands $100.
>
> If in addition Robert owed John $250 from a previous transaction, the complaint would have three causes of action; the third would ask for the additional $250.

Every cause of action is based on some legal authority. The facts in each case must be proved, either by documentary evidence or by the sworn testimony of witnesses at the trial. If the plaintiff does not prove these necessary elements to the satisfaction of the court, then as a matter of law, he cannot win. He has not established a "prima facie" case. He has not shown that he is entitled to a trial of the issues. The court may then dismiss his complaint before the defendant introduces any evidence.

The bringing of a lawsuit is a technical and complicated procedure. A plaintiff must determine first against whom he wants to bring it. When several parties are involved, all indispensable and necessary parties must be made parties defendant.

The court in which the action is to be brought must have jurisdiction over the defendant and the subject matter of the lawsuit.

Illustration: Ellsworth, living in California, was sued by Preston in the Civil Court of the City of New York for $11,000. Unless Ellsworth is personally served with process in New York or has property there, he cannot be brought within the jurisdiction of the New York Courts. Furthermore, the New York Civil Court only has authority to try cases under $10,000.

Finally, of course, the complaint must allege all of the necessary elements which must be proved in that particular type of action. Only those facts which are alleged in the complaint will be eligible for argument at the trial. If a necessary element is excluded from the complaint, it cannot be brought up at the trial and there can be no recovery. The courts now tend to be lenient with mere irregularities, but the correction of such errors may be costly and time-consuming.

A party is not compelled to have a lawyer and may proceed to try his own case. However, despite all of the leniency of the court, he will find himself at a disadvantage. The procedure of a trial is technical and requires a thorough knowledge of the rules of evidence. These are the rules which guide the court in determining which evidence is legally admissible. Evidence must be "relevant"; that is, it must bear a relationship to the fact that is to be proved. It must be "competent" in that it must be legally proper, not in violation of the rules of evidence. It must also be "material" so that it bears directly on the fact in issue and will tend to prove that fact.

Many jurisdictions have "small-claims courts," involving limited amounts. A party may safely try his own case there since the rules of evidence are not strictly applied and substantial justice is rendered between the parties. Generally, the relief offered by these courts is not available to corporations.

When the defendant is served with a summons and complaint, he must serve an answer within the time required in the summons. If he fails to do so, a judgment by default may be entered against him. He may thus lose the benefit of a trial and the judgment may be enforced against him.

The defendant must not delay in getting legal advice when he is served with a summons. His answer must contain all defenses which will protect his rights and resist the plaintiff's claim. This may be done by a "general denial," also known as a "demurrer," by "affirmative defenses" or by a "counterclaim." If the answer contains a "counterclaim," the plaintiff has the right to respond by serving a reply to oppose that claim.

Both the plaintiff and the defendant have an opportunity to demand that a jury try the issues of fact between them. The side which makes the demand must pay the jury fee.

The case is now "at issue," meaning that it is ready for trial before a jury or before the court without a jury.

The plaintiff is usually anxious to get an immediate trial. He will file the necessary papers to get the case on the "calendar." A calendar is a list on which all cases are placed when they are ready for trial. Generally there are two such lists or calendars, one for cases in law and another for cases in equity. In areas where there is a great deal of litigation, the law calendar may be further subdivided into a "Tort" or "Personal Injury" calendar and a general calendar to include all other types of cases. Each of these will then be further subdivided into "Jury" and "Non-jury."

Preparation for Trial

While the case is on the calendar, waiting for trial, there are certain preliminary steps which must be taken by both sides to prepare for the day when all issues between them will be finally heard.

The defendant has the right to demand a "bill of particulars." This is a statement prepared by the plaintiff's attorney which elaborates on the facts presented in the complaint. In answer to specific questions submitted by the defendant, the bill of particulars contains more detailed information about the plaintiff's claim.

Each side may be allowed to examine the other under oath before trial. This "examination before trial" is an informal taking of testimony. Information may also be obtained by a deposition or affidavit, or it may be done by interrogatories. These are a series of questions presented to be answered by the party being examined for the purpose of making information available to the adverse party.

In an action for personal injuries, the defendant will be permitted to have a doctor examine the plaintiff to corroborate the claims of injury and permanent disability.

Many courts have instituted arbitration and pre-trial procedures to settle and adjust cases before trial in an effort to reduce the size of court calendars and the waiting time for trial. If no satisfactory adjustment can be reached, both sides will then proceed to trial.

Selection of a Jury

Jurors who will hear a case assigned from the "jury calendar" are usually selected by lottery from a list of qualified residents of the county. They are chosen by lottery so that the persons selected will be a random sampling of the citizens. As an imposed civic duty, they are required to hear and decide matters in dispute between their fellow-citizens, without fear, favor or prejudice.

Generally, the qualifications of a juror are that he must reside in the county for a specified period, he must be of acceptable age, legally mature but under 70, he must own some property and be possessed of his natural faculties of health, sight and hearing.

A group of 20 to 30 prospective jurors are picked to constitute the "panel." From these the required number will be selected for the trial. Generally, 12 jurors are required. However, some states have reduced that number by appropriate legislation to 6 in civil actions.

Each potential juror is questioned first by the plaintiff's attorney and then by the defendant's. This is called the *voir dire*. Its purpose is to give each side an opportunity to choose jurors

who will be fair and unbiased. Their task is to listen to the
evidence as it is presented at the trial. They judge the demeanor of the witnesses to determine their truthfulness. They
then apply the principles of law, as explained to them by the
court, and arrive at their verdict, based upon their determination of the facts.

A prospective juror who states that he cannot be impartial
may be "challenged for cause" by either side and he will then
be excused by the court.

Both sides are permitted a certain number of "peremptory
challenges" which they may use at will without giving any reason. The peremptory challenge is a safeguard afforded each
litigant to eliminate any prospective juror whose attitude indicates that he is incapable of being fair and unbiased.

When the requisite number of jurors, acceptable to both
sides, has been chosen, the jury is declared to be "satisfactory"
and the trial will proceed.

In some of the local municipal courts, there is provision for
6 instead of 12 jurors, although a party demanding a jury may
request and pay the fee for 12, if he so desires.

THE TRIAL OF A CIVIL ACTION

In the trial of a civil case, the plaintiff has the burden of
proving all of the necessary elements in his complaint by a
"fair preponderance of the credible evidence." This is to be
distinguished from a criminal case, in which the prosecution
must prove its case against the defendant "beyond a reasonable
doubt."

To give the plaintiff an advantage, he is given the right, in a
jury case, to make his "opening statement" before the defendant.
He has the first opportunity to present his side of the controversy and explain to the jury what he intends to prove.

When both sides have opened their cases to the jury, the
plaintiff will begin to present his proof. This is accomplished by
means of witnesses or documents. Documents which are ad-

missible in evidence are marked as "exhibits" for either the plaintiff or the defendant. Those which are not admissible but are referred to during the trial are marked "for identification." The "exhibits in evidence" are part of the proof and are to be considered by the jury in their deliberations. "Exhibits for identification" are not evidence and may not be shown to the jury.

Witnesses are brought into court by the service upon them of a "subpoena." This is a direction from the court that they are to appear and testify in the case. A *subpoena duces tecum*, meaning, literally, bring with you, is served on any witness who has books, papers or documents in his possession which are required for the trial.

The witnesses for the plaintiff are each in their turn sworn to tell the truth. A witness who has conscientious scruples against taking an oath may be permitted to "solemnly, sincerely and truly declare and affirm" that the testimony he will give in the case on trial shall be the truth. An "affirmation" is just as binding as an oath in the event of perjury.

The witness will first be examined by the plaintiff's attorney to elicit that information, which is necessary to establish his cause of action. When he has completed his questioning, the attorney for the defendant will cross-examine. He will, by means of his questions, test the witness as to his testimony and his credibility. If he is able to "impeach" his credibility, the testimony, of course, loses its probative value before the jury.

After each of the plaintiff's witnesses is examined both on direct and cross-examination, the plaintiff will "rest." He has submitted all of his proof and feels that he has established all that proof necessary for him to present in order to win.

The defendant may then test this proof. He will make a "motion," an oral application to the court, to dismiss the complaint, on the ground that the plaintiff did not prove the elements necessary for his case.

The court will then decide if the proof is sufficient, as a matter of law. If the judge grants the motion of the defendant, then he will dismiss the complaint and the case is over. If he denies the motion the case will continue and the defendant will be required to answer the evidence of the plaintiff.

The defendant's witnesses are then sworn and examined, both directly by the defendant and on cross-examination by the plaintiff. When all of the available facts have been elicited by the defendant, he too will "rest."

If necessary, the plaintiff may be permitted to call "rebuttal" witnesses, to disprove some of the evidence presented by the defendant. Both sides will then "rest." All of the proof in the case is then completed.

The defendant will then make his closing statement or "summation" to the jury. The plaintiff, again getting the advantage, has the last word before the jury. Each side, in its turn will try to persuade the jury by facts, reason, logic and rhetoric that its client is entitled to their verdict.

The court then "charges" or instructs the jury as to the applicable principles of law in the case.

Illustration of a "charge":

"The plaintiff brings this action to recover damages for injuries he alleges were sustained by him by reason of the negligence of the defendant. In order to recover a verdict, the plaintiff must prove that the negligence of the defendant was the proximate cause of the accident. . . . Negligence in law may be defined as the failure or omission to perform some act or duty which one person owes to another. More simply defined, it is the absence of such care as a reasonable and prudent person would be expected to use, under similar circumstances. . . .

"You have heard the testimony. The law places upon you jurors the burden of deciding the issues of fact from your recollection of that testimony. . . .

"Under the law, if the plaintiff is to recover he must not only show that the defendant was negligent, but that he himself was free from any fault which in any way contributed to the accident. . . .

"The plaintiff can only recover if the evidence produced by him outweighs the evidence produced by the defendant. By that I do not mean the number of witnesses. It is the quality of the testimony and not the quantity that counts. . . .

"If you find therefore that the plaintiff has sustained the burden of proof and that the defendant should be called upon to compensate the plaintiff for the damages he sustained, you will then determine how much in money you should award the plaintiff. . . .

"If the evidence in your minds is so equally balanced that you cannot make up your minds, then your verdict must be for the defendant. . . .

"That is what we call 'preponderance of the evidence.' So if the evidence of the plaintiff does not preponderate in his favor, he cannot recover. . . .

"With minds free from bias, prejudice or sympathy, you must determine from the facts, considering them fairly and impartially, who is entitled to a verdict. You can bring in one of two verdicts. If you find that the plaintiff has not satisfied you by the rules I have laid down, you will find for the defendant. If you find that the plaintiff has satisfied you and you believe that the plaintiff's testimony outweighs the defendant's, in quality, then your verdict will be for the plaintiff."

After the charge, the court will ask for "exceptions." Each side will state any objections it has to the court's charge. The court will rule as to each exception. He may amend the charge to include a correction or he may deny it.

The jury will then retire to deliberate on the facts of the case. Some jurisdictions require a unanimous verdict even in civil actions. Others have amended the law and only require five-sixths of the jurors to agree in order to constitute a legal verdict. If the required number cannot agree on a verdict, then the jury will be dismissed and the case tried all over again before another jury.

If the deliberations of the jury extend far into the night, the court may order a "sealed verdict." When the verdict is reached, it will be written down and signed by all of the members of the jury—those in favor and those against. The verdict will then be sealed and opened before the court and both litigants at its next session, usually the next morning.

The verdict of the jury will be either "for the defendant" or "for the plaintiff." If the case requires the jury to determine the amount of recovery for the plaintiff, the verdict may be "For the Plaintiff in the sum of $1,500."

In a non-jury case, the trial of a civil action proceeds in essentially the same manner except that there is no need for opening and closing statements. The determination of the court is called its "decision."

APPEAL PROCEDURE

If the losing party in a civil action, whether jury or non-jury, is convinced that some "error" of law was committed on the trial of the case, he may appeal to a higher court. He will serve the other side with a "notice of appeal." Within the required time, he will prepare and serve on his opponent the papers and documents necessary for such an appeal.

These include a "record on appeal" consisting of all the documents in the case such as the summons, complaint, answer and bill of particulars. It will also include a complete transcript of all the testimony at the trial, and copies of the exhibits. The "appellant" will also be required to serve and file a "memorandum of law" to sustain his claim that an error was committed. The "respondent," also known as the "appellee," will also serve and file a memorandum of law to defeat the arguments of the appellant.

The appeal will be placed on a calendar in the appellate court. When it is reached in its turn it will be heard in argument. The appellate court may not feel that argument is required and may request both sides to "submit" their papers for its consideration and decision.

The appellate court will either affirm the decision of the lower court or reverse it and send the case back for a new trial.

ENFORCING THE JUDGMENT OF THE COURT

When the verdict of the jury or the decision of the court is for the plaintiff, he will enter judgment in the sum awarded to him, in the County Clerk's office, or such other place as judgments are recorded. If payment is not made within a reasonable time, he will then take those steps necessary to collect that judgment.

An appeal stays the enforcement of the judgment. If the judgment creditor is served with notice of appeal he is stayed from proceeding until the appeal is denied, dismissed or defeated.

If there is no appeal, the judgment creditor may be entitled to examine the judgment debtor under oath in "proceedings supplementary to judgment" to determine the extent of his assets. In his further attempts to collect on the judgment, he may have "execution" issued to an officer of the court, directing him to seize and hold the debtor's property until payment is made or it is sold. When payment is made, the judgment debtor is entitled to have a "satisfaction of judgment" docketed to show that the judgment was satisfied. In those cases where a lawsuit involves real estate, and a *lis pendens* was filed as notice to prospective purchasers that litigation was pending, this too should be canceled of record when payment is made.

ADMINISTRATIVE AGENCIES

Because of the increasing complexity of government, motor vehicle bureaus, tax assessors, liquor authorities and similar government agencies have been given power to administer activities affecting personal rights and business interests. In the event of an adverse decision, a court proceeding "in certiorari" may review that determination. If it is shown that the decision was unreasonable, arbitrary or capricious, the court will order a reconsideration or will reverse that decision.

ARBITRATION

Although it is illegal to make any contract which will deprive anyone of the right to seek relief in the courts, contracts may provide for the settlement of disputes by arbitration. The contract will set forth the manner of choosing the impartial arbitrator or it may direct that the matter be submitted to the American Arbitration Association. An arbitration decision cannot be appealed or reversed in court unless it is shown that there was some impropriety in the proceeding or in the decision.

CHAPTER 2

The Contract

WHY STUDY CONTRACTS?

In our daily associations and activities, we all make agreements; some are social in nature and others commit us financially.

Contracts are agreements which create legal obligations and are enforceable in a court of Law.

In civil law, the contract is the basic legal concept, the foundation of all legal relationships. Every one of our daily acts creates, in some way, a legal obligation.

When we arise in the early morning of a winter day, turn on the light or the radio, we are a party to a contract with the electric company. It makes the electric current available to us and we pay for the amount that we use.

Those of us who are homeowners and don't have our own wells have a similar contract with the water company.

When our newspaper is delivered in the morning, we are purchasers under a contract, either express or implied, to pay for that paper when the newsboy comes around to collect.

We take a taxicab, get on a bus, go by subway; all of these acts are contractual relationships.

These are trivial, unimportant contracts and don't cost much. How about some of our more important transactions—buying a car, a washing machine, a house? Do we understand the principles which underlie our actions? Do we know the obligations we incur and the rights and privileges that we acquire?

More important, in making a contract, are we certain that it is as binding on the other side as it is on us?

In terms of law, a contract is a mutual obligation between two people with a mutual right by either to demand its performance. The breach of this right, the failure to perform that promise, creates in the other person the right to relief and redress in a court of law.

The Uniform Commercial Code was enacted to simplify the law governing commercial transactions and to continue the accepted commercial customs and practices. The basic concepts of contract law are thus not affected except that those contracts which are of a commercial nature are afforded the expanded benefits of commercial usage.

SOME TYPES OF CONTRACTS

A "unilateral" contract is a promise of commitment made by one party conditioned upon the performance of an act by the other. The contract does not become binding until the act is performed.

Illustration: "I promise to pay you a commission, if you will get me a buyer for my car." When the person to whom the promise is made brings a willing buyer for the car, he has earned his commission.

A "bilateral" contract is created when mutual promises are exchanged by both parties to the transaction. The failure by either party to perform his part of the contract in accordance with his promise may subject him to damages which result from the breach of the contract.

Illustration: "I promise to pay you 15¢ a gallon for 300 gallons of #2 grade fuel oil, if you will promise to deliver it tomorrow morning." "I'll deliver it."

An "executory" contract is one which is not fully performed. It has been partly performed but something still has to be done by either or both of the contracting parties.

An "executed" contract is one which has been fully performed by both sides. There is nothing further to be done. The transaction is complete.

Illustration: The 300 gallons are delivered in the morning as promised and the buyer pays in accordance with his agreement.

A "void" contract is one which is not legally enforcible and is not binding on either of the parties. The expression "null and void," so often used, is redundant. It actually means "non-existent and not enforcible."

Illustration: Contracts which are illegal in scope and in purpose are void and unenforcible.

A "voidable" contract is one which is valid, binding and enforcible. However, there is a right available to one or, in some instances, to both of the parties to avoid responsibility of performance. It may thus be enforcible against one of the parties but not against the other.

Illustration: A contract made with a "minor," also known as an "infant," a person legally under age, is enforcible by him against the other, the adult. Under certain circumstances, the minor may renege on his contract and demand the return of the money he paid. Of course, if he seeks to enforce the contract against the adult, he cannot then disaffirm.

An "express" contract is one in which all of the terms are agreed upon by the parties and are specifically set forth in detail, as in a writing.

Illustration: A lease or insurance policy is a good example of an express contract.

An "implied" contract is one which is created by law, imposed upon the parties because of their actions or their behavior, despite the fact that they had no actual or express agreement.

Illustration: Anna sued the estate of her deceased employer Gertrude. She claimed that she was hired by Gertrude, who was aged and infirm. She was told by Gertrude in the presence of other friends that she need not worry about getting paid, she would be well taken care of in the will. She worked as a companion for 11 years without pay, only for board and lodging. The will only provided for $100 to be paid to Anna. She claimed her rightful compensation. Despite the fact that there was no valid express contract between them, a contract was *implied* by law. Anna was awarded reasonable compensation for the services she rendered to Gertrude through the years.

A contract will be implied because of the particular relationship of the parties. A husband is obligated to support his wife, parents to support and care for their infant children.

A "quasi-contract," "as if there were a contract," will result and will be implied when one party in a transaction is in possession of money or property belonging to another. The law creates this implied contract to prevent that person from being "unjustly enriched."

Illustration: The previously described case of the unpaid companion, also applies here.

A person who pays money under a mistake of fact may be given the right to recover it under an implied or quasi-contract.

Illustration: Algernon, believing that he owned a certain parcel of real estate, paid taxes on it. When he found that he did not own it, he asked that the money be refunded to him. The city refused and he sued. The court allowed him to recover on the theory of implied contract.

ELEMENTS NECESSARY FOR A VALID CONTRACT

In all express contracts, as distinguished from those implied by law, the words and actions of the parties must reveal an intention to create a contract which the law will recognize. This intention can be determined from the provisions of the contract and the legal interpretation of those terms.

In addition to the terms of agreement, a contract, to be enforcible in a court of law, must have the following essential elements:

The contractual obligations must be voluntarily assumed. Therefore a contract must consist of an "offer" made by one party and an "acceptance" of that offer by the party to whom it was made. This is called consent, "mutual assent" or, popularly, "a meeting of the minds."

Each party must have contributed some consideration toward the creation of the contract. There must be a *quid pro quo,* a something in exchange for something else to make the deal a binding one. A mere gratuitous promise, not made in reliance upon a reciprocal promise, is not binding and not enforcible.

Each of the participants to the transaction must have legal capacity to enter into the deal. They must have no legal disability which would prevent them from making a contract.

Illustration: A person who has been legally declared to be insane cannot enter into a legal contract. He has no capacity to contract.

Finally, the purpose and subject matter of the agreement must be legal and not in violation of any law or contrary to the public policy or morals of the place where the contract is made.

Illustration: An agreement to rent a house for the specific purpose of operating a house of prostitution, where such is unlawful, is void.

OFFER AND ACCEPTANCE

The first essential elements of a contract are the "offer" and the "acceptance." This is an indication by both sides of a mutual intention to be legally bound and obligated.

The Offer

An "offer" is a promise which, by its terms, is conditional on its being accepted. This may consist of a reciprocal promise or an act specifically requested by the terms of the offer, from the person to whom it is made.

Illustration: "I will sell you my car if you will pay me $500."

An offer, then, is a promise or an act which, if it is accepted, ripens into a contract.

It must be clear, definite and specific, so that there will be no misunderstanding, no ambiguity.

Illustration: Peter, starting in his new business, needed a special type of glue. Dan promised to sell him "all the glue he would need" for the first year at 9¢ a pound. When the cost of the glue went up, Peter asked Dan to deliver. Dan refused, claimed there was no contract, no definite offer. The court agreed with Dan. The offer did not contain a definite quantity. There was no way of determining how much glue Peter would need during the first year, since he was just starting the business. There was no contract, so that Peter could not recover in his action for breach of contract.

There must be an obvious and unquestionable intention to be bound. A mere jest or attempt at humor will not be considered as an indication of such intention.

Illustration: Elmer was showing his new watch to the "boys." Everyone guessed at its value. To prove that Gene knew nothing about watches, Elmer offered the $100 watch to him for $15. Gene accepted the offer. There was obviously no intention to sell or to offer for sale under the circumstances. There was no enforcible contract.

The person to whom an offer is made must be aware that it was made to him. He cannot accept an offer unless it was received by him or communicated to him.

Illustrations: The Aywon Insurance Company sent a letter to Ansel advising him that his policy covering him for automobile collision insurance expired but would be renewed for another year. Ansel never received this letter and did not know of the renewal. However, after an accident he claimed coverage because of this letter. The court did not agree with Ansel. It held that since he had no knowledge of the offer to renew, he could not have accepted. Of course there was no contract.

Van sues Sherwood to recover a reward for helping to convict a murderer. Sherwood had offered a reward for the arrest and conviction of a suspected murderer. Van helped to apprehend the murderer before he knew of Sherwood's offer. He was not entitled to recover the reward because he had no knowledge of the offer and could not have acted on it.

Since the contractual relationship is a voluntary one, a person making an offer has the right to direct it to a particular person. Only the person to whom the offer is made may accept it.

Illustration: Sam offered to sell his car to Bill in the presence of Ted. Bill said nothing but Ted anxiously said, "I'll buy it." Ted's acceptance did not ripen into a contract since the offer was not made to him. If Sam accepts Ted's offer to buy the car, he may do so and have a binding contract. This however is a counter-offer made by Ted and accepted by Sam. It is not based on the original offer.

An offer made to a group of people gives anyone in that group the right to accept. Such offers, called "general offers," are usually made as rewards for the return of a lost article or for the arrest and conviction of a criminal. The first person who, with knowledge of the offer, acts on it thereby accepts it and a contract results.

Illustration: Olga in a newspaper advertisement offered $500 as a reward for the return of her lost diamond bracelet. Earl found the bracelet, read the ad and returned it to Olga. He claimed the $500 and she only offered him $50. He sued for the full amount and recovered.

ADVERTISEMENTS BY STORES OF ARTICLES ON SALE

Retail stores and other business establishments, to attract business, advertise widely that their merchandise is on sale at reduced prices. These advertisements are either in newspapers, on radio, television or in printed circulars. The decision of the courts has been that these advertisements are not offers to sell. They are only invitations to the general public to come to their places of business and make an offer for any particular merchandise that is then available.

Illustration: A store advertised a well-known brand of radios in certain models at a reduction of 25 to 40 per cent. Owen came into the store, demanded two radios of a certain model and tendered his check for the amount. This was refused. He sued the store, claiming the difference between the regular price of those radios and the advertised price. He lost because the court held that there was no offer. His tender of his check was actually a counter-offer which the store was at liberty to refuse.

AUCTIONS AS CONTRACTS

An auction is usually an invitation for offers from successive bidders. The bids made are really offers to buy. When a higher bid is made, it is an offer by another person. The bidder may withdraw his bid at any time before the fall of the auctioneer's hammer or before he indicates in any other manner that the sale is complete.

If the bids are not adequate for the value of the item he may withdraw it from sale. If, however, before putting an item up for sale he announces that the sale of this item is "without reserve," he is bound to sell it at any price offered by the highest bidder. Such a sale may be enforced in a court.

TERMINATION OF THE OFFER

An offer which is not accepted does not give the person to whom it is made any right. It may be withdrawn or revoked at any time before it is accepted.

Illustration: The Honta Silk Company sent out an offer to all of its customers that it had a quantity of a certain type of cloth available at a certain price. Before any orders were received the company advised its customers that the offer was withdrawn. The customers could not claim a contract because they had not accepted the original offer.

If an offer specifies the time within which it must be accepted, it is considered to have lapsed if not accepted within that time.

If no time is specified, then, if not accepted within a reasonable time, it will be considered to have lapsed automatically.

Illustration: Telegram from the Eurasian Fur Company stated, "Have just received shipment of cerulean mink offering 500 skins at $35. Accept by immediate reply." The acceptance was delayed by 24 hours. The offer was considered lapsed; the reply in this case was not deemed immediate.

Death or insanity of the person making the offer or the person to whom it is made, before acceptance, results in a lapse.

Illustration: Aldren offered to extend Bowan's lease if he would construct additional warehouse space. The death of Aldren before Bowan took any action to build constituted a lapse of the offer.

Acceptance of an offer by one of several people to whom it is made terminates it as to the others.

Illustration: Louis offered to sell his motorboat in a statement made to three men with whom he was playing golf. Ronald accepted the offer. The sale was thus consummated and the offer as far as the other two men were concerned was withdrawn and terminated.

Rejection of an offer by the person to whom it is made terminates it and it cannot be revived by him subsequently. An effort to accept the offer later is only a counter-offer and ripens into a contract only if it is accepted by the person who made the original offer. The same situation applies when an offer is made at one price and the acceptance is at a lower price. It is actually a counter-offer which rejects the original offer. It must be accepted to constitute a contract.

An "option" is a special agreement between an offeror and an offeree, to keep the offer open and irrevocable for a definite period. It must have the necessary elements as a contract. If the option is in writing or is included as one of the terms of a written offer, signed by the offeror, then it is enforcible, even though there was no added consideration.

Illustration: Baldwin wrote a letter to Sorner offering to sell him his house for $15,000. He added in the letter, "You don't have to rush into this, take your time. I will hold this offer open for two weeks, to give you ample time to consider it." Baldwin sold the house to Forester before the two weeks expired. Within that time Sorner accepted the offer. Baldwin was held responsible on the contract created when Sorner accepted the offer.

THE ACCEPTANCE

An "acceptance" of an offer is the compliance by the person to whom it is made with its precise terms and provisions. This act of compliance, whether it is the making of a promise or the performance of an act as required, creates the contract.

Any change in the terms of the offer which is made by the acceptance is considered a rejection of the original offer.

Illustration: In negotiating for a lease to certain grasslands for feeding his herd, Alston in his acceptance stated that he would pay the rental with a 30-day promissory note instead of in cash. This change in the terms was considered a substantial alteration and therefore a rejection of the offer.

If the offer contains a specific requirement, it must be complied with. An offer which requires that the acceptance must be received by the offeror to be binding is not effective until it is received. In such a situation, the offer may then be withdrawn at any time before the acceptance is received.

Illustration: Paul is a contractor. Dan considered moving his store to a new location and wanted Paul to give him an estimate on alterations to be made according to his plans. The estimate was satisfactory but Dan wrote to Paul: "On your agreement that you will finish the work in two weeks, begin at once." Paul bought lumber and was prepared to start work when Dan told him he did not want the work done. Paul sued Dan for breach of contract. The court determined that the offer by Dan required Paul to promise that he would finish in two weeks. Paul did not comply. The contract did not come into being until Paul promised to finish within the required time. This he did not do before the offer was withdrawn.

If the offer does not require the acceptance to be received by the offeror, a contract may result even though the acceptance is never received. Such a situation arises from the business practice that unless otherwise instructed an offer must be accepted by the same means as it is received. If this practice is followed, then the delivery of the acceptance to transmitting agency creates an effective contract, despite the fact that it may not be subsequently received by the offeror.

Illustration: Baxter sent Noitman a telegram offer of 50 bales of cotton at 5¢ a pound, making no reference to the means for reply nor to the fact that the acceptance must be received. Noitman accepted the offer and filed the telegram with the dispatch clerk. There was delay in transmission and before the wire was sent to

Baxter, a fire in the telegraph office destroyed the telegram. Noit-man contended that he had accepted the offer. He proved it by showing a copy of the wire he sent and the clerk testified that he had received it. The court held that since Baxter had chosen the telegraph as the transmitting agency, and had given no other instructions, he had in effect made the telegraph company his agent.

In similar situations, offers sent through the mails have been considered accepted when the letter of acceptance was dropped into the letter box.

A contract cannot be forced upon anyone. Merchandise shipped without request, where there were no prior dealings between the parties, need not be accepted or paid for. This applies particularly to those items sent to us in the form of books, gadgets and other unwanted objects, with a request for payment. There is no obligation to send the merchandise back. If it gets lost because it was not picked up within a reasonable time, there is no responsibility attached. The risk is entirely on the shipper.

Consideration is another necessary element of a contract. The common law requires all contracts to have consideration. Without it they are void and unenforcible. The only exception is a contract under seal. The presence of the seal on a written contract creates under the common law the legal presumption that there is a legally sufficient consideration as a basis of the agreement.

Consideration has been held to be either a promise or an act given or performed by a person who was not otherwise legally obligated to make that promise or to perform that act.

Illustration: If you will paint my house, I promise to pay you $200.

The consideration on the one hand is the painting of my house. The person addressed does not have any obligation to paint my house except for the offer made. The consideration on the other side is the promise to pay $200 if the house is painted.

A contract, then, is formed by the presence of a consideration. One side promises to do something if the other side will perform a certain act. "I promise to pay you $200 if you paint my house." This is an example of sufficient consideration to sustain an enforcible contract.

Each party to the contract then obligates himself to a promise or an act which he is not obligated to undertake in the absence of the contract to be created.

Illustration: At a family reunion, a prosperous uncle in an expansive mood promised his nephew $5,000, if he would refrain from gambling, drinking and profanity until he became 21. The nephew very scrupulously complied with his uncle's request. When he reached 21, he demanded the $5,000. The uncle attempted to renege. He claimed that abstention from those activities was for the benefit of his nephew's health; that there was not sufficient consideration on which to base a contract. The nephew sued and the court held in favor of the nephew. In reliance upon his uncle's offer, he had abstained from doing those things which he had an absolute right to do. There was sufficient consideration. He received the $5,000.

The consideration must be simultaneous with the making of the contract. Past performance or past promises are not enough and not valid as a binding consideration.

Illustration: Jonas asked for permission to use Olney's truck to move some of his furniture. This permission was granted without any mention of payment since they were close friends. Several weeks later, after an argument, Olney demanded $25 from Jonas for the use of the truck. His attempt to recover the money met with failure since he could not recover for a past consideration. There had been no contract, no promise of payment. The prior use of the truck was not sufficient basis for a payment or a promise of payment later.

The presence of consideration is sufficient to sustain the contract. The degree or value of the consideration is of no importance legally. The adequacy of consideration does not affect its legal sufficiency. Whatever is acceptable to the party making the contract as the basis for his obligation will be considered to be legally sufficient.

Illustration: Jules believes that a letter in Elmer's possession will help him establish a claim against Frank. He buys the letter from

Elmer for $100. The letter is not sufficient to establish his claim against Frank but it is sufficient consideration for the $100 he paid Jules for it.

By legislative enactment, the common law pertaining to consideration has been changed. When the terms of an agreement are incorporated in a writing signed by the parties who are to be bound by it, the existence of a consideration is presumed. The contract, by its written terms, sets forth the respective obligations of the parties.

WHO IS CAPABLE OF MAKING A LEGAL CONTRACT?

All persons not declared mentally incompetent are legally capable of entering into a contract. However, the contracts of minors and persons who are mentally incompetent, though not so judicially declared, will be discussed to explain their legal effect and their legal implications.

Once again we return to the basic concept that a contract is a voluntary act. A person who lacks the mental capacity to understand the effect of his actions cannot be considered to be performing a voluntary act. Any contract entered into by such a person is not enforcible against him because of this lack of capacity.

This particular subject is important in our everyday experiences because, in making a contract, we must make certain that the person with whom we contract has the capacity to make it enforcible against him.

This applies particularly to the contracts of minors, also called "infants." Each state, by law, determines the age of maturity of its minors. On reaching that age, be it 18 or 21, the person becomes legally responsible.

WHAT IS THE STATUS OF A CONTRACT MADE BY A MINOR?

As a general rule, a contract made by an infant is voidable by him. He can avoid responsibility under it. Since an infant is considered a ward of the court and under its protection, he is given every safeguard to prevent any adult from taking undue advantage of his tender years.

After he has made a contract in which personal property is involved, he has the right to disaffirm it at any time until he reaches maturity. He must, however, return any of the benefits that he received through the contract, if he is to be relieved from any further liability under it and recover any money paid.

Illustration: Reginald, age 20, was interested in a correspondence course in "Complete Steam Engineering." He registered with a correspondence school, gave his age as 21 and paid in $85 out of a total of $150. He received some books in the course. However, before using them he changed his mind and returned the books, advising the school of his disaffirmance. The school sued him for the balance of $65. The court found that he was entitled to the return of his $85 and was relieved of any liability for the course, despite the fact that he had lied about his age. The risk in such a situation is with the person dealing with a minor. He had not retained any of the benefits and was entitled to the protection of the law.

Although a minor may disafirm a contract at any time before maturity, he cannot ratify it until he attains it. As a minor, his act of ratification can have no meaning since it cannot affect its voidable status.

The only situation which may bind a minor in a contract occurs when he attempts to enforce that contract against an adult. He then becomes legally bound.

The protection of minority is only for the benefit of the minor, who, at the time when the contract was made, misrepresented his age or any other material fact.

An adult may be permitted to avoid a contract made with a minor who misrepresented his age at the time of the making of the contract because of the misrepresentation, not the non-age.

Illustration: Refer to the previous case. When the school found that Reginald was a minor, it had the right to avoid the contract because of Reginald's misrepresentation of his age. It could have returned his money and requested the return of its books. Instead, it attempted to enforce the contract against him and was, of course, defeated.

On reaching maturity, the minor has a final opportunity to disaffirm any contract that he made during his minority. If he fails to do so, within a reasonable time, then the contract is deemed to have been ratified by him.

In real-estate contracts, a minor can neither disaffirm nor ratify before he reaches maturity. This rule is effective because real property requires a chain of title involving persons who have no legal disabilities. It is for that reason also that a minor does not have the authority to dispose of real property by will.

Disaffirmance of a contract may be expressed by notice of such intention by the minor. It may also be implied from his conduct when it is clearly inconsistent with the existence or recognition of the contract.

Illustration: Alfred, a minor, gives a chattel mortgage on his car to guarantee payment of a loan. The sale and delivery of the car to another is a clear indication of disaffirmance of the prior chattel mortgage transaction.

Disaffirmance by the infant renders the contract void from the beginning. Once disaffirmed, it cannot thereafter be ratified. The parties are left as though no contract existed, and the consideration given by the infant is to be returned.

An interesting question arises when personal property sold by an infant is then resold to another. If a person buys in good faith and for value, without knowledge that the title was voidable due to the right of the infant to disaffirm, his right to the property cannot be challenged. A bona fide purchaser for value gets good title to personal property bought from a seller with a voidable title, provided that the contract has not yet been disaffirmed.

Illustration: Eddie, a minor, sold his old car to Vernon, a used car dealer. Vernon fixed the car up and sold it to Harris, a stranger in town. Harris had no knowledge of Vernon's deal with Eddie and paid a fair price for the car. Eddie changed his mind about the car and demanded it back from Vernon. He found that Harris was still in town and tried to get the car back from him. Harris had received a good and valid title from Vernon because he had bought the car before Eddie had changed his mind. Eddie could not get the car back from Harris.

An infant is liable for his torts. However, the court will not permit an adult to recover against an infant on a breach of his contract by treating the breach as a tort. Any tort which is related to a breach of contract cannot be held against a minor since it would deprive him of the protection under the law.

Injury to property by an infant because of his lack of care, discretion or skill in relation to a contract creates no obligation on the part of the infant. The infant's protection under a contract and his right to disaffirm apply because the breach may be due to his being immature and incapable of coping with the responsibility involved.

Illustration: Irwin, a minor, rents a horse and wagon to drive to town. Because of his inability to handle the horse, it runs away. When the wagon overturns, the horse is injured so that it has to be destroyed. Irwin is not liable for the loss of the horse since the damage was directly related to the contract of hiring.

However, when the infant willfully and intentionally misuses the property of the contract or uses it for a purpose other than intended, he is liable for any damage he causes. This obligation is not due to his breach of the contract. It is a tort, an act in violation of the contract and unrelated to it, for which he is liable.

Illustration: Adolph, an infant, hires a horse to ride into town. The owner warns him not to ride across country but to use the road into town. Adolph disregards these instructions. He does go across country, tries to hurdle a fence. The horse is injured and has to be destroyed. The court construed Adolph's act as disaffirming the contract and held him liable for his tortious act in willfully causing the damage to the horse.

A MINOR IS LIABLE FOR NECESSARIES SUPPLIED TO HIM

The law does not intend that its efforts to protect a minor shall cause him hardship. Nor is the infant to use this protection to his advantage and to the disadvantage of the people who deal with him.

An infant is held liable for any necessaries supplied to him or his family when there is no one who is able or willing to buy them for him. "Necessaries" have been defined as food, clothing, shelter, schooling and such other items which he may require according to his particular station in life.

The obligation upon the infant is not however as a contract, but as a "quasi-contract," a relationship created by the law to prevent the infant from using his infancy to his advantage.

If he has no parent or any person *in loco parentis* who has the means to supply him with these needs, he will be held responsible and be made to pay for them. However, he is only obligated to pay a reasonable price for them and not the agreed or contract price.

Illustration: Ernest, a minor, lived at home with his parents. To facilitate his transportation to and from school, his father bought him a car. One day he was involved in an accident. His damaged car needed repair and he took it into a garage. He agreed upon a price for the job, told the garageman he did not want his father to know about it and promised to pay for it himself. The garageman repaired and released the car to him. But when he demanded the money, Ernest claimed protection as a minor. The owner claimed that his repair job was a "necessary." The court held this was not a "necessary" for Ernest since his father, in giving him the car, was in a position to pay for the repairs. There was no recovery against Ernest on the agreed price. A minor is only liable for necessaries when there is no parent or guardian who can supply them to him.

EMANCIPATION OF A MINOR

The "emancipation" of a minor is the release of his custody and control from the domination of his parents. This may be accomplished by the express consent of the parents. It may result by implication from the acts of the parents or of the minor.

The failure of a parent to support a minor will create an

emancipated status. The marriage of a minor or his joining the armed forces will create that status.

An emancipated minor has the right to his own earnings. His new status widens the scope of those things which he must buy as necessaries. He becomes financially liable for the necessaries furnished to him, or to his wife and child.

Illustration: Paul, age 17, ran away from home, got a job in another town, met a girl and married her. He found that he needed a car to get to and from work so he bought one from the New Drive Auto Co. To secure payment for the car, he executed a chattel mortgage on the car. When he failed to make the necessary payments, the company took steps to recover the money or the car. Paul claimed his infancy as a defense in the transaction. Paul was an emancipated minor. He needed and did furnish certain necessaries for himself and his wife. The car was to him a necessity since it provided him with a means of getting to and from work. This transaction was binding on Paul. Infancy was not a defense.

It is interesting to note here that the earnings of an unemancipated minor belong to his parents. An employer who receives a demand from a father for his son's pay check, may be required to hand it over to him.

WHO ARE INCOMPETENTS?

An "incompetent" is a person who is not considered capable of handling his own affairs. He does not know the nature and the consequence of his acts. For his protection, he is also deemed to be a ward of the court. All efforts are made to protect his interests from improper transactions.

A person is considered insane when he is suffering from a mental condition or disease which impairs his will and judgment; causes his conduct to be irrational. To affect a person's capacity to make a contract, this mental impairment must be more than just weak-mindedness. It need not, however, be so severe as to dethrone all reason. The test of a person's mental condition is whether he understands the nature and the effect of any particular transaction, whether he is capable of transacting business and whether he is capable of seeing things in their true relation.

Any person who is mentally ill may by a proper judicial proceeding be declared insane. Such a proceeding is considered notice to the world that he is mentally incompetent and legally incapable of handling his own affairs. A "committee" is appointed to act for him, to handle all of his financial affairs and to take care of his person and his property.

All contracts subsequently made by a person so declared are void and unenforcible. The lunacy record—that is, the record of the proceeding—is conclusive evidence of his lack of capacity as long as it remains in force.

Illustration: Henry was declared mentally incompetent and unable to handle his own affairs. A committee or conservator was appointed for him. Although his acts were irrational, he did have certain lucid intervals. In one of those moments, he purchased by mail order a complete set of exercise and weight lifting equipment costing $150. He even sent a deposit of $5.00 by check. The equipment was delivered and the company requested payment. Since he had been adjudicated incompetent and no proceedings had been taken to vacate that determination, his contracts were void. The company took back the equipment and had no claim against Henry or his committee.

A contract made by an incompetent who, though not adjudicated, behaves in a manner which should put the other party on notice, may be avoided by him or in his behalf.

Illustration: Eric enjoyed going to auction sales. He attended this particular one held at the Beyall Auction Rooms. There were some particularly interesting things to buy. Eric bought 302 lots of merchandise. Among the items he bought were an auto body, 2 safes, a florist's icebox, some furniture and 50 bolts of cloth. He paid $1,706 for this rare collection. When the merchandise was delivered, his wife called the auctioneer and told him that her husband was ill, that he had no use for such a variety of items and that she wanted to return the entire purchase and get the money back. The auctioneer refused. When sued, he was compelled to return the money paid and was permitted to take back his merchandise. The court felt that the purchase of such a variety was an indication to the auctioneer that Eric was not completely aware of the nature of his actions.

An incompetent, or someone in his behalf, who seeks to avoid liability under a contract must restore any benefits that were received as a condition precedent to such relief.

As in the case of minors, these principles are for the protection of the incompetent only and not for the person dealing with him. The contract may be voided by the incompetent but not by the other side. If the contract is of benefit to the incompetent, it may be enforced in his behalf.

Incompetents are responsible for any necessaries which have been supplied to them. Here again the purpose is to protect persons dealing with incompetents and to prevent the defense of incompetency from being used to avoid valid obligations.

A contract made by an incompetent may be ratified by him when he regains his faculties and finds the terms to his benefit.

Ratification of such a contract is possible when the individual has had a reasonable time to understand the nature of his contractual obligations and benefits. If, after a reasonable time, he does not disaffirm this contract, he will be deemed to have ratified it.

A drunken person is liable for his contracts, unless his condition is apparent and thus affects his mental capacity. In such an instance, the contract which he entered into during that period is voidable. Slight intoxication does not affect the validity of a contract. The facts in each case govern, since any condition which tends to destroy a person's understanding will affect the volition necessary for a valid contract.

A habitual drunkard, if he has not been adjudicated an incompetent by judicial proceeding, may make a will, execute a deed and make a contract. The test is that, at the time he executed the document or made the contract, his reason and his understanding were not affected; that he knew the nature of his act.

Illustration: Greg was 50, and known to be a drunkard for at least two years. He called his lawyer one day and requested him to draw a deed to the house he owned to be given to his cousin Edgar. Edgar was being dispossessed from his home and had no place to take his family. The deed was prepared by the lawyer and Greg executed it in his presence. Two weeks later Greg was judicially declared a drunkard and a committee was appointed to handle his affairs. The committee attempted to set aside the deed to Edgar. This was defeated when the lawyer testified that, during the execution of the deed, Greg was sober, intelligent and competent.

There are proceedings to declare persons who are habitual drunkards as incompetent to handle their own affairs. A committee is appointed to take care of the person and the property of the incompetent so adjudicated. Contracts made by the incompetent after such adjudication are void.

If it is shown, in a legal proceeding, that a person adjudicated an habitual drunkard is able to manage himself and his affairs, he may be declared competent and the prior adjudication vacated.

A drug addict can be classified in the same category as the habitual drunkard with regard to his mental capacity to enter into a contract. Again the important factor is his ability to understand the nature of his actions and their consequences. If his mind is under the influence of the drug so that his reasoning powers are affected, then his contract is voidable.

A person who is so completely under the influence of alcohol or of drugs that he does not know what he is doing is in the same position as an insane person as to his liability for necessaries furnished to him. He is liable for the reasonable value of the necessary articles or services furnished to him. The liability is not on the basis of contract but on the theory of an implied contract.

A spendthrift is a person who is careless in the handling and spending of his money. Under the common law there were no restrictions placed on the freedom of a spendthrift to manage his own affairs no matter how badly he did it. Several of the states have provided by legislation for the appointment of a "guardian" for the handling of his affairs if it is shown to be necessary. A person so judicially declared has no capacity to make a contract and his contracts are void. Another proceeding is necessary to free him of this disability and vacate the prior adjudication.

Married women under the common law were subject to the disabilities of coverture. That is, they were under control and domination of their husbands. The husband was in all respects the head of the house. The wife could not own property in her own name, she could not enter into a contract in her own name, nor could she sue or be sued in her own name.

Present legislation in all states has removed all of these disabilities and restrictions. A married woman may now own property in her own name, she may sue and be sued; enforce her contracts. She is, of course, liable for her torts and her contracts.

Aliens are persons who are resident in this country but are citizens or subjects of a foreign country. Generally, when his country is not at war with the United States, an alien has the same power to contract that a citizen has. He may sue and be sued in our courts and may enforce his rights in the same manner as a citizen may.

Citizenship is obtained by application and qualification after 5 years of continuous residence in the country. The first step is to file a declaration of intention to become a citizen. Then after five years, application is made for final citizenship papers. Naturalization of the father includes in his papers all minor children. The mother must make application on her own.

Marriage to an American does not bestow citizenship on an alien, although it may make it easier for him to obtain naturalization papers.

An enemy alien is a person who is a citizen of a country which is at war with the United States. War suspends all commercial intercourse between the citizens of the hostile powers. All contracts made with citizens of belligerent nations after the outbreak of war are usually declared void. However, the courts will tend to preserve and not destroy contracts made before hostilities began. The effectiveness of these contracts will be suspended for the duration.

ENEMY ALIENS AS PLAINTIFFS

Generally an enemy alien cannot prosecute an action in the courts of this country during the progress of hostilities. However, there has been a trend toward recognizing and enforcing the civil rights of enemy aliens domiciled in this country, as long as they obey and respect the laws and observe the rules of conduct laid down for their guidance.

A CONVICT'S RIGHTS

A person serving a sentence of imprisonment, even for life, or awaiting execution for a capital offense is not deprived of his right to make a valid contract.

A person convicted of a crime and even while serving his sentence may dispose of his property by will or by deed. He may make contracts pertaining to his property. His estate will be liable for the breach of such contracts by him. He cannot enforce any contract on his own behalf because his civil rights are suspended. However, the rights of his creditors are not affected and they may reach any property that belongs to him.

CONTRACTS OF CORPORATIONS

Corporations are empowered by charter or certificate of incorporation, both expressly and by implication, to enter into contracts which are enforcible by and against them. A corporation can only function through its officers, its agents and employees, acting in the name of the corporation.

Those contracts which a corporation does not have the authority to make are called *ultra vires*, outside of its powers. They are not illegal, unless so designated by state law.

ASSIGNMENTS

Generally, only parties to a contract have a right to enforce the terms of the contract. However, obligations and duties under a contract which are not personal in nature can be delegated and assigned, on notice to the other party. The original party, the assignor, is not relieved of the obligations of the contract. He is still responsible for its performance if the assignee fails to perform. He can only be relieved by a specific agreement of the other side.

> Illustration: Prentiss and Allison entered into a contract for the manufacture and sale of lanterns. Prentiss assigned the contract to Erlands so that Erlands was to manufacture and ship the lanterns to Allison in accordance with contract. Allison breached the contract and refused to accept shipment from Erlands. He claimed that Erlands had no right under the contract. The court sustained Erlands in his suit against Allison on the ground that the contract was not affected by the assignment. Prentiss would have been liable to Allison if no lanterns were made or delivered. As long as the lanterns complied with the terms of the contract, Allison was compelled to accept them.

Contracts which require the special skill, knowledge or judgment of an individual party to a contract are not assignable.

ASSIGNMENTS IMPOSED BY LAW

When a person or a business is financially insolvent, when the liabilities are greater than the available assets or when the debts are not being paid when they become due, an assignment of all of the assets may be made to a designated person for the benefit of creditors. The assets are then liquidated and the proceeds are distributed by the assignee under the supervision of the court to all of the creditors in settlement of their claims.

In bankruptcy proceedings, under the federal laws, the assets of the bankrupt are assigned to a person designated to act as trustee. He gathers all of the assets, liquidates them and then distributes the proceeds to settle the claims of the creditors.

A person who dies and leaves a will has all of his personal property transferred to his named executor. It is the duty of the executor in administering the estate to gather all of the assets and distribute the proceeds in accordance with the provisions of the will.

If a person dies intestate, without a will to provide for the disposition of his estate, an Administrator is appointed on application to the Probate or Surrogate's Court. This Administrator then has all of the property transferred to him for the purpose of distributing it to the next of kin of the decedent in accordance with the laws of the particular state.

WHAT IS LEGALITY OF SUBJECT MATTER IN A CONTRACT?

The importance of a contract is its enforcibility in a court of law. If the purpose or the subject matter of the contract is illegal or against public policy and public morals, it will not be recognized and therefore is not enforcible. A contract which is not recognized in a court of law is void from its very inception.

Illustration: Many states have specific laws which declare that gambling within the state is illegal. Any contract in which gambling is the subject is thus expressly void and unenforcible.

A contract which is void because it is illegal in the state where it was created is void everywhere else. It cannot be enforced in the courts of any other state. This applies to gambling contracts, usurious contracts and all other contracts with an illegal purpose.

Illustration: A contract which is usurious in the state where it was made is unenforcible in all other states. Hilton agreed to pay Jensen 7½ per cent interest on a badly needed loan. Since the contract was made in New York, it was usurious and void because the legal rate of interest in New York is 6 per cent. Jensen sued Hilton to recover the loan and interest in Connecticut. Hilton used the defense of usury successfully. Jensen could not recover in Connecticut on a usurious New York contract.

Usury is a factor which may make a contract illegal. Each state has an established legal rate of interest to be charged for a loan of money. When that rate is exceeded in any transaction, it is considered to be usurious. The penalties against usurious transactions depend upon the laws of the state where the transaction takes place.

Some states consider a contract tainted with usury as void. In any state where such a law exists, a usurious contract is unenforcible. Neither the interest nor the money on the original loan can be recovered.

Other states are not so strict. They do not consider the contract void. It is enforcible to recover the principal sum. As to the recovery of the unpaid usurious interest, the states differ in their penalties. Despite the existence of a legal rate of interest, some transactions have by legislation been authorized to charge higher rates as in home mortgage loans and consumer credit sales.

Corporations have been in some states excluded from the protection of the usury laws. The interest charged for a loan to a corporation may be greater than the statutory legal rate and still be collectible without any penalties. Contracts of corporations containing an excessive rate of interest may be thus enforcible and not considered usurious.

Under this protection, and to avoid the usury prohibitions, corporations were used in the purchase of homes as residences. This practice was curbed when legislation was enacted making such corporations subject to the usury laws.

Certain businesses and professions are required by law to be licensed. This requirement is for the protection of the public because of the particular type of activity that is involved. A failure to obtain such a license may result in criminal prosecution as well as the civil penalty of not being able to enter into a legal, enforcible contract. This applies to plumbers, real-estate brokers, insurance brokers, doctors, dentists, lawyers and pawnbrokers. There are many others. Contracts made by such persons who are not licensed are not enforcible. Without having such a license, there can be no recovery for services rendered.

Illustration: A real-estate broker named Zackary produced a buyer who was "ready, willing and able" to buy a house which had been listed with him by the owner. The deal was consummated and the house was sold. Zackary claimed his commission from the seller, who refused to pay. It appeared that Zackary had failed to renew his real-estate broker's license and during this transaction did not have such a license. He sued the seller for his commissions but the court did not permit him to recover. He could only be entitled to his commission if he was an authorized broker. Without a license, he was not.

CONTRACTS IN VIOLATION OF SUNDAY OR BLUE LAWS

Under the common law, there were no restrictions or prohibitions against the making of a contract on Sunday. Present restrictions are based on laws passed by the legislatures of the various states.

If the law in the state expressly declares that all contracts made on a Sunday are void, then there is no ground for interpretation. Such contracts are void and unenforcible.

However, the statutes may not be so specific. The law may say, as it often does:

"All labor on Sunday is prohibited, except the works of necessity and charity, whatever is needed during the day for the good order, health or comfort of the community."

Illustration: A contract by an opera singer to perform on a Sunday is void, because the services are labor and, of course, prohibited.

However, paying a debt, making a will or settling a dispute is not condemned because that is not regarded as labor within the meaning of the Sunday Laws, also called Blue Laws.

Supplementing the Sunday statutes, there are special regulations which control the sale of food and refreshments or holding sports exhibitions or theatrical performances on Sunday. Some states permit these activities only during a designated time on Sunday.

CONTRACTS VIOLATING OUR CONCEPT OF GOOD CONDUCT, MORALS AND PUBLIC POLICY

There is no definition of public policy. There is therefore no absolute rule to test a contract to determine if it is contrary to public policy. Each contract is judged individually, not so much by the actual damage that is done but by the evil tendency which it reveals.

A contract to commit a tort is illegal and the courts will not entertain any lawsuit to enforce it.

Illustration: Frank hired Tom to write an article about Ellis which was false and libelous. Tom wrote the article and then attempted to sue Frank for the agreed price. This was illegal and not enforcible in court.

Agreements in fraud of creditors are void.

Illustration: Gordon secretly agrees to pay Frontane, one of his creditors, an additional 10 per cent of his indebtedness on the following condition: Frontane must persuade the others to agree to Gordon's offer of a composition agreement for all the creditors to settle their claims against him for 45%. After the settlement, Frontane tries to enforce this promise and fails. It is an illegal promise.

Contracts which tend to injure public service or good government are void.

Illustration: Prince promised Duke $250 if he would induce the purchasing agent of one of the government buying offices to give him some government business. Duke cannot legally enforce such a promise.

Agreements in unreasonable restraint of trade are against public policy and void.

Illustration: Johnson sells his small retail grocery to Reamer and promises not to engage in business of any kind in the city. The restraint is more extensive than is necessary for Reamer's protection and it is unenforcible.

Contracts by employees which unreasonably restrict their right to work after termination of their employment are against public policy and void.

Illustration: Bemis is employed as a manager of a cotton mill for a term of 5 years. His contract of employment restricts him from taking any job as a manager of any mill for a period of 3 years after his employment terminates. This was considered as creating an unnecessary hardship on Bemis. A restriction merely as a manager of a cotton mill within a reasonable area would be satisfactory.

Agreements which tend to create monopolies and prevent competition are a detriment to the public interest and are void.

Illustration: Danner is a coal distributor. He made a contract to purchase 2,700 tons of coal from the Blue Chip Coal Co. When he refused to accept delivery, the Blue Chip sued him. It appeared at the trial that Danner's plan was to make similar contracts with all coal companies serving the area in order to keep the price of coal high in that area. It was proved by Danner that the Blue Chip Co. knew of this plan when it entered into this contract with him. Since the contract and its purpose are illegal and against public policy, it is not enforcible by Blue Chip since they were a guilty party to the transaction. Blue Chip could not recover in its suit against Danner.

FACTORS WHICH AFFECT THE MAKING OF A CONTRACT

A contract which is completed to the satisfaction of both sides, creates no problem and never ends in a lawsuit.

It is only in those cases where one or the other of the parties wants, for reasons of his own, to be relieved of his obligations that he begins to look for those factors which, with the guidance of his attorney, may make such relief available to him.

Contracts in business are made for profit. Merchandise is bought and sold against a rise or a fall in price in the hope that added benefits will result from the transaction. If such anticipated advantages are not realized, and if sufficient legal reason is available for avoidance of contractual responsibility, the matter usually ends up in court.

As mentioned previously, if any of the necessary elements of consent, capacity, consideration or legality are lacking, the contract is void. This aspect would be the first for consideration in an effort to avoid contractual liability.

Under the element of consent—that is, the voluntary "meeting of the minds"—we find certain factors which prevent a true agreement. Let us examine these more closely.

The first of these is called "mistake." It is a legal term for the existence of a state of facts from which an assent was expressed by one or both of the parties. However, this consent may have been based on a misunderstanding. Either no contract was intended or the one created was not as intended by the parties.

Let us discuss the latter situation first. "Mutual mistake" results when there is an error in understanding by both parties as to the subject matter of the contract. The mistake must be mutual, on the part of both. No contract is created; it is void.

Illustrations: Jacobsen agrees to buy the boat called the *Betsy* from Salmonsen. It appears that there are two boats called the *Betsy*. One of them is owned by Salmonsen. However, Jacobsen thought he was buying the other. They were obviously not dealing about the same boat. There could be no meeting of the minds even though they both agreed. The contract is void.

Bettis has several cases in his warehouse which he believes contain apples. He sells them to Bidwell as apples. When the crates are opened it appears that they contain potatoes. Here again there is no contract. The mutual error by both rendered agreement impossible.

The legal effect of mutual mistake as stated is that the contract attempted to be created is void, as if no contract was ever made. Any attempt by one of the parties to enforce it can be defeated by the other. He does so by setting up the defense of mutual mistake in his answer to any complaint that is served in such an action.

The other situation discussed under mistake is specifically called "operative mistake." This occurs when one of the parties is induced by the fraud or misrepresentation of the other to assent to a contract where no such contract is intended. Without an intention to enter into a contract, there can be no contract. Any contract thus created is void.

Illustration: Alperson sued the telephone company and demanded that it remove its poles from his property. The company showed a document signed by Alperson which purported to give the company permission to place its poles across his property. At the trial, Alperson testified that he met one of the company men on the property. The man offered him $1. He explained that he had damaged one of the trees and wanted to pay for the damage. He asked Alperson to sign a receipt for it. Alperson could not read the paper because he had left his glasses at home. The man told him not to worry, that it was merely a receipt which would enable him to get his dollar back from the company. Actually this was the document which authorized the easement. It was declared void and unenforcible by the court. The company had to remove the poles or make a more adequate financial adjustment to pay for the easement of having its wires and poles cross Alperson's land.

WHAT RELIEF IS AVAILABLE FROM A CONTRACT VOID BECAUSE OF MISTAKE, MUTUAL OR OPERATIVE?

In an action at law, the injured party, the defendant, resisting the enforcement of the contract, may set up "mistake" as one of his defenses. If he paid money under the alleged contract he may sue as a plaintiff to get his money back, stating in effect that the contract is void.

He may also bring a suit in equity to have the court declare the contract void, and as incidental relief give him back his money. If he is sued for specific performance he may, of course, set up the defense of mistake.

FRAUD

Any person who can prove fraud in the making of a contract can be relieved from its obligations. Fraud has not been legally defined. It is determined from the facts in each particular case. There are, however, certain elements which must be present before fraud can be established.

To prove the existence of fraud, there must be a false statement of a material fact made by one person to another, knowing that it is false. It must have been made with the intention that the other rely upon it. This false statement must actually have induced the victim to act upon it, to his financial loss. This is the technical approach. However, any representation made in a contract transaction which prevents the free and complete consent of either party defeats its formation.

The law will not inquire into a man's contract to determine if it is a wise and prudent one. Nor will it permit innocent persons to be entrapped by the fraudulent contrivances or deceitful conduct of others to their advantage.

Illustration: Jones, a jeweler, convinced Harris, a wholesale jeweler, that he was from Tulsa and that his credit was unimpeachable. Harris sold and delivered jewelry to him worth $5,000. Harris subsequently found that the Jones to whom he gave the jewelry on credit was not from Tulsa but from Newark and that his credit was not acceptable. He proved the fraud and was able to recover his property.

The relief available to a person who claims fraud in the inducement of a contract depends upon his need. He has the right to avoid responsibility and recover damages.

If he paid money and wants to disavow the contract, he can declare the contract avoided because of the fraud and sue to get his money back.

If he wants to retain the benefits of the contract, continue it in effect, he can sue only on the damage he sustained due to the fraud. This action is in tort and is only available when the claim is fraud.

If he is sued by the other side to enforce the contract, he can set up fraud as a defense to avoid responsibility under the contract.

Finally, if he wants the court to declare the contract invalid, he may bring suit in equity to establish his right to avoid the contract and, as incidental relief, ask for the return of the money he paid and any other damages he sustained.

HOW DOES MISREPRESENTATION AFFECT A CONTRACT?

Misrepresentation is a false statement made concerning a material fact which induced the making of a contract. This differs from fraud because there is no need to prove any intention to mislead or to defraud. As a matter of fact, there may not be such an intention. The misrepresentation may be entirely innocent and unknown. However, since it is false and has been relied upon by the other party to the contract, the court will relieve the victim of his contractual obligations. The contract is voidable at the option of the injured party.

With the exception of intent, the defense of misrepresentation is similar to fraud. The type of relief available is also the same. In each instance, to obtain relief the injured party must declare his intention to avoid the contract promptly. If he fails to do so he may be deemed to have waived his right to avoid.

Illustration: Cahill was interested in buying a block of stock in a certain company. The seller misrepresented the financial condition and the earnings of the company. There was no fraudulent intention. When Cahill learned of the misrepresentation he sued for rescission of the contract. The court declared the contract avoided and awarded him the money he paid in as damages.

WHAT IS THE EFFECT OF DURESS ON A CONTRACT?

Duress is the use of force, either actual or threatened. If duress is involved in the making of a contract, then the victim has the right to avoid the contract, since obviously it was not a voluntary act. If the duress is the result of a threat, then the person making the threat must have at hand the means of carrying out the threat. At least, it must so appear to the person threatened, so that he is compelled to submit.

Where duress is claimed, it must appear that the will of the person was actually overcome and so influenced as to compel him to consent, even though it was not a voluntary expression of his will.

The effect of duress is to make the contract or the transaction voidable at the option of the victim. The contract is considered valid until it is avoided by the court or by some affirmative act of the party.

It is necessary that an act of avoidance be performed promptly as soon as the duress is removed. Failure to do so will be considered a waiver to assert this right and a ratification of the contract.

Illustrations: Injab, a city official, threatened to turn off Hollis' water, necessary to operate his foundry, unless he paid an illegal license fee. Hollis paid to keep the supply of water from being interrupted. He then instituted suit to recover the money since he paid under duress and recovered.

Allen paid excess freight charges in order to get possession of goods shipped to him. He later demanded and received a refund.

WHAT IS THE EFFECT OF UNDUE INFLUENCE ON A CONTRACT?

Undue influence is that domination or power which a stronger-willed person wrongfully exercises over a weaker-willed one. When such influence is exerted to effect the execution of a contract, then it can be avoided by the person victimized. The contract did not result from the voluntary act of the victim but was the expression of the will of the dominant party imposed upon the other. Such an effect is often produced by constant pressure and persuasion, which thwarts the natural intelligence and understanding of the victim.

Such a contract is valid and binding until some action is taken by the person who has been imposed upon to avoid it. This must be done promptly to eliminate any impression of waiver or ratification.

Certain relationships may create a presumption of undue influence because the parties are not on an equal footing in their transaction. One has an advantage over the other. These may occur in the relation between a patient and his doctor, a ward and his guardian, a client and his lawyer.

Illustrations: Aline, a nurse, was named as the sole beneficiary under the will of her patient, with no provision made for his two married children. The circumstances pointed to and were proved as involving undue influence to induce the patient to leave everything to his nurse. The will was not admitted to probate. Aline did not benefit from her relationship.

Jeff had been operating his father's business for 15 years since his father became paralyzed. He supplied his father's every need. A grant by the father of certain real estate and a share in the business, without any other proof, was not based on undue influence, despite his father's illness. He did not exert any influence on his father to obtain those benefits.

WHAT ARE "CONDITIONS" IN A CONTRACT?

A condition is an essential provision in the contract which, if breached, discharges the other party from performing his obligations under it.

Illustration: In the case where the uncle promised the nephew $5,000 if he refrained from drinking, gambling and carrying on until he reached 21. Each of the restrictions was a condition of the contract. If the nephew violated any one of them he would not be entitled to the money.

A "condition precedent" is a provision of the contract which must first be performed by one of the parties before the other side becomes obligated to perform. The contract does not become effective, does not begin to operate until that condition is fulfilled.

Illustration: Bidlow agrees to sell merchandise to Solon on credit, provided that Solon's credit rating is satisfactory to him. Bidlow did not ship the merchandise. Solon sues for breach of contract for failing to ship. Bidlow claims the contract was based on a condition precedent. Solon's credit was poor and hence there was no obligation on his part to ship. Bidlow had a valid excuse for failing to perform on the contract.

During contractual negotiations, each side has the right to impose, and the other to refuse, any conditions to the agreement. However, once the contract with those conditions is accepted, it is binding. If one of the parties by his actions prevents the other from performing those conditions, he thereby relieves him of the obligation to perform.

Illustration: Selwyn agreed to sell his house to Butterby. The contract of sale contained a condition precedent that Butterby obtain a loan secured by a purchase-money mortgage on the house, under certain terms to make up the difference between the purchase price and the cash that Butterby had. Before a loan commitment can be obtained, an appraisal of the house is necessary so that the bank can determine if the house is sufficient security for the loan. Selwyn, having changed his mind about selling the house, refused the appraiser permission to inspect. The loan was not approved. Butterby claimed that Selwyn breached the contract by preventing the appraisal. Selwyn claimed that the sale was based on a loan and mortgage, or no sale. The court sustained Butterby. The condition could not be fulfilled if Selwyn prevented it.

A condition precedent may be waived, its performance disregarded by the side who stands to benefit. He may proceed with the contract without requiring that the condition be performed.

Illustration: Bidlow, the seller, could have proceeded to ship the merchandise to Solon despite the fact that his credit rating was poor. Shipment of the goods would be considered a waiver.

A "condition subsequent" is a provision in the contract which gives a party the right to terminate his obligation under it upon the occurrence of a certain event, while the contract is actually in effect.

Illustration: Some policies covering insurance of automobile accidents, also called liability, provide that the car will not be used for business, or that it will not be driven by a person under 25. If an accident occurs when it is used for business or by someone under 25, they reserve the right to refuse to be obligated under the contract.

CAN YOU ENFORCE A CONTRACT WHICH CAN'T BE PERFORMED?

A contract which concerns certain specific goods or subject matter is discharged if that subject matter is destroyed before it can be delivered.

Illustrations: Dean rented a theater building from Eamon to present a play. The building was destroyed by fire. Eamon was relieved of responsibility for the breach of the contract. It was impossible for him to carry out his part of the agreement.

Johnson agreed to supply the Suntan Hotel with water from the spring on his land. During the hot summer the spring dried up. Johnson was not responsible for the breach of contract.

When a contract becomes illegal because of a change in the law affecting it, the obligation to perform is terminated.

Illustrations: Elson and Horton made a contract to construct a wooden building on Horton's land. A new city ordinance prohibiting the construction of such buildings went into effect before the plans for the building were filed and approved. Performance under the contract was impossible and the contract obligation discharged.

The School Board of Little City hired a teacher for a year. The school was closed by order of the Board of Health. The contract was terminated.

When performance of a contract depends upon the continued life or good health of a particular person, his death or illness makes performance impossible. He and his estate are relieved from its obligation.

Illustrations: If an artist who agrees to paint a portrait dies before it is completed, the contract is terminated.

A doctor agreed to pay one of his patients $1,000 a month during her life, if she would submit to certain experimental medical treatments. The treatments were completed. The subsequent death of the doctor did not relieve his estate from paying this obligation. The contract was binding because she had performed her part of the bargain.

WHAT IS THE "STATUTE OF FRAUDS"?

In England, about 1676, "An Act for Prevention of Frauds and Perjuries" was passed. This has come down to us as the "Statute of Frauds." It was felt that many fraudulent practices with relation to contracts are commonly substantiated by perjury. If a contract is of substantial importance it should be in writing. This would reduce the opportunity and the temptation to change the terms of oral contracts by perjurious testimony. The Uniform Commercial Code, as adopted, requires such contracts to be in writing or evidenced by a written memorandum to be enforcible. Partial compliance or part payment is an exception and may enable an oral contract to be enforced in the courts.

Generally, the states and the Uniform Commercial Code require the following types of contracts to be in writing:

Any promise by an administrator or executor of an estate to pay for damages or debts of the estate from his own property.

Any special promise by a person to pay for the debt, default or misconduct of another.

Any agreement which will not be performed within a year or which will not be completed within a lifetime.

Any contract for the sale or lease of real property.

Any contract for the sale of merchandise of substantial value.

WHAT IS THE "STATUTE OF LIMITATIONS"?

The "Statute of Limitations" is a series of enactments, pertaining particularly to the procedural part of the law, which control the time within which a lawsuit may be started.

When a person breaches a contract or commits a tort, his liability is the basis for legal action. However, this liability does not exist indefinitely. The legislatures of the states require the person affected to bring his lawsuit seeking relief within a reasonable time. This makes the defendant aware of the claim against him and enables him to assemble all available facts and witnesses to construct an adequate defense.

These periods of limitation have been determined by the type of situation involved. However, since the legislators in the various states are free to make their own determinations, the actual time within which any action must be started by the service of legal process depends upon the specific requirement within the state.

As an illustration, an action to enforce an obligation of a contract must be started in one state within 10 years from the date when the right accrues and within 5 years in another, while under the Uniform Commercial Code it is 4 years.

An action for personal injuries must be started within 3 years in one state and within 6 years in another.

If a right of action exists, it must be brought with reasonable promptness and expedition within the time specified by the state law, or that right of recovery will be lost forever.

HOW IS A CONTRACT TERMINATED?

First of all and most obviously, the obligations under a contract are terminated by performance in accordance with its terms. If it requires the payment of money, then it is discharged when payment is made. If it requires the performance of an act, the completion of that act extinguishes the obligation.

"Tender" is the term used when a party offers to perform his obligation under the contract but is prevented from doing so by the other side. When a tender is made and refused, the party making the tender is relieved of any further obligation to proceed or perform under the contract.

Illustration: Singer delivers merchandise in accordance with the terms of his contract with Petersen. When Petersen refuses to accept the merchandise, Singer is relieved of any further obligation to deliver and may consider the contract breached by Petersen.

A contract must be performed according to its terms. The courts require full performance on the part of the person who is suing to enforce it. The plaintiff suing under a contract to enforce his rights must allege and prove that he has performed all parts of the contract that he was obliged to perform. However, "substantial performance" will be found acceptable by the court, where the omission is trivial or innocent.

Illustration: Jelinko was obligated by contract to erect 1,400 signs of a specified type and size. He had erected 1,380 when he sued Roemer on the contract. The Court held this was substantial performance sufficient to entitle Jelinko to relief against Roemer.

Contracts which are conditioned upon the personal satisfaction of one of the parties are generally binding. If the contract involves personal taste, or the merchandise is specifically required to satisfy the buyer or be returned, then it must meet with the buyer's satisfaction or it is not considered sufficient performance.

If personal taste is not involved, the condition of satisfaction will not be enforced if the approval is unreasonably withheld, after the services and the labor have been performed. What is expected is a reasonable satisfaction, not based upon personal taste of the buyer but its acceptability by a reasonable person.

Illustration: Gerrad agreed to repair a boiler and install a new heating system to Zouter's satisfaction. After the work was completed, Zouter refused to pay, claiming that he was not satisfied with it. The court held that in such a situation it was not Zouter's personal satisfaction that was involved but rather the satisfaction by a reasonable person for whom the work was performed.

However, if by specific provision, the merchandise sold or the work to be performed must be approved by a designated third person, such as an engineer, or an architect, such approval is necessary before there can be any recovery.

Illustration: Contracts for the sale of real property sometimes contain a provision that the title will be considered good and marketable if acceptable to a named Title Company. If the title is not acceptable to that company, the buyer has a valid basis for refusing to accept the title.

A contract may be terminated by agreement of the parties. They may both agree to abandon their original contract, rescind its terms and release each other from its obligations.

They may both enter into a new contract which by its terms will supersede the old one and substitute new provisions. This is known as "novation."

The contract may contain a provision that it is to terminate on a certain date or upon the occurrence of a certain event. See Condition Subsequent.

Obligations under a contract may be terminated by operation of law when a contract is impossible to perform. It also may be merged or superseded in a subsequent document or proceeding.

Illustrations: The provisions of an agreement for the sale of real property are merged in the deed which is executed and delivered by the seller in full performance of the contract.

An obligation arising from the breach of a contract is merged, in the judgment of the court, when an action to enforce it has been instituted.

Any material alteration of a contract, whether made innocently or fraudulently, destroys and terminates the obligation created under it. This occurs when such alteration is made by one party without the knowledge or consent of the other.

Illustration: An alteration in the date, amount or rate of interest on a negotiable instrument will constitute a material alteration.

Bankruptcy of one of the parties will discharge an obligation created by contract when it is listed in the schedules of the bankrupt's assets and liabilities.

Finally, a breach of contract, or failure to perform in accordance with its terms, discharges the other side from his obligations, while making the person who breached responsible for any resulting loss or damage.

WHAT RELIEF IS AVAILABLE FOR A BREACH OF CONTRACT?

A party who has acquired a right of action under a contract breached by the other side is relieved of the obligation to proceed any further in his performance of the contract.

He may sue to recover damages which he sustained as a result of this breach.

He may set up the breach of contract as a defense to resist and defeat a lawsuit brought against him by the person who breached the contract.

In a situation where he can obtain no adequate remedy at law by the mere payment of money damages, he may sue in a court of equity for a decree of specific performance or an injunction.

Damages are the losses claimed and proved by a party which resulted from the failure of the other side to perform under the provisions of a contract.

"Liquidated damages" are those losses which have been assessed and agreed upon by the parties in advance of any breach. They are made a part of the contract. When a breach is

proved, the loss to be recovered has been determined and is
provided for by its terms.

The parties to the contract, with knowledge of the consequences of their transaction, are able to anticipate the losses
which may be incurred by either party in the event of a failure
to perform. However, if the amounts provided in the contract
· as liquidated damages appear out of line with the actual loss
incurred and are more in the nature of a penalty to compel performance, they will not be enforcible. The courts frown upon
penalties and will not give their judicial approval to such practices.

The injured party will be compelled to prove and will recover those damages which he actually incurred.

Illustration: A contract for the sale of a house provided that in the
event of a failure to perform on the part of the buyer, the seller
may keep the $5,000 paid at signing of the contract. The buyer
backed out. The actual loss to the seller consisted merely in
readvertising the house for sale. He resold the house at the same
price. The court held such a provision for liquidated damages as
a penalty. The seller had to return the $5,000, less any expenses
he incurred.

"Specific performance" as relief to enforce a breach of contract is available only in a court of equity. It is only available,
when the injured party has no adequate remedy at law. The
subject of the contract must be so unique, so different that it
cannot be available elsewhere. Mere money damages are not
sufficient to satisfy the damage which results from the failure
to perform. Usually, such a situation exists in contracts involving the purchase and sale of real estate. The law considers no
two parcels of real property the same, so that money damages
will not provide adequate relief to a buyer in lieu of possession
and ownership of the property he contracted to purchase. The
facts in a specific contract involving personal property may be
such as to warrant relief by a court of equity.

Illustration: Archer hired Ellsworth, an engineer and designer, to
draw plans and construct a machine in accordance with Archer's
specific and secret instructions. When the machine was completed,

Ellsworth refused to deliver it to Archer. Money damages alone are not sufficient to repay Archer for the loss of this machine.

"Injunction" is another remedy available in a court of equity where there is no adequate remedy at law. Money damages are not sufficient. The breach may require continuous litigation or successive lawsuits to give the injured party relief. An injunction will be granted to prevent a person from performing certain acts or carrying on certain activities which, under the contract, he agreed not to do.

Illustration: Ellsworth, the engineer, having completed the plans and constructed the machine, under his contract with Archer, is proceeding to build other machines to sell to Archer's competitors. A court of equity will interfere and prevent Ellsworth from doing so in violation of his contract with Archer.

Contracts for personal services can never be specifically enforced. Such enforcement by a court would violate the constitutional safeguards against peonage and forced labor. However, the courts will in certain instances prevent a person from doing work elsewhere which he should be doing in accordance with the provisions of the contract.

Illustration: Flugle, a concert singer, under contract with Salton to perform in a series of concerts, received a better offer from Englor. He breached his contract with Salton and signed with Englor for a series of concerts during the same concert season. The court could not compel Flugle to sing for Salton but they can prevent him from performing for Englor or for anyone else during the current concert season.

Summation

Points to Remember about Contracts

If you contemplate contractual negotiations, you are urged to consult your attorney. Discuss the matter with him. Make him aware of the problems peculiar to your transaction and to your line of business.

It is advisable to anticipate certain terms and conditions which will be most favorable to you. You should be well prepared before you reach the point of negotiation. Once you agree to certain terms and provisions in the contract, you will be bound by them.

However, as is usually the case, you may not have the opportunity of getting such legal aid in advance. It is of great benefit to keep some of the basic points of law fresh in your mind.

Here are some questions to ask yourself:

Are you certain that you have a definite offer?

Has the offer been withdrawn or terminated?

Can you get an option to keep the offer open?

Is there a valid and proper acceptance?

Does the contract have sufficient consideration?

Is it in writing and signed by the person you want to hold financially responsible?

Are there any parties to the contract whose obligation may be excused by law because of lack of capacity?

Is the subject matter of the contract legal?

Are all the terms of the contract clear and understood by all the parties, to eliminate any subsequent claim of mistake, fraud, misrepresentation?

Are there any special conditions in the contract which must first be performed before the contract becomes binding?

What provisions are there in the contract for damages in the event of a breach?

How may it be terminated, other than by performance?

CHAPTER 3

The Sale of Property

There are many kinds of agreements made and each of them differs in its special features. Yet as we have seen, no matter what kind of contract we deal with it must have the necessary elements discussed in the previous chapter. It is subjected to the same factors which affect its validity and its enforcement. The relief available in the event of breach is either in damages or in equity if damages are not adequate.

Of all the various kinds of contracts we meet in our everyday activities, none is as familiar, none as omnipresent, as the contract of sale.

In the introduction to Chapter 2, I mentioned some of the very commonplace contracts that we make many times daily. I used the example of the very insignificant act of buying a newspaper. That is indeed a contract of sale. The mere fact that the transaction is immediately completed and consummated does not make it any less a contract. The time of delivery or the time of payment does not affect the creation of a contract.

If we scrutinized our every daily act and movement, we would find that we buy some things for cash and others on credit. Our economy is geared to buying and to selling. It is the basis of a stable economy and to each of us it is the source of supply of our necessaries and our luxuries.

Now let us see what reasons stand behind the law which governs and controls this one very vital area of our everyday activity.

In sales, there are actually two types of contracts. The contract to sell and the contract of sale. These should be distinguished at once so that there will be no misunderstanding.

A contract to sell is a promise to transfer ownership of certain merchandise or property at some future time when it is manufactured or becomes available. One person obligates himself to sell and deliver at that time and the other to accept the property that is offered. When that delivery and acceptance occurs, ownership is transferred, "title" passes, and we have a contract of sale. Payment is to be made in accordance with the particular agreement. It may be required on delivery or at some later date.

A "sale," or contract of sale, then, is a present transfer of ownership or "title" to existing property by one person to another for a consideration called the "price."

> Illustration: The Ace China Company promises to deliver to Silas two carloads of dinnerware a month for 12 months at an agreed price and under definite terms of payment. This is a contract to sell. As each shipment of dinnerware is delivered and accepted a contract of sale is created; when it is finally paid for the contract is consummated.

Contracts of sale may be for real property or for personal property. Although the principles are the same, real property requires greater formality and greater preparation before actual delivery can be made. It will be clearer therefore to discuss contracts for the sale of real property together with the entire subject of real property.

The contract of sale is subject to the requirements of the Statute of Frauds. A sale of goods of substantial value must be in writing and signed by the party to be charged or held responsible. The amount which determines whether a contract to sell or a contract of sale must be in writing varies among the states. Some require all contracts in value of $50 or greater, while others place the minimum value at $500.

The provisions of the Statute of Frauds apply to every contract even though delivery is intended in the future, and the merchandise is not manufactured or ready for delivery. The contracts must be in writing and signed. The term "party to be charged" means that the person against whom the contract is to be enforced must have signed it. The fact that it was only signed by him and not by the other does not invalidate it. The person who signed it is responsible under its terms. Obviously then it is advisable that both parties sign a contract since no one knows which of the parties is going to be "the party to be charged."

There are certain exceptions when the contract is enforcible even though it is not in writing and not signed by "the party to be charged."

If the buyer has received and accepted all or a part of the goods under the contract or if he has made a part payment for them, an oral contract may be enforced. Acceptance here means more than mere receipt of the goods. It is receipt with the intention of becoming the owner and taking possession or dominion and control.

Illustration: Under an oral contract, Bradford bought, inspected and accepted lumber on the premises of the lumberyard. However, he did not take it away but merely allowed it to remain piled up as it was. The contract was held to fall within the Statute of Frauds. That is, it was not enforcible since it was not in writing. It did not come within the exception because there was no receipt of the lumber although there was an acceptance. Both receipt and acceptance are necessary.

Any memorandum which contains the essential terms agreed upon by the parties and signed by the party to be charged will take the contract out of the Statute of Frauds requirement, even though the memorandum does not contain all of the terms of the contract.

Illustration: Jurgenson signed a salesman's memo of his order which contained the quantity, the description, the price per item and the fact that it was cash on delivery. This was considered sufficient to be enforcible against him.

An oral agreement is removed from the provisions of the Statute of Frauds when it is fully carried out by both sides.

Goods which are to be manufactured especially for the buyer and are not suitable for sale to others in the ordinary course of the seller's business are not within the Statute of Frauds. A contract for their manufacture need not be in writing to be enforcible.

Illustration: The Blattner Bottle Co., which manufactures and sells bottles, made up a quantity of glass bulbs for Montner, under a special order. Although the order was in writing, it was not signed by him. He refused the shipment and claimed that the transaction was subject to the Statute of Frauds. He was sued on the contract and the court held that the bulbs were made especially for Montner. This was not the regular business of the Blattner Company and no writing was required. Montner was charged with the damages of breach of contract.

CONDITIONS AND WARRANTIES

A condition is a provision of the contract which must be performed. The breach of such a term results in a breach of the contract.

Illustrations: "Condition Precedent": Prentis sold a secret formula to Santis and was to deliver it before Santis was required to perform his part of the bargain. When Prentis failed to deliver, Santis was relieved of the obligation of going through with the contract. Delivery by Prentis was a condition precedent and he had breached it.

"Condition Subsequent": The contract provided that Zudak, the buyer, was to pay the freight and storage charges for the fuel oil he bought. When the oil was delivered he refused to pay the freight and thus breached the condition subsequent. The seller had performed his part by making the delivery. Zudak prevented the contract from becoming effective. He failed to comply with its terms.

A "warranty" is not a part of the contract itself. It is separate and collateral, although it may be directly related to it. It usually consists of some statement or promise made by one party which tends to induce the other to make the contract. It is more than a mere opinion. It is a positive assertion about the subject of the contract on which the other side relies.

An express warranty is an affirmative statement made by the

seller to the buyer. Since he relies on it, the buyer has a right to expect the merchandise to conform to the warranty. If it does not the buyer has the right to sue for breach of warranty and recover any loss sustained.

Illustration: Rosner sold his horse to Pulver as a "top horse, worth the money, sound, clever, well-trained and with a great record." This was a warranty; it was an assertion of several positive facts which induced Pulver to buy.

The seller may expressly deny any warranties with relation to the goods. He may state that he makes no promises as to contents or quality. If this provision is a part of the contract, the seller can not be held responsible for the failure to conform.

Illustration: Perkins sold Allsop 1,000 onion sets and the contract included the statement that there was no warranty as to their productivity. When they failed to produce onions in accordance with Allsop's anticipation he sued Perkins for a breach of warranty. He did not recover because the contract specifically eliminated all warranties.

A buyer must make claim for breach of warranty within a reasonable time after he discovers that the merchandise does not conform or he will be deemed to have waived his rights.

"Implied warranties" are imposed by operation of law on the seller to protect the buyer, even when not made expressly.

A seller is presumed by law to warrant that he owns or has the right to sell the goods. This includes an implied promise on the part of the seller that the buyer will enjoy the possession and ownership of the merchandise without any lawful claims being made against it by others.

A seller who is in possession of the goods impliedly warrants that he has title to that merchandise. He must make good to the purchaser all losses resulting from his lack of good title.

Illustration: Cantrel bought an automobile from Dunbar. It was subsequently taken by process of law as a stolen car. Cantrel recovered against Dunbar for breach of warranty of title.

In a sale "by description," the property is described in the contract. The goods delivered must comply with that description. If they do not, then the buyer may sue for a breach of warranty.

Illustration: Ersatly bought cantaloupes from Farmer described in the contract as "US No. 1" grade melons. It was found that they were defective because of rot infection. They did not meet the implied warranty as to description and quality. Ersatly was justified in rejecting the shipment.

If the buyer has an opportunity to inspect the merchandise, he is bound by the condition of the property which that inspection should have revealed.

A sale "by sample," shown to the buyer, creates an implied warranty that the bulk of the merchandise will comply with that sample in quality. The law gives the buyer a reasonable time after delivery to compare the bulk with the sample to determine compliance.

Illustration: Granote purchased 5,000 ladies' blouses in accordance with a sample. When the bulk of the shipment arrived, he inspected it. They did not conform with the sample. He so advised Hornden who claimed that having accepted the shipment he had waived inspection. The court held that Granote was entitled to a reasonable time to make his inspection.

A "Warranty of Merchantability" is implied in a sale by the sample. This applies when the purchase is made from a person who deals in merchandise covered by the contract. This is an assurance that the goods are free from any defect which would render them unmerchantable or unsalable. Further, it is a promise that such a defect is not apparent from a reasonable examination of the sample.

However, if the buyer inspects the bulk of the merchandise before buying it he waives the benefit of this warranty. By doing so, he no longer relies upon the sample but upon his own inspection.

Illustration: Ingram bought beer barrels by sample from Johansen. He went into the warehouse and personally inspected the entire shipment before the contract was made. When the barrels were defective he tried to claim a breach of warranty of sale by sample. The court held that by his inspection and subsequent acceptance, he did not rely upon the sample and was not entitled to the implied warranty covering it.

Generally, there are no warranties of quality or fitness for any particular use unless the buyer tells the seller the purpose for which he needs the merchandise. If the buyer relies upon the skill or judgment of the seller in making the purchase, then there is created an implied warranty that the goods will reasonably comply in quality or fitness with their intended purpose.

Illustration: Klaesman bought a washing machine from Louder. The machine did not wash properly. Klaesman sued Louder for breach of warranty of fitness for use. Louder's claim that he was not told the purpose of the purchase was not sustained. The Court held that a washing machine is purchased to wash clothes and failure to do that is a breach of implied warranty.

Foodstuffs purchased from a person in the business of selling similar products are covered by an implied warranty that they are fit for human consumption. It is understood that it is bought to be eaten by the buyer and his family. If there is any injury or illness to the buyer because of the defective condition of the food, an action for the breach of this implied warranty may be brought against the seller. This responsibility is based on their contractual relationship, known as "privity of contract."

A warranty, though collateral, is part of the contract of sale. Recovery for a breach of warranty therefore is dependent upon an existing contractual relationship between the parties. Recovery can only be had if there is "privity of contract" between the parties. There must be a connecting link because of the contract between the person injured and the one being held responsible for the breach of warranty.

Illustrations: Matson bought anti-freeze for his automobile from his filling station. It was defective and caused damage to his car. He sued the gas-station owner, the manufacturer and the distributor of the anti-freeze for breach of warranty of fitness for use. He recovered against the filling station but not against the distributor or the manufacturer. He had no privity of contract with them.

Both the owner and his driver of an automobile were injured

by the blowout of a tubeless tire. Both sued the manufacturer from whom the tire was bought. The owner recovered for his injury, the driver did not. There was no privity of contract between the driver and the manufacturer, hence no responsibility.

Mother bought some cake, which her son ate. He got sick. The son could not recover damages. There was no "privity" between the son and the seller.

The buyer can protect himself in his purchases by having certain express warranties included in the contract by the seller so that the product which he buys will perform in accordance with its intended purpose. He is protected by law by the implied warranties of title, sale by description, sale by sample, salability and in specific instances by the warranty of quality or fitness for purpose intended. In all other respects and situations, the principle of *caveat emptor* applies: "Let the Buyer Beware."

If he has an opportunity to inspect and examine the merchandise he is about to buy and fails to do so, or if he does examine it and fails to detect an apparent and obvious defect, he must stand the loss.

WHEN DOES "TITLE" PASS?

Usually the problems which arise in contracts of sale result from the failure of the seller to deliver or the refusal of the buyer to accept delivery. On occasion the destruction of the goods prior to delivery may be the subject of a lawsuit. In all of these instances the important question which determines the rights and obligations of the parties is, "When did title to the property or risk of loss pass?"

Title to property for our purposes here means the legal ownership with the right to possess, use or dispose.

When agreed upon by the parties, title passes at such time as is intended and expressed by them in their agreement. This creates no problem because the ownership at any particular time during the transaction can be easily determined.

When such intention is not expressed in the contract, then title passes as determined by law.

If the contract is for the sale of specific and ascertained goods, with nothing more to be done by the seller, then title and risk of loss pass to the buyer when the contract is made.

Illustration: Montrose sold 50 dozen eggs to Nieron but they still had to be candled. Fire destroyed the building and the eggs. Montrose claimed that title passed at time of sale. Court held eggs that had to be candled were not ascertained and not in a deliverable state.

The same ruling applied to the sale of potatoes of a certain grade out of an entire crop, which had to be selected and separated as to size and grade.

Unless agreed upon to the contrary, the risk of loss is upon the party who has title to the property at the time of the loss. With the transfer of title go the obligations and responsibilities of ownership.

Illustration: Opper sold his house to Porter. The contract of sale called for Opper to move the house to Porter's lot, the balance to be paid after the house was lowered on the foundation prepared for it. The house was destroyed by fire while on blocks on Porter's land but not yet on the foundation. Title did not pass; the risk of loss was still on Opper.

PASSING OF TITLE IMPLIED IN SPECIAL TYPES OF CONTRACTS, WHEN NOT EXPRESSLY PROVIDED

Goods delivered "on sale or return," indicating a present sale but with an option to return, are considered to have been transferred in ownership at the time of delivery. However, the title may be revested by the return of the merchandise within the time specified or within a reasonable time after delivery.

When goods are delivered "on trial" or "on approval," title passes when such approval is indicated by the buyer. If the buyer does not accept he must give notice of rejection within a reasonable time.

Illustration: Quateman bought electronic equipment "on trial." It was shipped to him and he gave no notice of rejection within a reasonable time after receipt. He was considered the owner with the concurrent obligation to pay for it.

C.F. (cost and freight) contracts require the seller to deliver the merchandise destined for the buyer to the carrier and pay the freight. The contract or sales price includes the cost of the merchandise and the freight. Title passes, if not otherwise agreed, when delivery to the carrier is made. The risk of loss is then on the buyer. The buyer may pay the freight if not paid by the seller. In this case the buyer will deduct the freight charges from the purchase price.

C.I.F. (cost, insurance and freight) contracts require the seller to deliver the goods to the carrier and pay the freight to the point of destination. He must then send to the buyer the invoice, an insurance policy covering the shipment, the bill of lading and a receipt to show that the freight was paid. When the seller has done all of these things, title passes.

A bill of lading is issued by a carrier to the shipper of goods.

A "straight bill" is a receipt for the goods and a contract of shipment.

A "negotiable bill" also serves as a document of ownership. The person presenting a negotiable bill at the point of destination is entitled to delivery. If the transaction requires pre-payment, then the bill is forwarded through the shipper's bank, attached to a draft. When the draft is paid, the negotiable bill of lading is delivered to the buyer who will then present it to the carrier and receive the goods.

An F.O.B. (free on board) contract or F.A.S. (free alongside ship) passes title to the buyer when the seller makes delivery at the point of destination, as named in the contract.

Illustration: When a contract called for delivery of a cargo of sugar "F.A.S. S.S. *Marimba,* Havana," title to the sugar passed when delivery was made alongside the S.S. *Marimba* in Havana. From that point on, the responsibility for shipping charges and risk of shipment is on the buyer.

Sale by a person without authority gives no better title to the buyer than the seller had. This is true even though the buyer is an innocent purchaser who paid a valuable consideration for it and had no notice of any defective title from the seller.

Illustration: A purchaser of stolen merchandise gets no better title than the thief, as against the claim of the true owner.

A seller who has voidable title to property may give good title to his purchaser. This might occur when an adult buys something from a minor or from a person who is mentally incompetent. It may also happen when the person who sold the property to the present seller has a claim of fraud, misrepresentation, duress or undue influence. Such a claim if proved would give him a right to rescind the contract. However, a seller with such voidable title has good title and passes good title to his purchaser before rescission by the original seller takes place.

Illustration: Softerman, an impostor, misrepresented his identity and persuaded Toner, a jeweler, to sell him some valuable jewelry on credit. Softerman convinced Toner that he was Softerman from Omaha, whom Toner knew by reputation as having a good credit rating. The jewelry was delivered to Softerman who immediately sold it to Ulrich and disappeared. Toner sued Ulrich to get the jewelry back. Ulrich proved that he did not know of the previous transaction and that he paid a valuable consideration for the jewelry. He also proved that the sale took place before Toner learned of the deception and avoided the sale. The sale to Ulrich was upheld as valid.

FRAUDULENT TRANSFERS OF PROPERTY

When a sale of merchandise is made for less than the market price it is considered to be in fraud of creditors if it renders the seller insolvent. A person is insolvent when the fair salable value of his assets is less than the amount he needs to pay his financial obligations. Such a fraudulent transfer may be traced, set aside and the proceeds used to satisfy the claims of the creditors.

However, a sale of goods to an innocent purchaser for a reasonable price, and without notice to him of any fraudulent intentions by the seller, is valid and protects the buyer.

BULK SALES AND TRANSFERS

Creditors' rights are further protected by Article 6 of the Uniform Commercial Code regulating bulk transfers. This controls the sale by a person in business of all or a major part of his inventory, fixtures and equipment for the protection of the rights of his unpaid creditors.

Such a transfer is ineffective against any creditor of the seller unless a list of the existing creditors has been furnished the buyer, signed and sworn to by the seller, an inventory of the property sold is prepared, notice is given to the creditors at least 10 days before the sale and the buyer retains the documents in his possession for 6 months.

The failure to comply with the requirements of the law may result in having the sale vacated and the buyer held to account to the creditors, as their trustee for the value of the stock and fixtures he bought.

RELIEF IN BREACH OF SALES CONTRACT

The seller who has not been paid for his goods is entitled to recover any loss resulting from the breach that he can prove. If title to the goods did not pass and the buyer refused to accept delivery, he is entitled to recover for a breach of contract.

Illustration: Vanner sold Worleib 10,000 flashlight batteries at 8¢ each, title to pass on delivery. Worleib refused to accept the batteries. Vanner was compelled to sell the batteries at a loss of 3¢ per battery, at the market price. He would be entitled to recover $300. His measure of damages is the difference between the contract price and the market price at the time of the breach.

If title to the merchandise did pass to the buyer and the seller has not been paid although delivery was made, the seller can sue for the contract price of the goods.

If the seller still has possession of the goods and title passed, the seller has a "lien" against it for the purchase price and the right to retain it until it is paid. A lien is a claim made by a person in possession of property against its owner. The property then becomes the security for the payment of the claim. He has the right to retain the property until the claim is paid. If it is not paid within a reasonable time, the "lienor" may foreclose on the lien under the appropriate provisions of law and sell the goods to satisfy his claim. The right of lien is based upon possession and control of the property of the debtor. When that possession is relinquished, the right of lien is lost.

If the goods have been shipped and, while it is *in transitu,* the seller learns that the buyer has become insolvent, he may stop the shipment by notifying the carrier. He may retake possession, even though title has passed, and acquire a lien against him for the contract price.

The seller may also rescind the transfer of title and resume ownership. He can only do that, however, if the contract provides for it and he gave the buyer notice of his intention to rescind. If he takes this remedy, he will not be liable to the buyer on the contract and will then be in a position to resell the goods. If he suffers any loss, he may sue the buyer for damages.

If the buyer has shown an unwillingness to perform his contractual obligations, the seller, if he has not delivered the goods, may rescind the contract on notice to the buyer.

If title passed, the buyer who has not received the merchandise in accordance with the terms of the contract may maintain an action in replevin to recover possession of the goods. Such an action, when it is authorized by the laws of the state, may even give a sheriff the right to seize the property and hold it pending the determination by the court of the rights of the parties.

The buyer may also sue in conversion, on the basis that the seller wrongfully converted the goods to his own use by withholding it from the buyer who had title. In such an action, the buyer would merely ask for and recover the money value of the property so wrongfully withheld.

If title did not pass to the buyer, he may sue the seller for

breach of contract and failure to deliver. He can thus recover
such damages as he is able to prove.

Illustration: Yahner bought 400 tons of sugar from Alder at 5¢ a
pound. Title was to pass on delivery but Alder failed to deliver.
His failure was understandable since the price of sugar went up
to 8¢ a pound. Yahner sued Alder in breach of contract and was
able to prove that he paid 8¢ a pound on the market. He was thus
entitled to recover at the rate of 3¢ a pound for 400 tons. His
measure of damages is the market price less the contract price.

REMEDIES TO THE BUYER FOR BREACH OF WARRANTY

The buyer, in claiming a breach of warranty of merchandise
delivered, may accept and keep the shipment, and set up a
claim for damages against the amount due.

He may, if he has paid for them, accept and keep the goods
and maintain an action for damages resulting from such breach
of warranty.

If title did not pass, the buyer may refuse to accept the shipment and maintain an action for damages due to the breach of
warranty.

He may rescind the contract and refuse to accept the shipment. If he received it he may return it to seller and recover
the price he paid for it.

If the buyer has a right to rescind the contract, he must do
so on notice to the seller advising him of his intention. If he
paid any money, he has a lien against the goods which he may
enforce by foreclosure and sale under the appropriate statute.

The measure of damages for a breach of warranty is the loss
which results directly and naturally from such breach in the
ordinary course of events.

In a breach of warranty of quality, the loss or damage is the
difference between the value of the goods at the time of delivery and the value they would have had if there had been
compliance with the warranty. In addition, if greater damage
is shown due to the breach than the mere difference in value,
whatever damage is proved is recoverable.

Illustration: Bolger sold Crater 300 dozen sweaters made of a

new fiber, expressly warranted as noninflammable. Crater sold 30
dozen and then found that they were highly inflammable and dangerous. He could not sell the others, had to refund the money for
29 dozen. In addition, he had a lawsuit on his hands when one
of the ultimate consumers suffered burns because of the dangerous condition of the sweaters. The measure of damages in such
a situation is not only the loss in sales of 300 dozen sweaters but
also loss of profits as well as damages which he had to pay in the
lawsuit.

SECURED CREDIT SALES

The mainstay of our economy is the credit purchase of
merchandise by the consumer and by the merchant for resale.
To encourage such credit transactions, the law gives to the
seller certain protection, in addition to his right to sue, to
secure payment of the purchase price. Obviously, if the buyer
is bankrupt, or financially distressed, suing for the money
would be futile. He is therefore given a "security interest" in
the merchandise itself, now in the possession of the buyer,
until it has been paid for.

Prior to the adoption of the Uniform Commercial Code and
the introduction of the "secured transaction," the conditional
bill of sale and the chattel mortgage were used for this
purpose. They are still so used in those states where the Uniform Commercial Code has not been adopted. They are of
course binding and effective if executed before the Code went
into effect until such time as they are satisfied by payment or
foreclosed in a court proceeding.

The "conditional sales contract" is an agreement for the sale
of merchandise which provides for delivery and possession to
the buyer but with title and ownership to be retained by the
seller until complete payment is made. The contract usually
provides for installment payments at regular intervals until the
entire purchase price is paid. Until that final payment is made
title does not pass to the buyer.

Illustration: Dahler purchased a printing press which was installed in his plant. He bought it under a conditional sales contract and was to pay it off by regular monthly payments until the entire price was paid. Title to it passed to him when the full amount was paid.

The "chattel mortgage" is a legal document which actually transfers title and ownership of described personal property by the owner to another until a designated event occurs. Since the chattel mortgage is used to secure the payment of money, this transfer of ownership is the means by which the security is accomplished. When the money has been paid, the title reverts to the original owner. Although the chattel mortgage is generally used to secure the payment of a loan, it has also been used in a credit sale transaction. The buyer, now becoming the owner, executes a chattel mortgage to the seller, giving him title until the purchase price has been paid.

Illustration: Landman bought a pizza-making machine, on credit. Under the purchase he becomes the owner of the machine. However, to secure payment of the purchase price, he executes a chattel mortgage to the seller, which is effective until full payment is made.

Both the conditional sales contract and the chattel mortgage are required to be filed as notice to the public that the seller retains a claim for payment of the purchase price. In each case, the filing protects the transaction for a period of three years with the right to file a renewal. When payment is made, the debtor is entitled to a written statement from the creditor that the debt was satisfied, so that the record of the transaction can be canceled.

Under the Uniform Commercial Code, the "credit sale" protects the seller of consumer goods, the wholesaler or manufacturer, who sells merchandise to the retailer for resale (inventory goods) and the seller of machinery and other items necessary for the operation of a business or profession (called equipment).

The "secured credit sale" is an ordinary sale of consumer

goods, "inventory" or "equipment" on credit, in which, by agreement between the buyer and the seller, title, possession and risk of loss pass to the buyer, but the seller retains a security interest in the merchandise (called "collateral") until payment is made.

This agreement, called the "security agreement," must be in writing and signed by the buyer, and it should describe the collateral so that it may be easily identified.

Because of the greater number of consumer credit sales, the Code makes a distinction in procedure between consumer goods sales and inventory and equipment credit sales. No filing of any kind is necessary in a consumer credit sale.

With the signing of the security agreement and the delivery of the goods, the credit seller acquires a "perfected security interest" until payment is made. As long as the buyer makes payment according to the contract of sale (the security agreement), he has all the rights of ownership that the cash buyer has. However, in the event of a default by the buyer, the seller may be entitled to the entire purchase price and may, peacefully or by legal proceedings, retake and resell the collateral, applying the proceeds to the amount due and holding the buyer responsible for the balance.

In the sale of inventory goods or equipment, the security agreement creates the security interest in favor of the seller. However, in order to protect the seller, a "financing statement" must be executed and filed. This document gives the seller a "perfected security interest" in the collateral and gives notice to the public that payment is still due. It must be signed by both the debtor and the creditor (buyer and seller). It must include their addresses and must indicate the type and description of the collateral.

Here again, as long as the buyer complies with the terms of sale, he has all the rights of ownership. In the case of inventory goods, of course, he has the full right to sell to his customers, without any restriction. The purchasers of merchandise from the buyer in the ordinary course of his business obtain good title.

The filing of the financing statement gives notice to all that full payment has not been made and that the seller retains a claim. Creditors of the buyer are put on notice that the described merchandise on his premises does not belong to him until payment has been made.

This protection may extend to a period of five years and if not paid may again be extended for another five years by the filing of a "continuation statement" by the secured party. When final payment is made, the secured party must give a "termination statement" to the debtor indicating that no further claim of security interest is made, and the financing statement will then be canceled on the record.

In certain installment transactions, the seller may require the purchaser to execute a "confession of judgment" or an "assignment of salary" to assure payment of the purchase price. However, under the consumer protection laws, the use of confessions of judgment, garnishments and assignments of salary is restricted unless there are provisions for a hearing.

The confession of judgment is a formal statement signed by the buyer which empowers the seller to enter a judgment against him without a trial if he defaults in his installment payments. This is prohibited in many states because it is too drastic.

An assignment of salary is a statement which authorizes the employer of the buyer to deduct a definite sum of money from his salary to be paid to the seller.

A "garnishment" or "garnishee" of salary is a direction of the court after judgment which requires the employer to deduct a percentage of the judgment debtor's salary to satisfy the judgment.

Summation

Points to Remember about Sales Contracts

As mentioned in the beginning of this chapter, most of our everyday transactions are based upon the contract of sale. If you are going to make an important purchase, there are some things which you should keep in mind.

The contract of sale must have all of the elements of a contract.

If the purchase involves a substantial sum of money, it would be wise to get a written contract or statement to include the terms of sale and the signature of the seller.

Any promise, condition or warranty which is made orally should be included in the written statement.

Here are some questions to ask yourself:

When will title pass? Will you be responsible for it before you get delivery? Who is responsible if it is damaged or destroyed before you get it?

Is the seller authorized to sell it? Is it his regular business to sell this merchandise? Will this sale in any way affect the rights of his creditors?

If the purchase is a credit transaction, have you signed a security agreement? What does it provide? Do you also have to sign a financing statement? Are there also promissory notes to be paid? Do the papers include a confession of judgment or an assignment of wages? Do you understand your obligations under the agreement or should you obtain the advice of a lawyer?

CHAPTER 4

Bailments

Most of our everyday activities involve either the purchase of necessary articles or the hiring of necessary services.

We take a bus to work, a taxi or the subway. These are the services of a common carrier.

We take our car to the garage to be repaired, our coat to the cleaners. These are just a few of the many contracts we make daily for services so important to our way of living.

What obligations and responsibilities do such contracts create? What rights and what benefits?

Services are easily divided into two categories. First there are those services rendered by an individual who is specially skilled because of his knowledge and experience in his particular field, either artistic or professional in nature. This would include accountants, painters, architects, lawyers, doctors. These services are personal in nature.

The other group consists of services relating to property, real or personal. The person rendering them is also skilled and experienced in his field. We hire him because of our confidence in his ability. However, the type of work that he does is not considered so personal that another could not accomplish it with the same results. A plumber who knows his business will do the required job without introducing any personal trait to distinguish it from the work of another competent plumber.

Since the greater portion of our experiences concerns services related to property, this subject of bailments will receive most of our attention.

BAILMENTS OR SERVICES RELATED TO PROPERTY

A bailment is a contract which provides for the delivery of personal property by the owner for some specific purpose. Only possession is transferred; title and ownership are retained by the owner. When the purpose is fulfilled, the property is returned. The owner is called the bailor; the person who receives the property is called the bailee.

Illustration: Leder is a farmer and Reimer is a dealer in chickens. Reimer furnished 5,500 chicks to Leder under an agreement which provided that Leder was to furnish labor and equipment to care for the chicks while Reimer would furnish the feed that was necessary. This is called a "broiler feeder agreement." Title is retained by Reimer and only possession is given to Leder. This is a bailment. Leder is to raise the chicks at an agreed price per head, and Reimer can regain possession at any time he wants them.

Bailments fall into three classes: those for the sole benefit of the bailor; for the sole benefit of the bailee; and those for the benefit of both, also called a "mutual benefit bailment."

FOR THE SOLE BENEFIT OF THE BAILOR

In an agreement of bailment for the sole benefit of the bailor, the bailee is to get no compensation for the services he is to render to the property of the bailor. He merely undertakes to do it as a courtesy to the bailor. As such there is no consideration as far as he is concerned. Since a contract is not enforcible unless there is a mutual consideration, the bailee cannot be held to his promise. However, once he has obtained possession of the property, his acceptance of it constitutes sufficient consideration to require him to perform.

Illustration: Eldridge offered to repair his neighbor's lawn mower. As a promise, it could not be enforced. However, once Eldridge took the mower and started working on it, he was responsible as a gratuitous bailee. This obligation requires him to discharge his promise in a proper manner.

A gratuitous bailee is liable for gross negligence in the fulfillment of his contract. Gross negligence may be defined as a complete failure to exercise care over the property of the bailor. It is the use of such slight care as to create a belief that there was complete indifference to the safety of the bailor's property.

Illustration: Zander offered to take care of Aiken's money. He promised to keep it in a safe place and return it on request. Zander, when he received the money, put it in his mattress, together with his own. The money was stolen by another boarder in the house. When Aiken claimed his money, Zander contended that he had it in a safe place and that it was stolen together with his own. The court found that Zander had not discharged his duty properly, had not kept the money in a safe place and had indeed been grossly negligent. The degree of care or carelessness that a person takes with his own property is not related to the care he is to give to the property of another.

Property left in the care of a bailee must not be used by him unless such use is necessary for its proper care and maintenance. Any unauthorized use may create a liability in conversion for its loss or destruction.

Illustration: Young left his horse with Beral for two weeks while he went on a trip. Beral promised to feed and exercise the horse regularly. Instead of riding him, Beral practiced jumping and impaled the horse on a fence. Beral was held responsible for the loss of the horse due to his unauthorized use.

TERMINATION

This type of bailment is terminated at will by either party. However, if the bailee agreed to keep the property for a designated time or to transport it to a designated place, he must complete his requirement or he will be responsible for the damages resulting when he fails.

Illustration: Williams offered to take Caswell's wheat to the mill when he took his own. He loaded Caswell's first and then loaded his own on the truck. When he found the load too great, he unloaded some of Caswell's and left it at his farm. The wheat was destroyed and did not reach the mill. Williams was held responsible for the portion of Caswell's wheat which was destroyed.

FOR THE SOLE BENEFIT OF THE BAILEE

Here the bailor delivers his property to be used and returned by the bailee without expectation of payment.

Here, too, a mere promise is not enforcible. It is only when the bailor surrenders possession and the bailee accepts that the contract becomes effective.

Illustration: Stone promises to let his neighbor, Arkright, use his power mower to cut his grass. This promise cannot be enforced. A bailment results when Stone permits Arkright to take the mower.

The use of the property is limited strictly to the purpose for which it is given. Any departure from such agreed use is at the peril of the bailee.

In an old case, one of the judges in his decision stated, "If a man lends his horse to another to go westward and the bailee goes northward, the bailee will be chargeable if any accident happens on the northward journey, because he used the horse contrary to the trust that it was lent to him under."

Illustration: Volper loaned his motor-powered lawn mower to his next-door neighbor, Dean. When Dean finished using it, instead of returning it, he let Ullan use it. When it was damaged by Ullan, Dean was responsible to Volper.

The bailee is required to exercise great care in using and keeping the property loaned to him. He is responsible for any loss caused by negligence on his part. The absence of the most scrupulous caution is regarded as neglect by the bailee. He will only be absolved of liability for loss, by damage or theft, if he can show that it was not due to any negligence on his part.

Unless it was created for a definite period, this type of bailment also is terminable at will by either party.

Return of the property must be made to the bailor in accordance with the terms of the agreement. Failure to do so may result in legal liability.

Illustration: Torrens borrowed a car from Evers, his garageman.

When he returned, Evers was out, so he left the car, with the key in the ignition, parked in front of the garage. The car was stolen and wrecked. Torrens was held responsible for the loss because he had failed to return the car to Evers.

WHAT IS A MUTUAL BENEFIT BAILMENT?

A mutual benefit bailment is an agreement by which one of the parties is given possession of another's property for a definite and specific purpose to their mutual advantage. This may occur when the bailee hires the property of the bailor or when the bailor delivers his property to the bailee for some specified services.

Illustration: Taylor rents a paint sprayer and compressor to paint the body of his truck, or he takes his truck in to an automobile body shop to have it done for him. In the first case, he is responsible for the sprayer; in the second, the repair shop is responsible to him for his truck. In the first case he is a bailee of the paint sprayer; in the second a bailor of the truck.

Responsibility is based on the lack of care and diligence in safeguarding the property of the bailor.

The bailee is responsible if he is negligent. He is required to use ordinary care, such care which a reasonable and prudent man would use in the care of his property. If he fails to exercise that duty and the property left in his care and custody is lost, stolen or damaged, he is responsible.

Any loss which results in spite of his care and diligence is beyond his control and relieves him of liability.

Illustration: Solon leaves a fur coat with Foran to be repaired. When Solon returns for the coat, he is told by Foran that there had been a fire and the coat was destroyed. The fire was not caused by Foran's negligence. Foran is relieved of responsibility for the loss of the coat.

The liability of a bailee is based on his negligence, his failure to use ordinary care with regard to the bailor's property. Unless such negligence is proved in court, the bailee cannot be held responsible for the loss of the property involved in the bailment

This risk is sometimes covered by the bailee in special insurance to make good any loss of merchandise in his care, whether due to his negligence or not. However, such insurance coverage is not compulsory. If it is not carried by the bailee it may result in a loss to the bailor, if no negligence is proved.

Illustration: Russell owned a Siamese cat which won several blue ribbons in pet shows. He agreed to exhibit the cat in one show and left it in the care of the person in charge. There was a fire and the cat was destroyed. Russell could not recover for the loss because the fire was not caused by the negligence of the exhibitor, who was not covered by fire insurance, for such a risk.

On the other hand, if the property, when used by the bailee, causes him injury, the bailor is responsible. The bailor should have kept it in good repair or he should have warned the bailee that it was inherently dangerous.

Illustration: Glidden rented a truck from Quinlan's garage to cart lumber. The brakes on the truck were defective. When Glidden took the truck from the garage, he had an accident because the brakes failed to hold. He was injured. He was allowed to recover from Quinlan for his injury. He proved that Quinlan knew that the brakes were bad and had failed to advise him.

A PLEDGE OR PAWN

A pledge is a bailment of personal property and documents given to secure the payment of a loan. This type of agreement is generally accompanied by a power to sell the property in the event that the loan is not repaid. The pledgor is the bailor who gives his property to secure the repayment of money he borrowed. The pledgee is the bailee who receives possession but no ownership. However, he may have the right to sell on the pledgor's default. As long as he retains possession of the property, the pledgee has a lien against it to the extent of his claim. When the pledgor fails to pay, he has the right to foreclose on the lien and satisfy his claim by a sale of the property.

The owner-pledgor is entitled to notice of the time and place of sale, unless their agreement dispenses with such notice. If the owner is not given such notice, then he may hold the pledgee liable for conversion in selling his property without authority. The notice gives the owner-pledgor an opportunity to redeem on payment of the amount due.

A loan made by a pawnbroker based on some security left with him is a pledge, governed by these principles. Usually the ticket given by the pawnbroker as a receipt of the transaction is also the contract which states the terms of the bailment agreement. The provisions on that ticket are binding on both sides and will protect the pawnbroker when he complies with them. A pawn then is a pledge of personal property only.

The pledgee is only responsible for the breach of his duty of ordinary and reasonable care of the property in his possession. If he is negligent in fulfilling this obligation he will be held responsible.

A storekeeper may be held responsible for the property of his customers if this property must be removed in order that his merchandise may be tried on.

Illustration: Mrs. Panner came to the Gem Store to buy a coat. She removed her coat and, seeing that there was no place designated for it, left it on the counter while she tried on several coats. When she made the purchase and looked for her coat, it was gone. The court held that it was the duty of the store to arrange for the care of clothing which necessarily must be removed. A failure to furnish such a service makes the store liable for loss.

Restaurants are usually not responsible for coats or hats, even if left on hooks especially provided for that purpose. There is no liability even though the waiter helps you to remove your coat and hangs it up on such a hanger. If the restaurant provides checking facilities then the extent of its liability is usually printed on the check given as a receipt. Ordinarily there is some limit of liability as to the value of a checked article, unless the person checking it makes specific mention of the value to the checkroom attendant.

A BAILMENT FOR HIRE

This is an agreement by which the bailor rents out his property to be used by the bailee for a specific purpose on payment of a rental fee. The bailor either expressly or by implication warrants that the article hired is suitable for the use contemplated. He is liable for any breach of this warranty and for any loss or injury which flows directly from such failure on his part.

Illustration: Otis rented a tractor to Hammer. There was a defect in the mechanism which caused the tractor to go out of control. It caused damage to Hammer's crop and Hammer was hurt in trying to stop it. Hammer recovered from Otis for his losses, because Otis failed to reveal the mechanical defect which caused damage.

Unless there is some other agreement, the bailee is responsible for repairs which are necessary during the usual care and use of the article or machine. The bailor is responsible for extraordinary and special repairs.

Illustration: A person who rents an automobile would be responsible for gas and oil as well as the repair of a flat tire, while the bailor is responsible for such special repairs as defective brakes, battery, fuel pump and similar unusual breakdowns.

Another type of bailment is the transfer of property to the bailee for services to be rendered to it.

These services may be repair, alteration or manufacture, as furnished by a jeweler in the repair of a watch, by a miller in grinding wheat into flour or by the manufacture of cloth into dresses.

They may be the hiring of custodial services as furnished by a warehouse for the storage of property or may consist of transportation of merchandise by a private or by a common carrier.

Generally the principles are the same as those which apply to the hiring of property.

In those instances where the services rendered to the property of the bailor change the form or the appearance of the property, some question may arise whether there is a bailment or a sale relationship involved. This can only be inferred from the provisions of the contract and the intention of the parties. If title to the property is retained and mere possession is transferred, the transaction can only be a bailment. A sale requires a transfer of title and ownership as well as possession.

Illustration: Norton delivered milk to Ingraham to be converted into butter and cheese. A fire destroyed Ingraham's plant without his negligence. Norton claimed the price of the milk on the ground that there was a sale. Ingraham claimed it was a bailment and, since the loss occurred without his fault, he was not responsible. Court agreed with Ingraham. Ownership was still with Norton, who controlled the sale of the butter and the cheese. The loss was not due to Ingraham's negligence and was not his liability.

HIRING OF CUSTODY

A hiring of custody arises when a person engages another to take care of his property for him. The bailee may perform no service on the property except to store it.

A warehouseman is one who engages in the business of storing the goods and merchandise of others for compensation. He is liable for any loss which results from his failure to exercise reasonable care. He is not an insurer of the goods he stores. In the absence of any other agreement, he is only responsible for the results of his own negligence.

Illustration: Manston, a warehouseman, stored frozen waffles owned by Jergen near frozen seafood. This resulted in the contamination of the waffles, which acquired an odor of fish. Manston was responsible for such damage because the proper storing of the merchandise was his primary obligation.

An agistor is a person who takes custody of cattle, horses and other livestock to pasture and feed on his lands at an agreed price. He is not an insurer of their safety. If the animals are stolen, lost, injured or killed through his carelessness, he is liable. If he uses reasonable care, keeps the animals in proper enclosures and free from dangerous conditions, he is relieved of any liability resulting from their loss.

A livery stable keeper is one who keeps a building where horses may be boarded and cared for. As a bailee, his liability is the same as that of an agistor. The same responsibility is incurred by persons who board dogs, cats and other household pets.

A garage or parking lot owner is subject to the same responsibility. He must take reasonable care to see that his patrons' cars are not damaged. He is liable for any damage caused by his negligence or that of his employees, even though his receipt states that he is relieved of all liability.

A wharfinger is a person who keeps a warehouse at or near a pier for the storage of goods. His liability is that of a bailee and in the same capacity as a warehouseman.

Safe-deposit companies with facilities available for their depositors to store their valuables are bailees offering custodial services. They have similar responsibilities and obligations for losses which result from the negligence of their employees.

HIRING OF TRANSPORTATION

The transportation of merchandise may be accomplished by a common or contract carrier. Although the services rendered are the same, their obligations and responsibilities to their customers differ because their status in the community differs. The contract carrier transports merchandise pursuant to a contract he makes with the shipper both as to rates and conditions of carriage. He does not hold himself out to the public as available for service. His is a strictly contractual relationship. He has the right to select the customers for whom he will carry merchandise and those by whom he wants to be employed. His responsibility is the same as that of a bailee for hire. He is only liable for loss which results from his negligence, his failure to use reasonable care in the performance of his task. The term private carrier may also be used for a contract carrier or to designate a company under contract to carry goods for one customer only.

The common carrier of goods undertakes to transport personal property for compensation at the request of all who choose to employ him. He advertises himself as willing and able to carry goods and merchandise for anyone who will hire him and pay the standard fee for his services.

Illustration: The railroad, as a common carrier of merchandise, cannot refuse to transport the property of any person who offers to use its services, provided that he complies with the requirements established by it.

A common carrier of freight may refuse to carry merchandise which he does not ordinarily transport; merchandise which is not properly packed; articles which are dangerous; goods which are perishable, if he does not have the immediate means of transportation or facilities for proper refrigeration; or if due to the unusual press of business he does not have the facilities.

He may also refuse to carry goods which are not presented in accordance with the reasonable rules, established for the operation of a carrier's business. He may demand the payment of freight charges in advance and may refuse to carry if such payment is refused.

The liability of the common carrier of freight begins when the goods, properly packed and ready for immediate shipment, are accepted by him. This is true even though he may be compelled to store the freight because he does not have the facilities for immediate shipment.

The common carrier is an insurer of the goods which he accepts to transport. His obligation is not merely limited to loss caused by the negligence of his employees, but extends to all cause of loss with the following exceptions:

This responsibility is excused if the loss is due to an act of God, a public enemy, the inherent nature of the goods, the act of the shipper or the act of a public authority.

The term "act of God" includes any cause which is completely without any intervention of a human agency.

Illustrations: Fire caused by lightning.
     Snowstorm delaying or derailing trains.
     Floods, tornadoes.

Loss by act of public enemy does not also include loss due to mobs, rioters, robbers and strikes.

Loss due to inherent nature of the goods is, in the absence of the carrier's negligence, not his responsibility.

Illustrations: Deterioration of perishable food.
     The bursting of a barrel of molasses due to fermentation.

Loss due to negligence of the shipper includes improper packing, not apparent or known to the carrier, and a fraudulent concealment as to the nature of the goods.

Illustration: Chinaware not packed with some cushioning material would constitute an act of negligence of the shipper. If properly packed and there is breakage, the loss is to be borne by the carrier.

Loss due to act of public authority relieves the carrier of responsibility. If an authorized government agency, with proper legal process, requests the shipment, the carrier is relieved of liability for such loss. The shipper may have some claim against the right of the agency to take the property, but the carrier is not implicated.

Illustration: This situation would arise if cattle or produce are impounded by authorities regulating interstate commerce in preventing the spread of some animal or plant disease from one area to another.

LIABILITY FOR DELAY IN DELIVERY

A common carrier is liable for any unnecessary delay in making delivery. In addition to being an insurer, he also undertakes to deliver within a reasonable time. Failure to do so is only excusable if caused by act of God or by strikes.

However, if the contract expressly calls for delivery by the carrier within a specified time, he is bound to deliver within that time, regardless of delay, or be responsible for any loss that is incurred.

A common carrier may limit his liability by contract if the limitation is not unreasonable. The bill of lading, which is the contract between the shipper and the carrier, may include a provision to limit the carrier's liability. If there is no fraud or other imposition, it controls the rights of the parties and is enforcible. The failure on the part of the shipper to read the contents of the bill of lading does not excuse him from his obligation under its provisions.

Steamship tickets have been held to be binding on the passengers as limiting the liability of the company, whether read by them or not.

On the other hand, similar limitations of liability on a baggage check have not been held to be binding unless the attention of the shipper has been specifically called to the contents of the baggage check.

A common carrier may set a certain rate for carrying certain merchandise, based on its weight. It sets the valuation of such goods at an established figure which is the maximum limit of its liability for loss. If the shipper gives the carrier the actual value of the goods shipped and there is an additional transportation charge, the full value of the goods is recoverable in the event of loss.

A carrier is entitled to know the nature and the value of the goods entrusted to his care for shipment. If the shipper conceals the true nature or value of the property to avoid the payment of increased freight charges, the carrier may be discharged from liability resulting even from his negligence.

Illustration: If the perishable or fragile nature of goods is concealed to avoid a higher charge, the carrier will be discharged from liability when such merchandise is damaged.

When a shipment reaches its destination, the carrier will either deliver it to the consignee or give him notice to pick it up, depending upon the carrier's facilities. If the consignee, the person for whom the shipment is intended, fails to pick it up, the carrier's liability as an insurer of the shipment terminates. His obligation from that point and thereafter is only that of a warehouseman. He is liable only for damage caused by his own negligence, his failure to use reasonable care.

As a warehouseman he is entitled to an additional charge for the storage services he renders. When the shipment consists of a full freight car and the failure to unload causes a delay in getting the car on its way, the charge is called demurrage. This term originated and is used in maritime transactions as charges assessed when a vessel is delayed from sailing.

THE COMMON CARRIER OF PASSENGERS

As with the transportation of freight, there are private and public carriers of passengers. The distinction here is the same. The private carrier operates on the basis of an express contract made with the person whom he desires to transport. Since he does not offer his services to the public, he has the right to choose the person with whom he will do business. His liability too is based on the terms of his contract.

The common carrier of passengers offers his services to the public. He may not discriminate. He must carry all persons who request his services. He may only refuse to transport any person whose behavior is objectionable or who does not have the money to pay. The rates for his services are standard for all. These principles of law may, however, be subject to local restrictive regulations.

A person is a passenger of the carrier when he enters the premises, intending to use the carrier's services. If his purpose is to use the carrier, he is entitled to all of the rights and privileges of a passenger, even though he has not as yet purchased a ticket.

The carrier has the duty to exercise reasonable care to provide his passengers with safe transportation to their point of destination. His responsibility is based only on his negligence in maintaining and operating his business. He is not an insurer of the safety of his passengers but is responsible for the acts of his agents and employees, if they cause damage or injury to his passengers. He is not responsible for any delay which causes his passengers to arrive late at their point of destination.

BAGGAGE

The common carrier is obligated to carry a certain amount of baggage for eacn passenger. Baggage is considered as those articles which are necessary for the personal comfort of the passenger during the trip.

The carrier is not responsible for the hand baggage carried by the passengers while in transit. This is within the control of the passenger and remains his own responsibility. The heavier baggage becomes the carrier's responsibility when it is checked with him. He is charged with the liability of an insurer for any loss or damage sustained while it is in his custody.

He may however limit this responsibility as to amount and contents by express contract with the passenger. These limitations are usually printed on the baggage check which is issued by him. These provisions, however, may not be binding unless it is shown that the attention of the passenger was called to them.

Common carriers are generally controlled and supervised in each state by an agency of government which sets rules for their business operation.

Those common carriers which operate across state lines in interstate commerce are controlled by the Interstate Commerce Commission. Certain rules and regulations must be complied with if the carrier is to continue in operation.

The baggage check issued by the common carrier to the passenger is a receipt for the baggage. It also is the contract between them setting forth the provisions of obligation and responsibility.

Usually the baggage check provides that the carrier is responsible to the passenger for the full value of the baggage lost with a stated maximum limit of liability for each check. Railroads have set that maximum at $150. If the value of the baggage is greater, it is the responsibility of the passenger to declare it to the carrier. An additional charge will then be made to cover the greater risk assumed by the carrier. If this is done, and the baggage is lost, the full value may then be recovered.

The carrier may limit the type of contents to be included and shipped as baggage. Among other things, jewelry is not accepted as an item of baggage and liability for its safety will not be assumed by the carrier.

THE RESPONSIBILITY OF A HOTEL OR INNKEEPER

An inn, hotel or motel is a public house, open to all and engaged in the business of furnishing transient living accommodations to all who request them and comply with its reasonable regulations on payment of reasonable compensation for such services which are rendered.

Under this definition, rooming houses and apartment hotels are not in this category since their tenants are not transient guests but reside on a more or less permanent basis. However, it appears that the distinction is not as to the type of accommodations offered but rather the specific relationship between the host and the guest. Thus a hotel for transients may have some permanent weekly or monthly tenants and a rooming house may also take in overnight guests.

An innkeeper holds himself out to the public as being ready to receive and accommodate all travelers and transient guests who are not objectionable and who are able and willing to pay the price of the accommodations. The responsibility of the host for the safety of the guest and his property will depend upon their relationship. The host owes a greater responsibility to a transient guest.

A traveler who requests accommodation at a hotel immediately becomes a guest, even before registering or entering the building.

Illustration: When a traveler delivers a baggage check to a porter of a hotel and subsequently registers, his status as a guest relates back to the time he gave the check to the porter. The liability of the hotel for that baggage is then established.

The relationship of host and guest terminates when the guest pays his bill and has a reasonable opportunity to remove his baggage. If he pays his bill but leaves his baggage to be called for later, his status as a guest terminates when he leaves the premises. The relationship as to the baggage thereafter is that of bailor and bailee.

The duties of a hotelkeeper are of a public nature. He must serve the public. He is bound to receive all reputable transient persons who are able to pay for their accommodations, provided that he has room for them. This duty, as are all obligations of an innkeeper, is imposed by law and not by contract. It relates back to the time when inns were the only places for stopover on a long journey, the only places where rest, food and lodging were available to the traveler on the road. For that reason the duty of the hotelkeeper includes an obligation to receive the goods, baggage, horses and attendants of the traveler.

His responsibility for the safety of his guests is limited to the exercise of reasonable care. He is not an insurer. A guest, when occupying a room, is entitled to protection and the proprietor is liable for any intrusion of such occupancy, unless it is necessary for the orderly management of the hotel.

Illustration: The manager of a hotel broke into the room of one
of the guests, wrongly accused her of immoral conduct and removed her and her baggage from her room and the hotel. The
act of the manager was proven to be wrongful and the owner was
held liable for the act of his employee.

The law as to the liability of the hotelkeeper in the care and
safety of a guest's property is not uniform in all states. The
greater number hold the innkeeper to his common-law liability
as an insurer of the goods and baggage of his guest against all
loss. He is only excused when the loss is due to an act of God,
a public enemy or the negligence of the guest himself. This
harsh rule originated during the days when travel was dangerous and the traveler needed all the protection he could get from
bandits, brigands, road agents and unscrupulous and dishonest
innkeepers. The burden was then placed upon the innkeeper to
furnish the traveler with protection as well as hospitality.

Goods lost or destroyed by any cause other than those excused, even though not due to the fault of the hotelkeeper, are
still his responsibility. This responsibility extends not only to
money and baggage but to all property brought to the inn by
the guest.

The hotelkeeper's responsibility may be limited by contract
and in some states it is limited by special statute. If the limitation of liability is by contract, it must appear that the guest was
made aware of it and consented to it.

Illustration: The provisions limiting the hotel's liability were
printed on the hotel's register. There was proof that this was
called to the guest's attention, that he read them and signed the
register. The court held that a valid contract was created limiting
the hotel's liability. The hotel was not responsible for any loss in
excess of the agreed limitation.

By statute, a hotelkeeper's liability is limited by allowing him
to provide a safe in the office for the safekeeping of money,
jewels and ornaments. A notice must be prominently posted
calling attention to the safe and its availability. If the hotel
complies with the requirements of the statute, its liability for
all money, jewels and ornaments deposited in the safe by the
guest is limited to a definite sum, usually $500 per guest. If the

value deposited by the guest is greater than the amount established by the statute, it must be so declared by the guest at time of deposit. A special agreement is then made to take the greater value into consideration. Failure by the guest to deposit such valuables in the safe relieves the hotelkeeper of all liability in event of loss.

If the safe is burglarized and there has been no negligence or responsibility on the part of the hotelkeeper, he is responsible as an insurer for the value of such items on deposit in the safe, not to exceed the maximum established by law. If the negligence of the hotelkeeper can be established, then the statutory limitation does not cover him and he is liable for the full value of the loss.

Illustration: Jewels left in the safe, not declared in value, were proved to be worth $5,000. Proof was also introduced that the safe was kept open and unlocked throughout the day. The bandits, aware of this, merely walked in and took the contents of the safe, including these jewels, at gunpoint. The Court held the hotelkeeper negligent not covered by the statutory limitation and responsible for the full value of the stolen jewels.

Articles of value worn as a part of ordinary attire are not considered jewelry and if stolen from the room are the responsibility of the hotel in their full value.

Illustration: A gold watch, a pigskin bag, a silver comb-and-brush set were stolen from the room of a guest in a hotel. He asked the hotel to reimburse him for the loss. The hotel claimed that they were jewelry and should have been deposited or there was no liability. The Court held that such items are not jewelry but items necessary for a person's everyday use. The innkeeper was held responsible as an insurer for their safety or return.

If a guest has not had an opportunity to put his money or his jewelry in the safe and it is stolen, the hotel becomes liable under its common-law liability as an insurer of the property of its guests. The same principle applies when jewelry and money are removed from the hotel safe to be packed with the baggage before checking out.

Illustration: A guest preparing to leave the hotel took his jewelry from the safe, packed it in his trunk. He gave instructions to have the trunk and his baggage brought down while he went down to the office to check out. When the trunk was not brought down with the rest of his baggage he went up to the room and found that it had been broken open and the jewelry stolen. The hotel was held responsible for his loss, under its common-law responsibility.

HOTELKEEPER'S LIEN

A hotel has a lien on all property brought in by the guest for all charges and obligations owed by him. When a guest has run up a large bill for services rendered to him, the hotel may retain any property on the premises belonging to the guest as security for the payment of its claim. Some states have enacted legislation which extends to boarding houses and lodging houses the right of a lien against property of a guest who has not paid for his accommodations.

Illustration: A guest who ran up a bill of $100 and was not financially able to pay it had a portable television set in his possession which was not fully paid for. The claim of the hotel to the set as security was held superior to the claim of the person who sold the set.

THE CONTRACT FOR PERSONAL SERVICES

The contract of personal services is made with one individual in preference to another because in his field, his performance is distinctive and different. For this reason, contracts for personal services are not assignable. The patient chooses his doctor carefully and wants that doctor and no other. There can be no substitution without the consent of the patient. The same principle applies in all such services.

The contract is dependent for its performance upon the continued good health of the person whose services are required. If illness or death make it impossible to perform, the contractual liability is discharged. However, if the partial services rendered were in substantial completion of the contract or were of some value in themselves, then a claim for the reasonable value of those services would be maintainable by the estate of the deceased artist or professional.

Illustrations: If an artist, hired to do a portrait, dies before the picture is recognizably completed, there can be no recovery for the work he did. However, if the painting is substantially completed and merely requires some technical finishing, it may be considered as substantial performance.

An architect and engineer was hired to draw plans and build a factory. If he completed the plans to the satisfaction of his client and died before he completed the building, estate could recover for the value of the services in the drawing of the plans.

Contracts for personal services do not have to be in writing to be enforcible. However, if the services to be rendered will not be completed or performed within a year or a lifetime, then such a transaction falls within the requirements of the Statute of Frauds. Since an oral agreement will be difficult to prove after a year or after one of the participants is dead, a writing is required. To prevent any lapse of memory, fraud or perjury, such a contract must be in writing and signed by the person who is to be held responsible.

Summation

Points to Remember about Bailments

Of all the contracts we make in the course of our day-to-day living, the number of contracts we make creating a bailment relationship is second only to our contracts of purchase and sale.

We take our clothes to the cleaners, our car to the garage for repairs, our shirts to the laundry. We borrow our neighbor's lawn mower or she borrows our vacuum cleaner.

For that reason it is a good idea to keep some of the following in mind:

What is a bailment for the benefit of the bailor?

What is one for the benefit of the bailee?

What is a mutual benefit bailment?

What are their responsibilities and obligations?

What is the responsibility of a common carrier? For freight, for passengers, for baggage?

What is the obligation of a hotelkeeper for the safety and welfare of his guests, for their property, their jewels?

What is a contract for personal services?

CHAPTER 5

Insurance

INTRODUCTION

The frequency of our contacts with insurance—agents, brokers or companies—depends upon the nature of our employment and our financial condition.

However, most families do have insurance of some sort. There is life insurance, usually taken out on the life of the breadwinner of the family to assure some sort of financial security in the event of his death. Then, for those families who own an automobile, there is the liability policy in the event of accident, comprehensive damage coverage and coverage for damage due to collision. Anyone who owns a house is confronted with fire insurance, extended coverage, public liability insurance and title insurance.

This list is intended to make you realize that you do deal in insurance and you should know something about it.

We often hear the slogan, "Read your insurance policy." I agree with that statement wholeheartedly. However, I suggest that you *know* more about your policy before you buy it and before you receive it.

I can assure you that the type of policy your agent or your broker sells you will be the one you will receive from the company. Agents and brokers are men of honesty and integrity. They have to be licensed to carry on their work and they will certainly not jeopardize that license. However, they will try to sell you such insurance as they believe you need. As a purchaser, you should know the type of merchandise you are buying, whether it is insurance or any other product. You should also make certain that you need the insurance you buy, that the insurance coverage you are getting is the coverage you want.

I plan to discuss some of the more common types of insurance which people ordinarily require. I will not give you any insurance advice; that is the broker's job. I shall point out those factors which are important to legally protect your interests.

WHAT IS INSURANCE?

Insurance is a contract relationship entered into by the insurer and the insured.

Such a contract, more commonly called the policy, usually provides that, on payment of the premium, the insurer promises to indemnify and reimburse the insured for any loss incurred by him from certain stated causes. The policy, as a contract, must contain all of the elements necessary for a valid contract. The mutual considerations here are the premium paid by the insured and the promise of coverage made by the insurance company.

The causes of damage as provided for in the policy are also called "risks." The company specifically stipulates those risks which are covered under the particular policy. Any risk that is not stated is not included. This fact is of particular importance because we often find that after a loss has occurred due to a risk not included in the policy, we have a tendency to be bitter about the omission. In insurance, as in every other transaction, we get only what we pay for. There are no extras, no bonuses. Each coverage you want included has an additional premium to take care of the greater risk assumed by the company.

In life insurance, the person whose life is insured is generally called the "insured." The person named in the policy to benefit from the death of that person is called the "beneficiary."

In property insurance, the person whose property is insured may be called the "assured." He is in most instances also the beneficiary, since he will recover for the loss to his property.

The term "loss" is used to designate the damage or injury sustained as a result of the risk covered by the policy.

ADDITIONAL INGREDIENTS OF AN INSURANCE CONTRACT

A policy must have a subject which is to be insured. It may be the life of a designated person; it may be a house; it may be a ship or the cargo aboard ship.

The risk or peril against which the life or property is to be insured must be specified in the policy: the death of a person, injury resulting from accidental means, fire damage to property, loss due to the peril of the sea, liability which results from the negligent operation and control of an automobile.

The amount for which the policy covers the loss must be indicated. This is in effect an agreed value on the basis of which the loss and the recovery of that loss will be determined.

The term or period during which the policy will be in effect must be stated.

INSURABLE INTEREST

Since a contract of insurance is one of indemnity, it will reimburse or make good any loss incurred. It must be founded on some interest or ownership right which is affected by the loss.

In property insurance, this insurable interest must be present in the assured, both at the time when the policy is taken out and at the time of loss. If there is no insurable interest present in the assured on both occasions, there can be no recovery. If there is no property right, there is no insurable interest and hence no right to insurance.

Any interest or part ownership in property is sufficient to create an insurable interest, provided that it is accurately described in the policy.

A bailee has an insurable interest in the property left in his possession. In the event of loss, he may be held responsible. He thus has the right to insure the property, although he does not own it.

In life insurance, the subject of insurable interest is not involved when the insured takes out a policy on his own life and makes someone else the beneficiary. The beneficiary in such a situation does not need to have any insurable interest in the life of the insured. He may be a complete stranger.

The question of insurable interest arises when a person takes out insurance on the life of another and makes himself the beneficiary. He must then have an insurable interest in the life of the insured. This relationship must exist at the time when the policy is issued. It need not exist at any time thereafter to make the policy enforcible.

FACTORS AFFECTING THE INSURANCE CONTRACT

The Statute of Frauds does not affect a contract of insurance. Contracts have been held enforcible though oral. However, since there are many terms and conditions involved in the policy, it is usually in writing.

Concealment and failure to disclose facts which are material to the risk affect the contract's enforcibility. If the facts which were concealed would have influenced the insurer against issuing the policy, then the company may avoid its obligation under it. This applies particularly in life and health policies where information as to the health of the insured is not available to the company. It also applies in marine insurance where there is no opportunity for the company to inspect and the insurer must rely upon the statements of the insured.

In fire and other types of property insurance, when the property is located in a designated place, the company has the opportunity of making its own inspection and determination. It cannot then be claimed that the company relied upon the statements of the insured. However, any unusual peril which enhances the risk must be disclosed.

Illustration: Noonan withheld the information, in an application for fire insurance, that one of the buildings had recently been fired by an incendiary. This was considered by the court as concealment of a fact which would have affected the acceptance of coverage by the company. The contract was voidable at the option of the company.

In life insurance, it must appear that the insured knew that the facts he withheld from the company were material. It must be shown that the concealment was made with intent to have the insurance company accept coverage. The company may under such circumstances avoid the policy.

However, if the application puts the company on notice that further investigation may reveal vital information concerning the applicant's health and the company fails to make such investigation, the policy when issued cannot be challenged.

As distinguished from concealment, the misrepresentation of a material fact, regardless of intent, whether it is innocent or fraudulent, renders the policy voidable. Concealment, to be effective, must have a fraudulent intent, which must be proved by the company. Misrepresentation, on the other hand, is a positive act of the applicant, so that his intention is of no consequence. When the misrepresentation of a material fact is relied upon by the company, it becomes actionable. The policy may then be avoided by the company.

A waiver is the voluntary abandonment of a right by a person with knowledge of its existence.

Illustration: The policy of the Seaside Insurance Co. covered the ship *Tremaine*. It specified that such coverage would terminate if it carried incendiary materials. The company was notified that the *Tremaine* carried such incendiary material. It nevertheless accepted the premiums on the policy. By such acceptance, it waived its right to cancel the insurance coverage.

Estoppel is an attitude on the part of a person or a company which is contrary and inconsistent with his or its subsequent action. In insurance, it is an act on the part of the company which is inconsistent with its previous attitude.

Illustration: Buxton, an agent for the Fulton Fire Insurance Co., knew that Hiller's house was unoccupied, yet he issued fire insurance to cover it. After there was a fire loss, the company attempted to avoid liability on the ground that the house was unoccupied. The company was estopped from asserting such a claim since the policy was issued with full knowledge of the situation. Hiller recovered for the fire damage he sustained.

WHO MAY BE AN INSURER?

Insurance companies are regulated, controlled and licensed by the state in which they do business. Companies organized in one state must obtain permission to do business in other states.

The failure of a company to have such a license makes its contracts of insurance void and unenforcible. It is important therefore to make certain that the company which is to issue your policy is either a domestic corporation, one organized in your state, or one licensed to do business in your state.

There are some insurance companies which do business through the mails. They solicit your insurance through a circular, request you to fill out their application and mail it back to them. The contract is consummated in the home state of the company. It is a valid and enforcible contract. However, to enforce it you will be required to sue in the company's home state, or in the federal court. You will not be able to obtain jurisdiction of that corporation in your home state, since it is not authorized to do business there.

WHO MAY BE INSURED?

Any person who is legally capable of making a contract, who has an insurable interest in the subject which he wants protected, may enter into a contract of insurance.

A corporation may insure the life of its officers or key employees and be the beneficiary, since it has an insurable interest.

A partnership may be the beneficiary in the contracts of insurance covering the lives of the partners.

Insurance is not considered a necessity, and therefore a contract made by an infant is voidable if it is not completed. If it is executed, he must pay the premium for the coverage he received. The infant is the only one who has the right to avoid the contract. The insurer can only avoid if the infant induced the contract by means of fraud or misrepresentation.

A person who is mentally incompetent may enter into a valid contract of insurance, unless he has been judicially declared insane. Adjudication subsequent to the issuance of the policy does not affect it, as long as the premiums are paid when they fall due.

Insurance is a personal contract dependent upon the character and acceptability of the assured to the insurer. When property is sold, the new owner is not automatically covered by the existing insurance. He must get new coverage or have the insurance company approve an assignment of the policy to him.

In the absence of a valid assignment with the consent of the company, the buyer of property is a stranger to the insurance contract and does not have any claim of recovery against it.

Illustration: Reiner bought Handel's car. He did not obtain a policy to cover his liability in the event of accident. Handel notified the company of the sale and his policy was terminated. When Reiner had an accident, he was unpleasantly surprised to find that he was not insured.

A claim against an insurance company after a loss is sustained is assignable. The claim may be transferred to a third person for collection. This does not require the consent of the company. It is not the policy which is assigned. It is the matured claim which is transferred. Such a claim, in legal parlance, is called a "chose in action."

Insurance agents are persons in the employ of an insurance company authorized to represent it in its dealings with brokers and applicants for insurance. Commitments made by its agent bind the company and are enforcible against it.

Adjusters are special agents of the company either employed by it or hired for the specific purpose of investigating and reporting a loss under the policy. They may be empowered to negotiate a settlement of the claim but are not empowered to bind the company. If an adjustment is reached, they report it to the company. It must be approved by the company to be binding. Their primary job is to obtain the information as to the loss from the insured. They make their own estimate of loss from their experience and submit their recommendations to the company.

Insurance brokers are not agents of the company. They do not represent it. They are usually independent businessmen who solicit insurance from their clients and then place it with a company of their choice. Legally, brokers are considered the agents of the insured.

Illustration: Parner returned his policy of collision insurance to Gebhart, his broker, with instructions to have it canceled. Gebhart wrote the word "canceled" across the policy and mailed it to the company on Friday. On Sunday, Parner had an accident and demolished his car. The "canceled" policy reached the office of the company on Monday morning. Parner claimed that he was covered under the policy. The company claimed that it had been canceled by Gebhart. The court agreed with Parner, held that Gebhart was not the agent of the company and directed recovery for Parner under the policy.

The insurance broker owes his client a duty of reasonable care, skill and judgment in obtaining a valid contract of insurance with a solvent company that is authorized to transact business in the state. He can be held liable by his client for failing in this duty. Brokers are licensed by the state and their activities are regulated so that they will act in the best interests of their clients, the applicants for insurance.

Illustration: Brown, an insurance broker, was requested to obtain fire insurance coverage of property located in Pennsylvania and owned by a New York resident. The company which issued the insurance was not licensed in either state. After a fire loss, the company refused to pay the claim on the ground that the policy was unenforcible. The broker was sued by the client and was held liable for the loss which resulted from the fire.

FIRE INSURANCE

The binder is a memorandum or note which is issued by the company or its agent, pending the issuance and delivery of the permanent fire insurance policy. It is as binding on the company as actual coverage. Any loss sustained during the period when it is in effect is recoverable. The binder becomes ineffectual when the policy is issued or when the company notifies the applicant that it refuses to accept the risk.

In burglary insurance, the company issues a binder to cover the property while the company investigates the applicant and its anticipated liability. The binder is then superseded by a "corrected" policy when the company agrees to accept the risk. However, if the company refuses to accept the risk, it must give the applicant written notice of cancellation.

Illustration: Colter applied for burglary insurance through his broker, who placed it with an agent of the company. After investigating, the company decided against accepting the risk. While the broker was in the office of the company, the agent told him orally that the company had decided not to accept the risk. A loss occurred. Colter claimed under the policy. The company contended that it had refused to accept the risk and had notified the broker. The court held that the company was bound. Oral notice of cancellation is not sufficient when written notice is required.

THE STANDARD FIRE INSURANCE POLICY

Most states have adopted the New York standard fire insurance policy consisting of 165 enumerated lines which set forth standard provisions. The result of this is to make uniform the terms and conditions which are included in a contract of fire insurance. All contracts of fire insurance issued in these states must contain the provisions of the standard form.

Illustration: Dinsmore applied to an agent of an insurance company for fire coverage on one of his buildings. The agent agreed orally that the contract was to be in effect for one year from that date at a designated premium. He promised to issue the policy within a few days. Three days after the oral agreement was made, a fire loss occurred. The company claimed that there was no contract since all of the terms and provisions were not included in the oral agreement. The court held in favor of Dinsmore, the assured. The terms of the insurance contract were those of the standard insurance policy which the law required to be used in all fire insurance coverage.

The standard fire insurance policy provides that the insured becomes liable for the premiums when the policy is delivered to him. The face amount of the policy is the maximum for which the company can become liable in the event of loss. All policies become effective at noon of the date of issue and expire at noon of the date of expiration.

Illustration: Payne had a fire loss in one of his buildings. The fire started about 15 minutes before noon. The policy terminated at noon of that day. The policy was still in effect when the fire started, and the loss was covered.

The policy covers property directly destroyed by fire. It also covers damage from smoke and from water used to extinguish the fire. The term "fire" is defined in its usual ordinary meaning. It must have glow and luminosity.

Illustration: The slow oxidation or "burning" of wool in fleece which was submerged during a flood, without any visible light or flame, was not considered a "fire."

To be covered, it is not necessary that the property be burned or even charred. If the damage is the result of a fire which is direct and hostile and the articles are blistered or smoked or water-soaked, it is considered a "fire loss."

Illustration: When a fire occurred on the third floor of a building and the water used to put the fire out poured down to the floor below and caused damage, it was covered.

The fire must be the direct cause of the damage.

Illustration: A clerk in a store went down to the basement to bring up some merchandise. In lighting his way with a match, he exploded gasoline fumes which had accumulated there. The building collapsed as a result of the explosion. The owner of the building claimed damage under his fire insurance policy. The court dismissed his complaint on the ground that the damage was caused by the explosion and not by the fire.

The fire must be hostile and out of control of its usual and ordinary use.

Illustrations: The match used by the clerk in the last illustration was not a hostile fire, even though it caused the fumes to explode.

Dunne, a servant of the assured, made a fire in the furnace but used a highly inflammable material, not intended for such use.

As a result, the heat became so intense that it cracked the chimney, charred the furniture in the building and burned the wallpaper. This fire was hostile.

Sheenan put his jewelry in a velvet bag and hid it in his stove for safekeeping. His wife, unaware of this, lit the stove. The jewelry was destroyed. This was not a hostile fire and there was no recovery.

Description of the property covered by the policy is usually brief and informal, but it must be comprehensive because only such property as is described in the policy will be covered in the event of a fire loss. The policy covers those items specifically mentioned and those which can be reasonably included.

Illustrations: Cahil applied for fire insurance to cover cement in bags located in a brick building 150 feet from the corner of a certain intersection. Actually, the cement was located in a wooden building, located 200 feet from that corner. The court held there was no coverage. A correct description in the application and in the policy is necessary before coverage and liability will apply.

A description of a "steam sawmill" can reasonably include the machinery and fixtures which are part of the steam sawmill.

Property which is moved from a designated and described location will not be covered unless notice of the transfer is given to the company and the change is noted.

The standard fire insurance policy contains a printed list of stipulations and conditions on the back which are a part of the contract. Each line is numbered and all policies contain the same information, as required by state law.

Fraud, misrepresentation and concealment by the insured of any material fact concerning the subject of insurance or after loss will render the policy void.

Illustration: A policy covering an automobile for fire at a face value of $1,800 was obtained by Elgin. When a fire destroyed the car, the proof at the trial brought to light the fact that the invoice on the car had been altered from $800 to $1,800. The court found against Elgin and for the insurance company on the ground that fraud as to this material fact had rendered the policy void.

The standard policy specifically excludes business accounts, bills, currency, deeds, notes or securities. Even if these items are included in the policy they will not be covered.

Illustration: An insured cannot include bonds in his fire insurance policy coverage.

Bullion, manuscripts, mechanical drawings, dies and patents can be insured only if these items are specifically included in the contract.

Illustration: A policy covering machinery to manufacture tinware includes dies to form the tinware. The dies are necessary for the proper use of the machinery.

The fire policy excludes loss caused by invasion riot, insurrection and civil war. These are specifically included under an extended coverage policy.

Unless stated otherwise in the policy, the insured must be the sole owner. The policy is void if the ownership of the property is shared with someone else and this fact is not disclosed to the company.

Illustration: A policy issued to a husband can be considered void by the insurer when the property is actually owned by both husband and wife.

Any extra hazard to the property within the knowledge or control of the assured will suspend coverage of the policy. The presence of prohibited and dangerous articles on the property will increase the hazard.

Illustrations: The presence of a still or quantities of alcohol have been held to increase the hazard.

·Fireworks brought into an insured building on July 3rd to be used the next day caused a fire that night which destroyed the building. The presence of the fireworks, as prohibited articles, prevented recovery under the policy.

When an insured building is left unoccupied for more than 60 consecutive days, coverage is suspended, unless notice is given to the insurer.

Illustration: A house used as a summer home but not labeled as such in the policy was held to be vacant under the terms of the policy. The furniture was left in the building and the caretaker slept in another building on the premises, yet coverage under the policy was suspended.

However, when an agent with knowledge that a building was unoccupied issued a policy to cover it, the company was estopped from claiming a forfeiture under the vacancy clause.

Cancellation by the insured becomes effective at once on receipt of notice by the insurer. The company will then refund the unused portion of the premium based on "short term" rates for the period when the policy was in effect.

Cancellation by the company becomes effective 5 days after written notice is given to the insured. Refunds here are made on a pro-rated basis for the period when the policy was in effect.

Illustration: A policy in effect for one fourth of its term if cancelled by the company would entitle the assured to a refund of three fourths of the premium paid. If canceled by the insured under the same circumstances, the refund would be less. The charge for the used portion is greater under the "short term" rate.

In the event of loss, certain requirements must be followed to recover under the policy. The assured must give immediate notice of loss to the company. He must furnish a list of the items lost or damaged and the amount claimed for each. Failure to comply with these conditions of the fire insurance policy may defeat the claim for recovery.

Coinsurance is a provision in the policy which does not come into play until there is a fire loss. The policy requires the insured to be covered for a designated minimum amount. This amount bears a definite relation to the value of the property. The policy may require coverage of 80 per cent or 90 per cent of the value of the property. When there is a partial fire loss, the company will pay the full amount of the loss only if the amount of insurance coverage is as required by the policy.

If the insurance is less, the company will pay that proportion of the loss which the existing policy bears to the coverage required. The insured will be a coinsurer for the balance because he will bear that portion of the loss.

Illustration: In a policy which contained an 80% coinsurance clause, there was a fire loss of $4,000. The value of the entire property was $10,000. The amount of insurance on the house was $6,000. The owner should have had $8,000 worth of insurance (80% of $10,000). The company paid only $3,000 and the owner was a coinsurer for $1,000 of the $4,000 damage he sustained.

The formula to be used in an 80 per cent coinsurance clause computation is as follows:

$$\text{The amount of insurance to be carried on the house} = 80\% \text{ of its value}$$

$$\frac{\text{The existing insurance}}{\text{The required insurance}} \times \frac{\text{The amount of the}}{\text{partial fire loss}} = \frac{\text{The amount of recovery}}{}$$

Using the figures of the illustration in the case above we have:

$$\frac{\$6,000}{80\% \text{ of } \$10,000} \times \$4,000 = \$3,000, \text{ the amount of recovery from the company.}$$

The coinsurance provision does not apply when there is a total loss of the insured property. Then the company will pay the face amount of the policy. If the coverage was less than the value of the property, the loss is borne by the assured, not because of the coinsurance clause but because he was underinsured.

The amount of insurance a person should have either on his house or on the furniture and personal property in the home depends, of course, upon their market or replacement value. The insurance broker is the most competent person to advise you on such matters.

Extended coverage policy is a separate and distinct agreement. It is usually made a part of the fire policy by attaching an extended coverage endorsement on payment of an additional premium. This coverage includes the perils of windstorm, hail, explosion, riot, civil commotion, aircraft, vehicles and smoke.

The policy does not cover loss by frost or cold weather, ice, snowstorm, tidal wave, high water or overflow, whether driven by wind or not. It does not include damage to the interior unless there was damage to the roof or to the wall by the direct action of the wind or hail.

Explosions are included if they are from gases or unconsumed fuel, but not from bursting steam boilers or pipes.

Damage caused by aircraft or vehicles is included only if the loss is directly due to actual physical contact. Smoke damage must be due to faulty operation of cooking or heating units.

LIFE INSURANCE

A contract of life insurance provides that, in consideration of the premium to be paid, the insurer promises to pay the beneficiary an agreed sum upon the death of the person whose life is to be insured.

A life insurance contract is not one of indemnity. It is not intended to reimburse for the loss sustained. It is, rather, one of investment. The company becomes liable to the beneficiary for the face amount upon the death of the insured, regardless of financial status or financial loss. The full face amount of the policy is paid whether the death occurs after the payment of the first premium or the 20th, as long as it is still effective.

There are several types of life insurance policies. These depend upon the number of premiums to be paid and the type of coverage desired.

The "whole" life policy is to be in effect during the entire lifetime of the insured. The same level premium is paid each year. In the event of his death, the face amount of the policy is paid to the named beneficiary. At any time during the life of the policy, the insured may turn it in for the cash surrender value listed in a schedule which is a part of every policy. The insured also has the option of turning his policy in for paid-up insurance in a lesser amount. A paid-up policy gives him insurance coverage with no further premiums to pay. He may also convert the policy to term insurance in the same amount as his original policy. The term policy will continue in effect until the cash fund has been exhausted in paying the premiums on a term basis. Although he will not have to pay any more premiums during the effective period of his policy, the cash fund will be consumed.

The 20-payment life policy requires that premiums be paid for 20 years while the coverage continues for the life of the insured. At the death of the insured, while the policy is in effect, the company will pay the named beneficiary the face amount of the policy.

The 30-payment life policy calls for 30 annual premium payments. The premiums on this policy are less than on the 20-payment, since they extend for a longer period, but the policy and the benefits are esssentially the same.

The term policy is written for a definite term or period, generally varying from 5 to 10 years. The premiums are paid annually at a level rate for the term of the policy, based upon the age of the insured. At the end of the term, the policy may be renewed. The premium to be paid will be based on the age of the insured at renewal. In the event of death during the term, the company will pay the face amount of the policy. Premium rates are lowest because this is considered pure insurance and there is no cash surrender value fund to be accumulated.

An endowment policy is a contract written for a definite term of years; 10, 20 or 30. The premiums are level and based upon the age of the individual at the time of application. At the death of the insured during the term of the policy, the face amount will be paid to the beneficiary. If the insured survives the term stated in the policy, he receives the full amount and the policy is terminated. If he wants to continue his insurance coverage, he may then make other arrangements with the company.

An annuity is another form of insurance. It is an agreement with an insurance company which provides that the company will pay the annuant or his beneficiary a fixed sum of money for life or for a definite number of years, if he will pay an agreed lump sum at the time the annuity arrangement is made.

Some states require all life insurance policies to contain

standard provisions relating to insurable interest, reservation to change beneficiary, incontestability clause, suicide, nonpayment of premiums, nonforfeiture and options. These terms are explained in greater detail below.

A person who applies for insurance as a beneficiary on the life of another must have an insurable interest in that person at the time when the policy is issued.

A husband and wife have an insurable interest in each other during their married life. If they are divorced, that insurable interest is terminated. However, if the husband is to pay alimony to the wife, she has been considered to have an insurable interest in his life to that extent. She may take out a policy of insurance as beneficiary on his life and pay the premiums herself.

A partnership has an insurable interest in the lives of all of its partners. A company has an insurable interest in the lives of its executives and technical personnel. A policy taken by the company, with itself as the beneficiary, is valid and enforcible.

The mere existence of a family relationship does not create an insurable interest, except if that relationship is that of parent and child. In some cases it has even been held that an adult child living independently and away from home does not have an insurable interest in his parents.

In those states which have "poor laws," which require a person to support his indigent relatives, the poor person may have an insurable interest in the life of his benefactor who is obligated to support him. If grandparents or grandchildren have legal obligations to support each other, then there is an insurable interest.

A beneficiary named in a policy does not need to have an insurable interest if the policy is taken out by the insured himself.

A beneficiary in a life insurance policy gets a vested interest in that policy, and the insured does not have the right to change that beneficiary without his consent. In order that the insured may retain the right to change his beneficiary at will, he must reserve this right in the policy.

If such reservation has not been made in the policy and the

beneficiary dies before the insured, the proceeds of the policy at the death of the insured are payable to the estate of the beneficiary. The estate of the insured has no right to the proceeds of that policy.

An insured may name his estate as the beneficiary of his life insurance and then distribute the proceeds of his entire estate, including the policy, by will.

Generally, the proceeds of a policy paid to a widow are not available to the creditors of the deceased husband. However, if it is shown that the premiums paid on the policy were from funds drawn in fraud of creditors, then the amount of such premiums may be recovered from the insurance proceeds and applied to the claims of the creditors.

The incontestability clause is a provision in the policy to the effect that after two years, misrepresentations made in the application shall not be the basis for avoiding liability by the company.

The contestable period gives the company an opportunity to investigate the information given by the insured in his application. It may then assert its claim to terminate the policy because of any fraud or misrepresentation discovered.

Illustration: Anders, the insured, fell from the roof of a building and was killed. An autopsy revealed that he had virulent tuberculosis. Since his death occurred within the 2-year contestable period, the company sued to rescind the policy and avoid payment. There was no proof of fraud, nor was there any proof that Anders knew he had this disease. The company, during its physical examination, had sufficient opportunity to discover the existence of this disease. The court refused to permit the company to avoid liability and directed that the face amount of the policy be paid.

The following defenses to paying on the policy are not limited by the incontestability clause and may be interposed at any time to defeat recovery:

The company may, at any time, prove that it did not consent to the contract. Since consent is a basic and essential element in the formation of a contract, if there is no consent, there is no contract.

Illustration: The person who applied for insurance had someone else take the physical examination in his place. This fraud prevented consent. There was no enforcible contract since it was fraudulently induced.

The company may always show that the policy was issued to the beneficiary and that he had no insurable interest, at the time it was issued, in the life of the insured.

Liability under the policy will be avoided if the company can prove that the cause of death was due to a risk not covered by the policy.

Suicide is the willful taking of one's own life. The policy may specifically exclude coverage of death by suicide. However, in the absence of a definite provision, some courts have construed that suicide is governed by the uncontestability clause. If the suicide occurs within the 2-year period, the policy may be terminated by the company. After the 2-year period, death by suicide is covered under the policy.

If the suicide is unintentional or results from an insane impulse, it is not considered as suicide but as accidental death.

Illustration: Buhler, the insured, was under a delusion that he was being chased by imaginary "little people." He was drowned in a well while hiding there to escape from them. This was considered as accidental death by the court and not suicide.

However, although under an emotional strain, if the insured knew the consequences of his actions, his act of self-destruction would be held to be suicide.

Illustration: Kohlman, in an effort to frighten his wife, drank carbolic acid and died. The court held his death as suicide.

Failure to pay premiums when they fall due terminates the company's obligation under the policy. This applies at any time during the life of the policy. It is not subject to the incontestability clause.

Generally, there is a 30-day grace period available to the insured to give him an opportunity to pay the premium without affecting his rights under the policy. After the expiration of such grace period, the policy may be considered lapsed by the company.

To protect the insured, some states have passed legislation which requires the insurance company to send a notice advising him when the premium is due. Unless such a notice has been sent, the company cannot consider the policy lapsed until one year after the failure to pay the premium.

If the insurance company accepts the payment of premium after the grace period, it cannot consider the policy lapsed.

Illustration: Poler failed to pay his annual premium which was due May 1st, although he had received a notice. He sent his check in on June 10th. The company accepted it and credited him with the payment. He died on June 20th. The company was unsuccessful in its claim that the policy had lapsed. The court held that the company, by accepting payment, had waived its right to lapse the policy.

No policy of life insurance, except term insurance, can be forfeited because of nonpayment of premium.

Since only a portion of the premiums of a life policy pay for the cost of the insurance, the balance is accumulated as a savings fund. This is the basis of the cash surrender value of the policy. The premiums of a term policy pay only for the cost of insurance and have no savings or cash surrender fund.

It is this fund which prevents the policy from being forfeited. The insured is entitled to the benefits of his cash surrender value, despite his failure to pay the premium.

The policy gives him certain options.

He can take the cash surrender value of his policy and thus terminate his insurance.

He may take a fully paid-up policy of insurance for an amount less than the original.

He has the right to make a loan from his cash fund, pay the premium for the year and continue to be insured.

Finally, he has the choice of converting his policy to extended term. He thus gets a term life insurance policy in the same amount as the original policy. However, the term of such a policy depends upon the money available in the fund, since the annual premiums will be deducted from it.

When a person applies for life insurance, he is usually given an application to be filled out. This contains a series of questions concerning the state of his health. If the applicant conceals or misrepresents his true condition to obtain the insurance, the courts have determined that these misrepresentations are subject to the incontestability clause. If at any time within 2 years the company discovers any fraud or misrepresentation, it has the right to rescind the contract and avoid its liability.

One of the questions applies to previous applications for insurance which were refused. The answer gives notice to the company that the applicant may be unacceptable.

A statement by an applicant that his health is good must be substantially true, to his knowledge. He may be suffering from an incurable disease, yet may know nothing about it. He cannot be presumed to know the nature of his illness or its possible effect upon his life, until he has been so advised by a doctor.

His answer to the question concerning medical treatment within the past 5 years must be true and must not conceal or withhold information. However, the question must be direct and specific, since his failure to answer correctly may be due to poor memory.

Illustration: Ajax Insurance Company sues to rescind a policy of insurance with Terry on the ground of fraud within the 2-year period. In his answer on the application, Terry stated that he had not been treated by a doctor in the last 5 years for any serious illness. The policy contained a disability clause so that if he became disabled he would be entitled to certain weekly payments. After the policy was issued, Terry was involved in an automobile accident. He claimed that as a result of the accident he suffered a heart attack and was unable to work. Investigation by the company revealed 12 treatments within the past 5 years with medication used in cases of heart disease. The court declared the misrepresentation was material and affected the risk. The policy was rescinded within the contestable period.

The applicant for insurance, when he misrepresents his age, may do so because of his vanity. More often, however, he does it to pay a lower premium. Premiums are based on the age of the applicant in accordance with an established rate schedule. Recognizing this tendency, the legislatures of several states have provided that when age is misrepresented it should not be a basis for avoiding the policy. The insurance coverage is reduced to that amount which the paid premium will buy at the true age of the insured.

Illustration: The application showed Duncan's age to be 30 while his true age was 35. The premium he paid for age 30 was $30 per $1,000 of insurance. At age 35, the rate was $40 per $1,000. The amount paid in premiums would only purchase $750 of insurance at Duncan's true age. The adjusted insurance coverage is $750 face value instead of $1,000.

The occupation of the insured is of material importance to the company. This may determine the hazard involved in the risk to the company. To avoid its obligation, the company must show that the statement as to occupation is false.

Illustration: Kingsley stated that he was a chauffeur for a private employer. He failed to declare that in his spare time he was also a stock-car racing driver. This occupation is, of course, much more hazardous.

Double indemnity is a separate and collateral agreement to the policy of life insurance. It provides that on payment of an additional premium, usually comparatively nominal, the insurer will pay double the face amount of the policy if the death of the insured results solely from external, violent and accidental means.

Illustration: Rodney, insured under a policy which contained a clause of double indemnity, slipped on the icy pavement, struck his head. He died of a brain hemorrhage as a result of the fall. The company paid twice the face value of the policy under the double indemnity clause.

ACCIDENT INSURANCE

An accident may here be defined as the unforeseen happening of an event without the aid or design of the person who is injured. The injury is unintended, unexpected and unusual.

Illustration: An infection resulting from a tooth extraction is an accident. The extraction was intended, but the result, the infection, was not intended or expected.

Accident policies do not insure against accident as such. They cover death or injury resulting from violent, external and accidental means. The risk covered is similar to that of the double indemnity indorsement in a life insurance policy.

Illustrations: Sunstroke caused by overexposure to sun while performing a necessary task was considered "accidental means."

Sunstroke caused by playing golf, in the noonday sun, was not considered "accidental means."

When the insured choked while eating a piece of steak, his death was caused by "accidental means."

A clause in an accident policy which excludes coverage for suicide committed "while sane or insane," is binding. There can be no recovery for suicide no matter how or when the suicide was committed. Contrary to the decisions in life insurance policies, such a restrictive clause continues during the term of the accident policy. There is no incontestability clause here to affect it.

Illustration: There was no recovery for death caused by an accidental drinking of a strychnine mixture by the insured.

HEALTH INSURANCE

The policy of health insurance may be written separately or it may be in conjunction with accident provisions. The terms of such a policy must be read carefully to determine the coverage. Generally, it provides that in consideration of an agreed premium, based upon the age of the insured, the insurer agrees to pay to the insured a stipulated sum weekly during any illness or temporary disability, as specifically listed. It may also cover the cost of hospitalization under certain specified terms. Further, it may cover the loss of life or any limb of the insured, according to an agreed schedule. Finally, it may contain a commitment to pay certain weekly payments in the event of total or partial disability for the lifetime of the insured.

Total disability has been construed by the courts to be the inability of the insured to be employed in the same or a reasonably similar occupation.

The policy may designate a certain period of time as a criterion of permanency. If the disability continues for that designated period it shall be considered permanent.

Illustration: Tyler, a tailor, suffered the amputation of his right hand. Such a loss was considered a permanent disability for which he was paid at the rate stipulated in the policy.

There are thus two provisions for disability payments: those which are temporary pending recuperation and those which are permanent and continue for life.

AUTOMOBILE INSURANCE

Insurance relating to automobiles can be divided into three categories: liability, collision and comprehensive coverage. They are each separate and distinct. They cover different risks.

Liability insurance covers the owner of a specified motor vehicle for any liability which results from his negligent operation of the vehicle. The policy is usually written for one year with a stated limit of liability by the company. Such a policy usually includes a promise to defend any lawsuit brought against the insured on any claim for damages relating to the operation of the motor vehicle.

Of course, the responsibility of the company to defend and to pay damages is dependent upon the receipt of timely notice of any incident which may involve liability. This is intended to give the insurer ample opportunity to investigate and prepare to defend the claim. Further, the insured is obligated to appear and testify in any action, so that the insurer will be able to defend it.

Some states have now enacted legislation which requires that all automobiles driven on the roads within the state be insured. Failure to comply may result in severe penalty, including the suspension of the driver's license and the automobile registration.

Out-of-state drivers using the highways, who cause property

damage or personal injury may be sued within the state by service of the summons and complaint upon the Secretary of State. By law, the use of the state highways by the out-of-state driver gives the state jurisdiction over him.

No Fault Insurance is a modification of the method for recovery for injury sustained from a motor vehicle. To facilitate compensation of medical expenses and loss of earnings, the car owner or his passengers will recover from his insurance company. If the injury is severe or permanent, or if the injured person is not a passenger, recovery is based on negligence and is the responsibility of the wrong-doer and his insurance company.

Collision insurance is a contract to reimburse the owner of a motor vehicle for any damage to his car resulting from a collision with another object.

To reduce the mounting premiums on this type of insurance, especially in congested cities, companies have been offering $50 and $100 deductible policies. This means that, for a lower premium, the insured must bear the burden of all accidents below $50. If his loss is greater than $50, the company will pay him the amount of his damage less $50.

This policy also provides that, upon payment to the insured, the company will be subrogated, or substituted, to his rights against the person who was responsible. If the company, after investigation, determines that the other person was responsible, it will have the right to proceed against him to recover the loss, in the name of the insured.

If the company recovers the damages from the other party, the insured will then receive the $50 originally deducted by the company.

Comprehensive insurance coverage protects the owner of a motor vehicle against damage resulting to his own car from certain stated risks such as falling objects, fire, theft, explosion, earthquake, vandalism, riot and civil commotion. It includes breakage of glass but specifically excludes collision or upset.

Illustration: Zane, the insured, drove his car into a deep puddle of water, lost control and went into a ditch. He claimed that his damage was caused by the impact of the water on his tie rods, which were bent. He did not have collision insurance, but he claimed under his comprehensive coverage policy. The court held that this accident was not due to the action of water but due to collision. Since collision is specifically excluded in a comprehensive coverage policy, Zane could not recover.

As in collision insurance, the company is entitled to be subrogated to the rights of the insured if there is reason to believe that the damage was caused by the fault of another. The company may institute suit, and the insured is obligated to help and co-operate as requested by the company.

Due to an increase in damage claims in congested areas, some companies now offer $50 and $100 deductible policies in comprehensive coverage, under the same terms as in collision policies.

PUBLIC LIABILITY INSURANCE

This type of insurance covers the owner or tenant of real estate against any claims for injury to persons on his premises, up to an agreed maximum amount.

In addition to paying any sum awarded by the court, the insurer is obligated to defend any action against the assured relating to his use of the property. The wording in the contract determines the extent of the company's obligation.

Illustration: Venner, the assured under a comprehensive personal liability policy, owned and operated a dog kennel in the back yard of his home. His neighbor brought suit to prevent him from continuing in this business. Venner notified the company and requested that it defend the suit in his name. The company refused. Venner retained his own attorney and defended his case successfully. He then sued the company for the costs in defending the suit. The court awarded him a judgment for the amount he expended.

LIABILITY FOR SIDEWALKS

Primarily, the liability for the construction, repair, and maintenance of sidewalks is on the municipality since they are a part of the highway to be used by pedestrians. However, by ordinance of each municipality, this responsibility is usually passed on to the owner of the property fronting on the sidewalk, known as the abutting owner. He is obligated to keep it in good repair and is responsible for any injury sustained by a pedestrian.

If the abutting owner uses the sidewalk in front of his premises for his own special purpose and this use causes a dangerous condition to exist, he is liable for any injury incurred.

Illustration: Delivery of beer in kegs to a bar and grill created a broken and dangerous condition on the sidewalk. When a pedestrian was injured, the tavern owner was held responsible under an ordinance which required him to keep the sidewalk in repair and because the sidewalk was used for his specific benefit.

Generally, a public liability insurance policy will cover claims for injuries sustained on the sidewalk in front of the premises of the insured, as well as on the property itself.

MARINE INSURANCE

This type of insurance covers damage to ship and cargo caused by "perils of the sea" and other risks specifically listed in the policy. Each policy, according to its terms, describes the risk against which the property is to be insured. The damage must be caused by the sea and not merely resulting while on the sea.

Illustration: A storm which was not unusually violent caused cattle in the ship's hold to be thrown against each other and killed by the tossing of the ship. It was held by the court to be a "peril of the sea." Therefore the owner of the cattle collected.

To recover on a claim, the insured must prove that the ship was seaworthy, properly operated and maintained, that the cargo was properly loaded and stored, and that the damage was caused by the risk included in the policy.

In applying for marine insurance coverage, the insured warrants that the ship is seaworthy, the voyage legal and the route direct.

TITLE INSURANCE

Title insurance covers against any loss to the owner of real property which results from any defect in his title. When such insurance is obtained, the company will investigate and search the title of the property to determine what encumbrances, liens or other claims exist against it. It will then agree to indemnify the owner for any claims not listed against the property, up to the value of the property. Only one premium is paid at the time the policy is issued and the policy continues in effect as long as the assured owns the property.

If a claim is made against the property, the insurance company is then obligated to defend the claim and pay any award that may be made to satisfy it. If the claim is such as to defeat the valid title of the insured and deprive him of ownership of the property, the company will then pay him the maximum amount on the policy.

OTHER TYPES OF POLICIES

Burglary, robbery, theft, larceny and pilferage policies cover and indemnify the insured against any loss caused by these specified risks. In essence they are based on the wrongful taking of the property of the assured by others with intent to deprive the owner of its use and possession. If the property is taken from a building, the policy will usually require that there be some visible evidence of a forcible and violent entrance. The assured must keep records to show the company what property was wrongfully taken.

Any change or increase in the hazard will tend to defeat recovery. Any conduct on the part of the assured which results in an increase of the risk of loss without notice to the company may be considered a release of its responsibility.

Flood insurance has been made available pursuant to the National Flood Insurance program through a cooperative effort between the federal government and private insurance companies under the supervision and control of the United States Department of Housing and Urban Development.

SURETYSHIP. WHAT IS A SURETY?

A surety is any person who for a consideration promises to make good for the debt or default of another.

This relationship comes into existence when the surety says to the creditor, "If you don't recover from the debtor, I will pay his debt."

As the term signifies, the surety is brought in to bolster the credit of the debtor. It may be that he wants additional credit or he wants to prevent the creditor from pressing him for payment of the money he owes. The creditor is satisfied because he thus gets the promise of payment from a person who generally has a much better credit rating than that of the debtor.

If the creditor accepts the promise of the surety and extends credit or continues the obligation, the contract of surety is made. However, to enforce this obligation the creditor must have obtained that promise in writing signed by the surety. This contract is subject to the requirements of the Statute of Frauds as one which "answers for the debt, default or miscarriage of another."

Illustration: Swanson repaired Adams' boat. He refused to release the boat until his bill was paid. Jergens, a friend of Adams, promised Swanson that he would pay the bill. Swanson released the boat. Adams did not pay, so Swanson sued Jergens on his promise as a surety. He did not win because the promise that Jergens made was not in writing. The promise of a surety must be in writing to be collectible.

When the debt now becomes due, the creditor will make his demand upon the debtor for payment. If he is not paid, he must institute suit to recover it. Then, if he does not collect, he may sue the surety. However, in practice, when the creditor notifies the surety that he has not been paid, the surety will pay to avoid a lawsuit.

When the surety pays the obligation of the debtor, he becomes subrogated to the right of the creditor. He can then proceed against the debtor to recover the money he paid.

The defenses of a surety against a suit by the creditor may

include the claim that the original debtor was discharged or released of his obligation by the creditor. The discharge of the debtor relieves the surety of his contractual responsibility. He may also prove that the creditor was guilty of fraud or collusion with the debtor as against him and thus be discharged.

A more commonly known use of the surety relationship occurs in criminal actions. A surety bond is often used to release a person from custody when arrested for a crime and awaiting trial. Generally, a person arrested and charged with the commission of a crime, except if it is a capital offense, is entitled to bail in an amount determined by the court. Bail is a deposit of money or securities to assure his presence for trial. If the person has the money or can get someone to put up the money for him, he is released. Persons owning real property may be acceptable as sureties to have someone released on bail.

However, if none of these possibilities is available, surety companies issue bail bonds acceptable to the court on payment of a premium and on the assurance by a reputable person that the defendant will not leave the jurisdiction of the court before his trial. This assurance to the bonding company often takes the form of a promise that, if there is a default in the amount of the bail bond, he will pay any loss to the company. We thus have the situation of a surety company in turn getting a promise from a personal surety.

Surety bonds are also used in civil actions when compliance with necessary court procedures is to be assured.

An out-of-state resident bringing suit may be required to give some assurance that if he loses the case he will pay the costs of litigation. The usual procedure is for that plaintiff to obtain a bond from a surety company which will guarantee such payment.

When two people claim ownership to the same personal property, one may institute a proceeding to obtain possession of the property before the matter is adjudicated at the trial. He must post a bond to assure the court and the other side that, in the event he loses his claim, the property or the value of the property will be available to the winner. Here again, a bond is obtained from a surety company on payment of a premium.

Summation

Points to Remember about Insurance

Almost every family in this country has some form of insurance coverage. The most common, of course, is life insurance. Then there is fire insurance covering household goods and the home. Those who own an automobile or truck usually have liability insurance. They may also have comprehensive coverage and collision as well. Persons who own their own homes may have public liability coverage and title insurance.

The following basic factors about insurance should be kept in mind:

The additional necessary ingredients of an insurance contract are important. What is insurable interest? Just when is it necessary in life insurance and in property insurance?

What risk does a fire policy cover? What are come of the provisions of a standard fire insurance policy? How is a policy canceled and how is the refund of premiums computed?

What types of life insurance policies are available? What are some standard provisions of a policy? What is the incontestability clause? How does it operate? What happens when you fail to pay your premiums? Can you forfeit your policy? What is double indemnity?

What risk is covered in an accident policy?

What are the three distinct types of automobile insurance? What is the purpose of each?

Why is public liability coverage necessary for anyone who owns property or operates a business?

What is the surety relationship? How is it created? How is it enforced?

CHAPTER 6

Negotiable Instruments

HOW DO NEGOTIABLE INSTRUMENTS APPLY TO EVERYDAY TRANSACTIONS?

There is a general impression that the very technical term "negotiable instruments" is of no concern to us in our personal lives; that negotiable instruments are used only by people in business and that they should be studied only by students of commercial law.

We should realize that we are constantly using negotiable instruments in our personal transactions—when we pay a bill by check or when we buy something on time. A check is a negotiable instrument, as are the promissory notes that are used in installment transactions.

SOME DEFINITIONS AND DISTINCTIONS

The negotiable instrument, now controlled by the Uniform Commercial Code, was devised by merchants to facilitate commercial transactions by eliminating the use of money and gold bullion.

It is a writing or a document which conforms to certain legal requirements. It can be negotiated from one person to another as a means of exchange or credit in place of money.

To be negotiable, it must contain a definite or ascertainable time for payment. It must be an unconditional order or promise to pay money in a definite sum. There must be special negotiable words used. These are: "Pay to the order of ____," "Pay to ____ or order," or "Pay to bearer" or "Pay to ____ or bearer." Finally, it must be signed by the person making or drawing the instrument.

A negotiable instrument is distinguished from all others by the use of the negotiable words "order" or "bearer." The failure to use them will defeat the purpose and will not create a negotiable instrument.

A negotiable instrument is easy to carry, easy to transfer and easily available. It is secure in its collectibility because of the legal safeguards. A person who acquires such an instrument in the proper manner for a valuable consideration without knowledge of any defects can collect the face amount without any defenses against it.

Negotiable instruments in use are the check, the promissory note, the draft, or bill of exchange, and the trade acceptance.

THE CHECK

A writing which by its terms directs a bank to pay a certain sum of money to the "order" of a definite person is a check.

The person who writes and signs the check is the "drawer." He has money on deposit with the bank, known as the "drawee," and therefore has a right to make such a demand. The person named on the check is the "payee."

There is no prescribed form to be used in drawing a check, but it should contain the date, a direction to the bank to pay to the "order of the payee" a certain sum of money and the signature of the drawer.

Illustration: Dallas, Texas, Jan. 5, 1975
                         Oilwell National Bank
                            Dallas, Texas
Pay to the order of Peter Payee $1,000.00
One thousand and no/100 .... Dollars
                         David Drawer (signed)

Instead of a named payee, the check may be made payable to "Cash" or to "Bearer."

When presented, the check must be paid by the bank if it contains all of the necessary information.

A "postdated" check is one which is presented for payment

before the date stated on its face. The bank is not authorized to pay on a postdated check.

Illustration: Chalmers drew a check payable to Elton on the National Bank for $150, dated June 25th, 1975. He gave the check to Elton on June 10th and asked him not to deposit it until the 25th, since he did not have the money in his account to cover it. Elton disregarded this instruction and deposited the check for collection on the 20th. The check was returned to Elton unpaid because it was postdated. When he deposited the check on the 25th, it was paid.

The bank is the agent of the drawer. It is only required to pay a check when it is properly drawn and when there is enough money in the account to cover it.

If there are no funds, the bank may refuse to pay. It will not be obligated to the payee for such refusal. The payee has a claim against the drawer on the original debt and on the unpaid check. A person who draws a check when he does not have the funds to cover it may be liable to a criminal prosecution. This is a safeguard to protect the trustworthiness of a negotiable instrument.

The drawer may order the bank to stop payment of any check before it is presented. The bank must follow his instructions. Here again the payee can have no claim against the bank but must proceed against the drawer on the check. As between the two, the maker may interpose any defense as against the payee.

However, if the check was negotiated by the payee to a "holder in due course" and payment is stopped when he presents it, the defenses of the maker may not be sufficient. The maker will be responsible for its payment to the holder in due course.

If the bank fails to pay on a check issued by the maker, or if it pays on a check when payment is stopped, it will be liable to the maker for any loss that he sustains.

A certified check is one which has been presented to the bank to have the account verified. The certification consists of an indorsement on the face of the check by the bank to indicate the date on which it was presented.

A check certified at the request of the maker, and before delivery to the payee, makes known to all subsequent holders that the check is genuine and that the drawer has an account with the bank. It is not an assurance that there will be sufficient funds in that account when the check is presented for payment.

A check presented for certification by a payee or a subsequent holder, however, creates a new relationship between all the parties—the drawer, the payee and the bank. The bank may refuse to certify if the funds are not sufficient. However, when it does certify the check, it becomes the primary debtor on the face amount of the check. The certification stamp on the face of the check in this case assures all subsequent holders that there is enough money to cover the amount, that it has been set aside by the bank and that it will be paid when it is presented for payment.

These are the legal distinctions as to certification. Practically, the procedure used by some banks is to certify all checks so presented and to set aside sufficient funds to cover the amount of the check as soon as it is presented for certification.

After certification, the payee will negotiate the check by indorsement and delivery to another, secure in the knowledge that the bank and not the drawer is responsible for its payment.

The effect of certification is to permit its continued use in business transactions with the facility of a negotiable instrument and the security of money.

THE PROMISSORY NOTE

A written promise by one person to another that, at a definite time, he will pay a stated sum of money to the proper person who presents it for payment is a promissory note.

The "maker" is the person who writes and signs the note. The "payee" is the one in whose name it is made payable.

Here again there is no definite required form as long as it contains an unconditional promise to pay a stated sum of money to the order of a named person.

Illustration:
                    $1,000.00
                                        Monterey, Calif., Jan. 5, 1975
Thirty days after date, I promise to pay to the order of Peter
Payee . . . . One Thousand and no/100 Dollars.
Payable at 5200 Oceanside Road
Interest at 10%
                                        Mervin Maker (signed)

The note may also contain the place where the note is to be
presented for payment. If no such place is designated, then it
is to be presented at the maker's home, office or bank.

It may contain the agreed interest rate between the parties.
If the rate agreed upon is the legal rate, it need not be included, since it will then be understood. However, if the rate
agreed upon is other than the legal rate, it must be stated on
the note. Some states do not recognize an interest rate higher
than the legal rate and will consider it usurious. However,
some states, such as California, permit parties to a written
contract to agree to an interest rate higher than the legal
rate and will enforce it. California has a legal rate of 7 per
cent, but will permit parties in an express written contract to
agree to 10% in their transaction.

A negotiable instrument is a contract and must be legal to be
enforcible. The effect of usury on a negotiable instrument differs in the various states. Pursuant to legislation, the legal rate
of interest depends upon the type of transaction involved. An
illustration of this change is the rate of interest permissible in
consumer open end credit plans, credit card purchases and
home mortgage loans. If it is drawn by a corporation, then it is
valid since New York does not limit the interest rate as charged
to a corporation. California penalizes a usurious transaction by
the forfeiture of all interest, and allows recovery of three times
the amount of usurious interest paid. Yet it will permit the recovery of the principal in a usurious transaction.

An "acceleration clause" may be included in each of a series
of notes payable at regular intervals. Default in payment of one
will cause all of the others still unpaid to become due and
payable. This is to eliminate the need to sue on each note as
it falls due. If you have signed a series of such notes and it
contains such a clause, you must be prepared to pay the entire

amount of your obligation if you fail to pay one of the notes.

The payee of the note may keep it until it falls due or he may negotiate it to someone else.

If he keeps it, presents it on the due date, and it is not paid, then he can sue the maker both on the note and on the original debt.

The benefits of a negotiable instrument are lost by the payee if he keeps it, since any defenses the maker has are available as against the payee and the note.

Illustration: Perkins bought Archer's car and gave him his note payable in 3 months for the sum of $500. Archer kept the note and presented it on the due date. Perkins refused to pay. He claimed that the car did not operate properly, that Archer had misrepresented its condition to him and that he had been after Archer all this time to take back the car. When Archer sued on the note, the defenses that Perkins set up were sufficient to defeat Archer's recovery.

THE DRAFT OR BILL OF EXCHANGE

Another form of negotiable instrument used in business and commerce is known as the "draft" or "bill of exchange." In form and substance, it is similar to a check. However, instead of being drawn on a bank, it is drawn on an individual or a firm.

It is an unconditional order in writing addressed to another to pay a stated sum of money to the order of a designated person. The draft is based upon some prior relationship between the drawer and the drawee which enables the drawer to demand that payment.

No definite form is required, but the essentials should be included: an unconditional order to pay to the order of a named person a stated sum of money at a stated time, addressed to the drawee and signed by the drawer.

Illustration:

$1,000.00   Phoenix, Arizona, Jan. 5, 1975

At sight pay to the order of Polly Payee, One Thousand and no/ 100 Dollars and charge to my account.

To: Daniel Drawee
      Bangor, Maine   Dorothy Drawer

The time for the payment of the draft is a term of the contract and must be stated on its face. "At sight" is the same as "on demand." It means when presented to the drawee. However, the drawee is given 24 hours to determine whether there are sufficient funds due to the drawer to enable him to accept the obligation.

The time specified may be "at 10 days sight." This would mean that the amount of the draft will be due and payable 10 days after it has been presented to the drawee for acceptance.

The drawee may refuse to accept or honor the draft. By doing so, the drawee has created no obligation between himself and the payee or the person who has presented it for acceptance. He may be accountable to the drawer on the debt due between them but he will then be able to interpose such defenses against the drawer as he has to defeat his claim.

If the drawee accepts the draft and agrees to pay it, he will write "I accept" across the face of it, then sign his name and add the date of such acceptance. He will become primarily liable for its payment when such payment is due. In the example given above, he is obligated to pay the amount of the draft when it is again presented 10 days from the date of acceptance. He is now known as the "acceptor" and any holder of that draft must first present the draft to him for payment on the date when it is due for payment.

As indicated above, a draft must be presented for acceptance when there is no determinable due date. The presentation then has the effect of fixing the date of maturity, the date when payment is due after acceptance. However, when the date of maturity is stated on the face as "30 days after date," it need not be presented for acceptance. It need only be presented for payment on the date when it falls due.

In certain situations, a draft may expressly require that it be presented for acceptance. This must be complied with to assure its collection.

The bank draft or the traveler's check is a good illustration of our personal use of the draft. When we take a trip and don't want to carry cash, we usually take a bank draft or a traveler's check. It is an order directed to a bank to pay a designated sum of money to our order. Any bank to which this draft is presented will honor it because it is drawn by a bank with unquestioned financial credit. No one can cash the traveler's check but the person named on it. It does not require an acceptance because it is payable when presented.

THE TRADE ACCEPTANCE

A trade acceptance is a draft. Its only distinction is a written demand for the amount of the purchase price drawn by the seller of merchandise on the buyer, payable to himself or his bank. It will usually contain a statement that the source of the obligation is the purchase of certain merchandise by the drawee from the drawer. In all other respects, it is like a draft.

Not all states consider a trade acceptance as a negotiable instrument. If your transaction involves a trade acceptance, you should first determine whether your state and the state in which it was drawn recognize it as such. The rights, obligations and responsibilities of a negotiable instrument differ from an ordinary contract, as we shall see. To make certain that your interests are protected, you should obtain competent legal advice.

Here again, no definite form is required as long as the necessary elements are present.

Illustration:

$1,000.00   St. Paul, Minn., Jan. 5, 1975
Ninety days after date, pay to the order of OURSELVES, One Thousand and no/100 Dollars. ....
The obligation of the acceptor hereof arises out of the purchase of goods from the drawer. The acceptor may make this acceptance payable at any bank or trust company which he may designate.
To: Duncan Drawee   Ditmars Drawer (signed)

The terms of the transaction may require that it be presented for acceptance. On presentation, the acceptor will then note his acceptance by writing "I accept, payable at State Bank, St. Paul. Duncan Drawee" (signed and dated).

A "certificate of deposit" is also considered a negotiable instrument. It is a written statement in the form of a receipt given by a bank for a sum of money it has received on deposit. Generally these are in the form of promissory notes payable to the order of the depositor. If they are so worded, they are, of course, negotiable. The negotiability of the certificate of deposit depends upon the terminology used. If it is drawn payable to the depositor or his assigns, it is not negotiable, because it does not have the words "to the order of" as required.

Illustration: A certificate of deposit which stated "Baldwin deposited in City Bank $1,000 to the credit of himself, payable on return of this certificate properly indorsed" was held to be negotiable though not made payable to the order of Baldwin.

Bills of lading and warehouse receipts are negotiable but they are not negotiable instruments. To be negotiable instruments, they must contain an order to pay money. Both bills of lading and warehouse receipts are mere orders to deliver merchandise.

They are negotiable because by custom and usage they can be transferred from one person to another when properly indorsed. A purchaser in good faith will get title to the merchandise represented by them free from any claims which may have existed as between the original parties.

WHAT IS NEGOTIATION?

Negotiation is the transfer of title and ownership to a negotiable instrument in a prescribed manner.

HOW IS NEGOTIATION ACCOMPLISHED?

A negotiable instrument which is payable to "bearer" need only be delivered to be negotiated. "Bearer" paper does not have to be indorsed. By means of this delivery, the new owner acquires all of the rights of a "holder in due course."

A negotiable instrument which is payable to the order of a "payee" is negotiated by the indorsement of the payee on the back of the instrument and the delivery of the instrument by him to the person who is to receive it.

If made payable to "the order of" the payee, delivery alone or indorsement alone do not suffice to accomplish a proper negotiation. There must be both indorsement and delivery. The act of indorsement is in the nature of a contract with the person to whom it is negotiated and to all subsequent holders. In effect, the indorser obligates himself as follows: "If you, the holder of the instrument, make a proper presentment for acceptance and for payment, and it is refused, then I will pay the face amount of the instrument when you give me proper notice."

TYPES OF INDORSEMENT

The "blank" indorsement is accomplished by having the payee or any subsequent indorser sign his name on the back of the instrument without any other comment or notation. This converts the instrument into "bearer" paper. All subsequent negotiation of this instrument can be made by mere delivery from one person to another. There is no further need for an indorsement by any subsequent holder.

The "special" or "full" indorsement is made by the payee or any subsequent holders by writing the words, "Pay to ____," "Pay to the order of ____," or "____ or order" on the back of the instrument and then signing his name under it. To further negotiate, the transferee will endorse to the person getting it from him, with his signature. No title to the instrument passes without the indorsement and delivery by the holder.

A "qualified" indorsement, also known as an indorsement "without recourse," limits the liability of the indorser. When he writes the words "without recourse" on the back and then signs his name, he says, in effect, "I am merely assigning my title to this instrument, but I refuse to incur any liability as an indorser." Such an indorsement transfers title to the instrument but does not affect its further negotiability.

A "restrictive" indorsement does not pass title to the instrument. According to its name, it restricts any further negotiation. It makes the indorsee a holder for a specific and designated purpose.

Illustration: Brown is the holder of a negotiable instrument. On the back he indorses, "For Collection, National Bank & Trust Company," and signs his name, "Cornelius V. Brown." He then delivers it to his bank, the National Bank & Trust Co., to present and collect. Such an indorsement is notice to all that the holder, the National Bank & Trust Co., has a restricted and limited authority in the instrument.

A "conditional" indorsement transfers title to a negotiable instrument only when the condition which is stated there is fulfilled. The negotiability of the instrument is not affected by such an indorsement if the condition is written on the back as a part of the indorsement. However, if it is written on the face, it creates a condition of the instrument and not of the indorsement. This automatically defeats its negotiability.

Illustrations: John Ellis wrote the following on a sheet of paper: "On my election as President of the Whizzers, I promise to pay to Jonah Fixer the sum of One Hundred Dollars. John Ellis (signed)." This promise to pay money is conditional on his being elected. It is not negotiable. In trying to collect on it, Jonah Fixer may find Ellis interposing many defenses which may defeat his efforts.

On the back of a promissory note, Joe Jay wrote, "On delivery of 1958 Ford 4-door sedan, pay to Joe Cromton. Joe Jay." (signed). This is a conditional indorsement. It does not affect the negotiability of the instrument, but the title to it, so transferred, is subject to be defeated if the condition is not fulfilled.

An accommodation maker, also known as a comaker, is a person who appears to be primarily liable on the face of the instrument, but is actually lending his name and credit for the benefit of another. He may appear as the maker on a promissory note, or he may be an accommodation indorser. He may indorse the note before it is delivered to the payee. The maker is considered a poor credit risk. The accommodation indorser bolsters the maker's credit so that the paper will then be acceptable to the payee. He has received no consideration for his indorsement but is nevertheless liable to a holder in due course by reason of his indorsement. However, he is not liable to the party whom he accommodated.

Illustration: Jack Holley wanted to buy a car but had no funds and no acceptable credit. He asked Jody to become an accommodation maker on a note. Jody drew a note with "Jack Holley" as payee and signed it. Holley then negotiated it to buy the car. Jody is the debtor and is liable to any holder in due course on the note. He is not, however, liable to Holley because he was the accommodation maker.

The "holder in due course" is the last person in possession of the instrument, the person who presents it for payment. All benefits of negotiation are in his favor and for his advantage. He holds this status because he is not a party to the original transaction. He acquired the instrument in good faith for a valuable consideration and without knowledge that it was defective in any way. When he presents it for payment there are only three defenses which can be interposed to defeat his recovery.

These are called real defenses and attack the validity of the original contract as to the issuance of the instrument. Proof that the original parties, the maker, drawer or the acceptor did not have the necessary legal capacity to make a contract will defeat recovery on the instrument. Proof that there was no consent, no mutual assent to the contract or that it is void by law will bar the collection on the note or draft by the holder in due course.

No other defenses can be used by any of the persons liable on the instrument. Lack of consideration or fraud, though available as between the original parties, cannot be sustained as against a holder in due course.

LIABILITY OF THE PARTIES

The maker is primarily liable on a promissory note. He received the original benefit for it when he drew it. He must subsequently pay it when it becomes due. Each subsequent holder in the chain parted with some consideration on obtaining it and then in turn got some consideration when he passed it along by negotiation. The holder of the note at the date of maturity, the day when it is to be paid, presents it to the maker. If this holder qualifies as a holder in due course, then there are only the three real defenses that the maker may interpose to defeat payment. No other defenses will be available to him and he must pay the note.

The drawer of a check, draft, bill of exchange or trade acceptance impliedly guarantees to the payee and all subsequent holders that the instrument will be accepted and that it will be paid when it is duly presented. If it is not accepted or is not paid, then, if he is given notice of dishonor, he will pay.

The drawee is the person upon whom the order is made. He is directed to pay money to the payee or to any subsequent holder. If it requires acceptance, he is obligated to the drawer alone for failing to accept. If no acceptance is required, then again he is obligated only to the drawer for failing to pay. If an acceptance is required and he does accept, then he becomes liable.

By accepting the obligation, he becomes primarily liable for the payment of the instrument. He thus promises to any subsequent holder that he will pay according to his promise of acceptance. If he qualified the instrument by his acceptance, he will then be responsible only to the extent of his acceptance.

Illustration: Danny Dunlap drew a draft on Dalrymple to the order of Peterson for $5,000. Dalrymple only owed Dunlap $3,000. He wrote across the face of the draft, "Accepted only in the sum of $3,000, payable at my office on due date, Jan. 20, 1958. Dennis Dalrymple" (signed). If accepted by Peterson, this is the limit of Dalrymple's obligation on the draft.

Each indorser is liable to all indorsers subsequent to himself and to the last owner or holder. This liability is based on the contract of negotiation and on his warranty. On the contract his obligation is conditional and secondary, based on notice that primary debtor did not pay. He is liable on the warranty to protect the holder in due course against real defenses asserted by the primary debtor. He thus warrants that the instrument is genuine, that he has title to it and that it is valid and subsisting.

This does not apply to the qualified indorser. He signed "without recourse." His only responsibility is that he has good title, that the instrument is genuine and that he has no knowledge that it is invalid. He is not bound to any contract by his indorsement and does not promise to pay.

The owner of "bearer" paper who negotiates by delivery is responsible only to the person to whom he transferred it. He, in effect, states that he has title, that the instrument is genuine and that he has no knowledge of any fact which would make it invalid or valueless. He is not responsible on any contract, since he did not indorse and did not promise to pay on notice of dishonor.

NOTICE OF DISHONOR

If a negotiable instrument is dishonored—that is, if it is not accepted when it should have been, or is not paid—notice must be given by the holder to the drawer and to each indorser. The purpose is to make them aware of their obligations and to give them an opportunity to take such action as will protect their interests. Failure to give such notice to anyone entitled to it will discharge him. By giving notice, the holder of the instrument complies with the condition in the indorser's contract of liability and makes it absolute.

PROTEST

Usually a negotiable instrument is presented for acceptance or payment by a bank or in person by the payee. However, to eliminate all doubt that a presentment was made, especially when any of the parties is from another state or another country, a more formal presentment is necessary. To give assurance and formality that due presentment was made, it is delegated to a notary public. He makes the presentment, and then, if it is refused, he certifies in a formal declaration, which he draws and signs, attesting to the dishonor. This is known as the protest. It is authentic proof that the instrument was dishonored and that those secondarily liable may expect to become responsible for payment. The protest may also be made by a private individual in the presence of two or more creditable witnesses.

Notice of protest must then be sent to all parties whose responsibility on the instrument is to become absolute as a result of the dishonor. As stated, the failure of anyone entitled to such notice discharges him from obligation.

It is important to note here that, since each indorser has the right to proceed against the indorser before him on the instrument, the discharge of any indorser in the chain will discharge all of those subsequent to him.

MATERIAL ALTERATION

Any change or material alteration in the terms of a negotiable instrument without the consent of all prior parties invalidates the instrument. It may also extinguish the obligation for which the instrument was given, against the person making the alteration.

If the alteration is not apparent on its face and is in the hands of a holder in due course, he can recover according to the original terms. Parties who obtain an instrument subsequent to the alteration are responsible under the new terms.

Illustration: Hurley is the holder in due course of a promissory note in the sum of $4,000. On presenting it for collection, he finds that it was originally for $1,000 and had been altered. He can only recover $1,000 as against the maker. However, he can proceed against his immediate indorser both on the note and on the indorser's warranty; on the note because it was $4,000 when it was indorsed and negotiated; on the warranty because an indorser warrants that the instrument is genuine and that it is valid and subsisting.

Forgery is an intent to defraud. No legal or equitable title can be obtained through a forged signature. Not even a holder in due course can recover on a forged signature. The holder can, however, recover on the warranty of his indorser that the instrument is genuine and that it is valid and subsisting.

Illustration: Sumner found a promissory note payable to another person with the same name of Sumner. He indorsed his name and passed it on. This was held to be a forgery. He was not entitled to it and had no authority to indorse since he was not the person intended. The holder in due course of that instrument could not recover against the maker because there was no delivery to the payee and his signature was forged. He did recover against the prior indorser on the warranty.

The theft of an incomplete instrument from the possession

of the maker or the drawer will not create a valid instrument when it is completed by the thief. There was no consent and no delivery of that contract. There was no valid contract created. It was void *ab initio*, from the beginning. This is one of the real defenses as against the holder in due course.

Illustration: Deevers had a signed blank check in his drawer. It was stolen by one of his employees. The sum of $150 was inserted as well as the name of Owen Mann as payee. The check was then certified by the thief and negotiated and paid. Deevers claimed the bank had no right to certify or pay since the check was void. The bank therefore credited his account and proceeded against the person who had cashed it. The court found that the bank, having paid out on a void check, was entitled to recover.

The discharge of a negotiable instrument means that the contractual obligation which was begun when it was first drawn has ceased to exist. A discharge then relieves all persons of their liability, whether it is a primary or a secondary one.

If for any reason the holder of the instrument releases the maker or the acceptor, who are primary obligors, then all others, secondarily responsible, are released too.

When the maker or acceptor becomes the holder and owner at or after maturity, all others are discharged. It is to be presumed that the one primarily responsible had paid his obligation.

However, if the maker of a note is an accommodation maker, the note is not discharged if it is in his possession because he is given the right to proceed against the person for whose benefit he became obligated on the note.

Summation

Points to Remember about Negotiable Instruments

We now use negotiable instruments in our daily and personal transactions. They are no longer relegated only to the business and commercial world. We pay our house bills by check. We borrow money and sign a promissory note to assure its payment. We take traveler's checks along on a trip if we don't want to carry too much money with us.

The following facts, if kept in mind, will make the advantages of using a negotiable instrument more meaningful.

The check and the draft are orders to another to pay money. The promissory note is a promise made by the maker to pay money. What is the distinction? Who are the parties involved? What are their reciprocal obligations and responsibilities?

What is negotiation? How is it accomplished? What types of indorsements are there? How does each indorser assume his obligation?

Who is the holder in due course? What are the requisites for becoming one?

What is notice of dishonor? What is a protest and notice of protest? What is its purpose?

How is a negotiable instrument discharged?

CHAPTER 7

Agency

HOW DOES AGENCY FIT INTO OUR EVERYDAY LIVING?

At first flush, the average man will scoff at the thought that we create agency relationships without knowing that we do, and much more often than we expect.

The wife is the agent of the husband when she shops for the family, whether it be for food or clothes. When we let someone use our car to drive the kids to school, we have made him our agent. Every time we get someone to do something for us, we may be creating an agency relationship.

How are we responsible? To the agent? To others with whom the agent comes in contact because of our relationship?

Agency is a legally created relationship. It is either the result of an express contract or it is implied because of the conduct of the parties. The agent acts for and represents the principal with the same legal effect as though the deed were done by the principal himself.

Illustrations: Alfred is authorized by written agreement to collect rents from a building which Peter owns. For this he is to receive 2 per cent of all amounts he collects.

Alice buys meat and other food items at the local store, which she charges. Her husband is sued when he does not pay. By law, Alice is the agent of her husband when buying necessaries for the home.

As in any other contract, its obligations cannot be imposed. They must be consented to and the terms of the agency agreed upon. However, consent may be evident from the actions and behavior of the parties.

The main reason for determining the existence of an agency relationship is to charge the acts of the agent to the principal. If an agency relationship is established, then the transfer of liability can be accomplished.

Illustration: Conway was responsible for the injury which Mrs. Eggers sustained when she fell while entering the Thrift Shop. When it was proved that Conway was employed by the Thrift Shop, the responsibility for the injury was then shifted to the owner of the store. Recovery was assured because the owner was insured and the injury was severe.

The contract of agency may create authority in the agent to represent the principal generally in a particular line of business.

Illustration: Terhune, as manager of Akin's store, had the power to represent Akin in all transactions pertaining to the operation of the store. When he purchased merchandise for the store, Akin was responsible to pay for it.

In some cases, an agency relationship may be created for a specific purpose. The agent may only be authorized to do a specific job.

Illustration: Vogel sent his foreman into town to buy four new tires and have them charged to him. This was a specific agency. Vogel had no right to buy anything else.

SOME PARTICULAR AGENCY RELATIONSHIPS

An "attorney in fact" is an agent who is authorized by means of a document called a "power of attorney" to represent the principal to do a specific act. He does not have to be a lawyer. He may be any person who has the physical and legal capacity to act in place of the principal.

Illustration: Bradley expects a payment due him in cash while he is in Europe. He executes a power of attorney authorizing Shore to receive the money for him. Payment to Shore is equivalent to payment to Bradley.

There are occasions when the principal is not available to carry on his business. He may then execute a general power of attorney authorizing an attorney in fact, as his agent, to carry on his business for him. There may be some legal requirement in your state which provides that a general power of attorney must contain certain specific provisions and must be drawn in some particular way. Such documents are executed when the owner of a business is ill and may get worse. It is necessary that someone be legally clothed with the right to carry on the business.

A broker is an agent of the person who employs him. It may be to sell a house or to buy one. A person who wants to buy or sell a business may retain a broker to accomplish the transaction. The extent of his power depends upon the agreement. If he is merely to find a buyer then he cannot bind the principal. However, if he is authorized to negotiate for his principal, then his commitments are binding. The fee of the broker depends upon his agreement with the principal or, if none was made, then upon the custom and usage in that particular business.

A factor is a merchant who takes goods from his principal, sells them in his own name and then is paid either on a commission basis or as per their particular agreement. A new aspect of factoring involves the purchase or collection of accounts receivable by the factor under an arrangement with the principal. The factor may collect the amounts due the principal on a commission basis or he may pay the principal an agreed price in advance and keep all that he collects.

An auctioneer is an agent because he undertakes to sell the property of others at a public competitive sale which he conducts. He acts as the agent of the seller in making the terms of sale. At the fall of his hammer, he indicates his and the seller's acceptance of the offer made by the highest bidder.

WHO MAY BE PRINCIPAL OR AGENT

Any person or company qualified to enter into a legal and enforcible contract is legally competent to be an agent or a principal.

An infant may act as an agent if the principal believes he has the ability to represent him. As an agent, he will bind the principal in all acts he is authorized to perform under the agency. However, as a minor he has the right to avoid his contract of agency with his principal.

Corporations may act as agents or as principals in all transactions which are within the scope of their authority as prescribed in their charter or certificate of incorporation.

Illustration: The Chaser Corp. was organized to manage real estate as an agent and can negotiate with owners of real estate to act as their agent.

Partnerships are controlled in their activities by the agreement among the partners. Unless there is some specific restriction upon any one partner, each may act as an agent of the partnership in the transaction of its business.

Persons who are interested in a business transaction cannot act as agents for parties with adverse interests. An agent owes his principal the utmost loyalty. He cannot serve two masters and serve them both well. Thus, he may not make any financial benefit from his agency relationship without the knowledge and consent of his principal.

Illustration: August retained Borden to act as a broker in the sale of his house. Borden obtained a corporation to buy the house. When August found that Borden was an officer of that corporation, he had the right to avoid the contract of sale.

If a license is required by an agent to carry on his particular business, and he does not have one, he will not be authorized to act, nor will he be able to enforce the payment for his services. He may even be subject to criminal prosecution for acting without a license.

Illustration: Real-estate brokers, insurance brokers and auctioneers have to be licensed, and if they do not have such licenses they cannot practice their business.

An agent may be appointed to perform any act which the principal can lawfully perform. If the act required of the principal is personal in nature, requires his personal attention and participation, he cannot delegate it to an agent.

Illustration: Black was retained to paint a portrait. His personal ability was required and he could not delegate this act to an agent.

If the act is required by law to be performed personally by the principal, it cannot be delegated to an agent.

Illustration: Voting, taking an automobile driving test or taking a civil service test are acts which by law are required to be performed by the principal.

The authority of an agent is based upon the contract and the authority granted to him by its terms. This is called the "express authority" of the agent.

However, every agent also has an "implied authority," that power intended to be given to the agent to enable him to carry out and perform the duties that he is expressly authorized to do.

If the express authority is clear and unambiguous, then there is no need to imply any additional authority, since there can be no question as to the scope and the extent of the agent's powers. It is only where there is some doubt as to the extent of the express powers that additional authority must be implied to enable the agent to perform the tasks for which he was hired.

Illustration: Kernan left his car with his garageman to see if he could sell it. He wanted $200 for it. The garageman sold it for $100 in cash and $100 to be paid in 30 days. The sale was binding as against Kernan. He had given the authority to sell and the garageman was acting within his implied authority as to the terms of sale.

Custom and usage often control the authority which is implied in certain agency relationships.

Illustration: Clerks and bellboys in hotels have certain authority, and a traveler, unless advised to the contrary, may rely on this implied authority. When he pays his bill to the clerk, he may rely on the implied authority that the desk clerk has the right to accept money.

However, if the agency is more limited than implied by custom and usage, then persons with knowledge of such restrictions are bound by them.

Illustration: If a hotel has a sign prominently displayed at the desk to the effect that all bills must be paid to the cashier, a person checking out must abide by that restriction and cannot pay the desk clerk instead.

The principal is bound by and is responsible for the acts of his agent within the scope of his authority. This includes his real or express authority as well as his apparent or implied authority. This applies particularly to agents who have general powers and not those who have specific authority to perform a certain specific act.

Illustration: A managing agent of a building who rents apartments in the building has the apparent authority to take a deposit on an apartment when he rents it.

If the principal wants to limit the apparent authority of his agent, he must give notice of such limitation to third parties dealing with the agent. If there is no notice of any limitation, a stranger dealing with the agent has the right to rely upon the apparent authority of the agent to bind his principal.

Illustration: The owner may post a notice in a store to the effect that all purchases are handled in the main office. This is an indication that the manager of the store does not have the authority to purchase. Anyone selling the manager is acting in contravention to the notice, and cannot expect to recover from the principal.

The agent cannot bind his principal by acts which are beyond the scope of his authority. It is, of course, the responsibility of a person dealing with an agent to make certain that he is acting with authority to bind his principal.

This can only be accomplished by some indication from the principal that the agent has such authority. It cannot be done by relying upon the word of the agent that he has the necessary authority.

The importance of ascertaining the extent of an agent's authority cannot be overlooked. If the agent has overstepped the bounds of his authority, then whatever contract you have made with him is not binding on the principal. This will defeat your purpose in making the deal. Of course, you may have recourse as against the agent, but in many cases the agent is not financially responsible and can give you no satisfaction.

A principal may ratify the act of his agent even though it was originally outside the scope of his authority, and unauthorized.

Illustration: An unauthorized person ordered five doors from Parker, a carpenter, to be delivered together with the invoices to Zakin. The doors, though not ordered by him, were accepted and used by Zakin. Parker demanded payment and was told that the price was too high. Parker sued and recovered the full price according to his invoice. Zakin had ratified the act of the unknown and unauthorized agent and was responsible for the price as charged.

RIGHTS AND OBLIGATIONS OF THE PARTIES

Generally, as long as the agent acts within the scope of his authority and makes contracts in the name of his principal, he is not personally liable. He obligates his principal and not himself. This applies as well where his original act was unauthorized but was subsequently ratified and accepted by the principal.

The agent becomes personally liable only when he acts beyond his authority. He also is liable if he fails to disclose the fact that he is acting as an agent for a principal, even though his acts are within the scope of his authority.

An agent who deals with others on behalf of his principal warrants that he has authority to transact business. If it subsequently appears that he had no authority, he violated that warranty and may be held liable for any damages which result. In such a situation the principal is not bound by the act of the unauthorized agent. The person acting as an agent is not responsible under the agency relationship. However, he will be held personally accountable under a breach of warranty of authority to the extent of the damages.

An agent is liable in tort jointly with his principal if he committed the tort in furtherance of his duties as an agent.

Illustration: Manners represented the Ace Vending Co. in placing vending machines in various business plants. While visiting a plant, he was responsible for the injury of one of the employees because of the negligent manner in which he drove the company car. Both Manners and the Ace Vending Co. were responsible in torts to the person injured.

OBLIGATION OF AGENT TO PRINCIPAL

The agent owes his principal the duty to obey his instruc- tions, to exercise care and diligence in discharging his obligation as an agent, to act in good faith and to account for all money received by him for the principal.

The agent has an absolute duty to follow the express instructions of his principal and is liable to him for any loss if he deviates.

Illustration: Roark was instructed by his principal to ship certain merchandise at a definite time, by a designated carrier. Roark shipped by another carrier because he thought he might save money. The merchandise was lost. Roark was responsible to his principal for the loss. He had violated his duty.

An agent is only justified in disobeying his principal's instructions if they are illegal, immoral or against public policy. In the event of a sudden emergency he may disobey if to follow instructions would threaten the safety of his principal's merchandise.

An agent is not an insurer of the safety of merchandise in his care belonging to his principal. He must only exercise such care, skill and diligence which the circumstances demand, the same care, skill and reasonable diligence which persons of ordinary capacity possess in the same business.

Compensation does not affect the duty and obligation of an agent. The fact that he is not to be paid for the work that he undertook to do, does not reduce his obligation as an agent. He was not obligated to accept the responsibility. However, once assumed, he must apply all of his skill and ability that the specific task assigned to him requires.

An agent may not attain any personal benefit from his relationship as an agent, without the knowledge and the consent of his principal. He must apply himself in the interest of his principal without any motive of personal gain.

If the contract between the agent and the principal specifically prohibits the agent from divulging or using any trade secrets obtained during the agency relationship, the agent may be restrained from doing so. However, if the contract does not so specify, then the agent, after the termination of the relationship, may only be prevented from using such information if fraud or dishonesty can be shown in his acts.

OBLIGATION OF PRINCIPAL TO AGENT

Generally the principal must pay the agent for the services he rendered in accordance with their agreement. He must reimburse him for any expenses he incurred.

Illustration: A real-estate broker hired to obtain a buyer for a house has earned his commissions, by custom and usage in the real-estate business, when he produces a buyer who is "ready, willing and able" to buy. Some brokerage contracts specifically require that a sale be consummated before commissions are earned.

OBLIGATION OF PRINCIPAL TO THIRD PARTIES

A principal is not bound and not responsible on a negotiable instrument if it is executed by an agent and the principal is not disclosed. It will be considered the personal obligation of the agent.

A principal is obligated when his agent enters into a contract with a third party and discloses that he is acting for his principal. The third party too is bound by the contract which he has made with an agent for a known principal.

If the principal is not disclosed and the third party subsequently learns of the agency relationship, he has a reasonable time to elect to hold either the principal or the agent.

Summation

Points to Remember about Agency

We often create an agency relationship without realizing that we have done so. We ask others to do something for us or we do something for them. When we represent them in dealings with others we are their agent. When they represent us, we are the principal. We ask our neighbor, who is going to the store, to buy something for us. We are the principal, the neighbor is our agent.

The agency is an agreement, a contract. It may also be implied by law. What are the obligations which are thus created?

The agent's authority is expressed in the contract. It may also be implied as necessary to accomplish those acts he is authorized to do.

What duty does the agent owe his principal? What can he expect in return?

What is the obligation of the principal and the agent to the third party dealing with the agent?

How is the third party obligated?

CHAPTER 8

Forms of Business Ownership

Statistics show conclusively that only a minority of our population is in business for itself. Most of us are employed, working for others.

The question then arises, why would a study of some of the principles and problems involved in organizing a business be of interest to the average reader?

The statistics mentioned only disclose the manner of earning a living. They do not reveal the other interests which most of us have. Some of us are contemplating some business venture, either on our own or with a partner. Many of us have some financial interest in a corporation. Others own stocks, bought on the stock exchange.

These are sufficient reasons to look into the law which governs the formation and the existence of a business.

TYPES OF BUSINESS OWNERSHIP AND CONTROL

Generally, there are three types of business structure. Each has its own advantages and disadvantages. It is selected by people contemplating the formation of a business from the standpoint of financial responsibility, control of operation, possibilities of growth and expansion, and the possibilities of capitalization and financial development. These three types are individual ownership, partnership and corporate ownership.

INDIVIDUAL OWNERSHIP

The individual ownership as a type of business organization is probably the oldest and most common of all three.

Any person with an inclination toward individual enterprise usually "goes into business for himself." This form of business ownership may be an indication of the independence and initiative of the individual.

The individual owner is his own boss. He makes all of the decisions, negotiates his own contracts. He establishes the rules by which he wants to operate his business. He plans the layout of his store or factory. He directs its establishment. He initiates all business procedures, hires all of his own help and generally maintains direct control over all of the activities of his business.

Depending upon his ability to delegate authority, he may establish some departmentalization and hire key personnel to handle some of the more detailed activities of the business. He will nevertheless retain close over-all supervision.

The one-man business can only grow if the owner has the ability to pick and retain competent key personnel to help him in the operation of all of the aspects of his business.

The growth of the business is dependent upon production and profit. The original investment of the individual owner is limited to his own capital and to the money which he may be able to borrow from his bank, friends or relatives. He can look to no other source of funds because he will not permit anyone to share in his business.

From the legal standpoint, he alone is responsible for the obligations of the business. All of his capital is pledged, all of his assets are subject to call in the event that his business reverses drain the money that he has invested. Obligations incurred in operating the business will have to be paid from his personal or even real property, if they are not satisfied from the assets of the business.

In a sole-ownership enterprise, there is no separation between the property of the business and the property of the owner. He has the right to draw any money he wants from the business and the business may drain all of his funds if it is not self-sustaining.

At this point it should be mentioned that if he draws money from the business in unusual amounts and if these withdrawals will make the business insolvent, the creditors will be able to trace those funds, follow them and recover them since they were taken in fraud of their rights and interests.

On the other hand, if the business is successful he derives all of the benefits of sole ownership. He does not have to share his profits with anyone. It is his investment, his risk and therefore his gain.

He may, as an incentive, establish some form of profit sharing with his key employees or with all of his employees. However, this would be a voluntary gesture on his part to improve the morale and will to work of his employees. He is not obligated to share his wealth in any way with anyone.

DOING BUSINESS UNDER A FIRM NAME

An individual may carry on his business in his own name or in the name of a company.

If he decides to do business under an assumed name, he must determine what the requirements are in his particular state.

Generally, there is no restriction against using a company name provided there is sufficient notice given to the public of the name and home address of the person who is the actual owner of that business.

The law may require that a person doing business under a firm name file a certificate to indicate that he is doing business under the name of a company. The certificate will then contain his name, his address and the name of the company which he has assumed. This certificate will then be filed, usually in the office of the county clerk so that it will be a public record and available to all who wish to see it. In addition, he may be required to obtain two certified copies of this certificate.

One of these may be required by his bank, to authorize him to have an account under that name, with himself as the signatory. The other he may be required to post prominently in his place of business, again to give the public the name of the person who owns the company.

Some municipalities may also require that the name of the proprietor of a business, if it is operated under an assumed name, be printed conspicuously on the door or window of the premises.

A person who conducts business under a company or an assumed name may sue and be sued in his own name. However, if the obligation has been incurred under the assumed or company name, such fact may be added to identify the transaction.

Illustration: John Olley is a shoemaker. He owns his own shoe repair shop which he calls the Parkside Shoe Repair Company. He was sued by the Apex Leather Corporation. The name of the action was "Apex Leather Corporation, Plaintiff, against John Olley, doing business under the firm name and style of Parkside Shoe Repair Company."

DISSOLUTION

A person doing business as an individual with sole ownership of his business may discontinue the business at any time he so desires. He may pay all of his debts and obligations, dispose of his stock and fixtures and wind up his business affairs. He needs no one's consent or approval. His only obligation is to make certain that he pays all of his business debts when he sells the assets of the business.

FORMATION OF A PARTNERSHIP

A general business partnership is created by agreement of two or more persons who decide that they want to carry on and operate a business enterprise for profit as co-owners.

The partnership agreement before it is signed should be carefully considered and scrutinized by each partner with competent legal guidance to make certain that his individual interests are protected. This agreement will govern the activities of the partners throughout their partnership relationship. It must be drawn in such a manner as to anticipate any problems that may arise. It should provide within itself the machinery to solve them. Friendship and optimism fade rapidly when business expectations are not realized and personalities clash.

Financial investment by the partners is dependent upon their agreed terms. The investment of skill and experience may be considered in lieu of money.

All partners have equal rights in the partnership business unless by their contract they agree otherwise.

Generally, the contract of partnership need not be in writing unless it specifically falls within the Statute of Frauds. It is strongly suggested, however, that all partnership agreements be in writing to avoid any future misunderstandings.

The partnership agreement must have all of the required elements of a contract to be enforcible. This relationship cannot be forced or imposed on anyone. One partner cannot be forced upon another without his consent. The association must be entered into voluntarily.

Illustration: Arthur, Benton and Carey were partners. Benton died. Arthur wanted to bring Daniels in as a partner. Carey refused. The partnership was dissolved and Arthur and Daniels then formed a new partnership.

The partnership is an entity in all of its business relationships. It makes contracts in the partnership name. Any change in the composition of the partners creates a new partnership and a new entity.

Illustration: Imre and Vigor were partners in a plastering business. They carried a policy of compensation insurance to cover their employees in event of injury. Renier bought Vigor's interest in the business. No notice of such change was given to the insurance company. Claims arising under the new partnership were not recognized by the company. The court sustained the contention of the company that a change in the partners creates a new partnership and a new party not entitled to any benefits under the old contract of insurance.

Partnerships may be required to file a partnership certificate in the county clerk's office, setting forth the names and home addresses of the partners.

If the partnership business is carried on in the name of a company not containing the names of the partners, then a certificate of doing business under that name may also be required.

Illustration: "Imre and Vigor" as a partnership must file a partnership certificate, but not a certificate of doing business. However, if they do business as the 'Excel Plastering Company" they may have to file both certificates.

RIGHTS AND OBLIGATIONS OF PARTNERS

Each partner is the owner of an undivided proportionate share of the partnership property, unless their agreement is to the contrary. This may be based on the proportionate share of the investment. It may be due to the fact that one partner supplies the money and the other the know-how. The one supplying the money, wishing to protect his investment, may request and obtain a greater interest in the business property.

Generally, all partners have an equal share and equal rights in the management and the conduct of the business. Here again, they may, by agreement, determine that the management of the business be delegated to one because of his special ability and experience.

Each partner is entitled to his proportionate share of the profits, unless they have a contrary understanding between them.

Each partner is obligated to share proportionately in the losses of the business.

On demand, a partner is entitled to full and complete information concerning the partnership business. He has the right to have access to the partnership books in order to inspect them. The books should be kept at the firm's place of business. As mentioned, he has the right to an accounting of the partnership assets and liabilities or he can obtain it by a formal court proceeding.

No partner is entitled to receive any pay or compensation for acting in the partnership business. However, if the partnership is dissolved, he may be entitled to reasonable compensation for services rendered in winding up the partnership business.

A partner is not generally entitled to any interest or reimbursement of the money he invested in the partnership. Reimbursement is dependent upon the financial condition of the company after dissolution.

However, he is entitled to interest and return of any money advanced, contributed or loaned to the business, over and above the initial investment.

Partners do not get compensation for their services. Any money drawn by them is charged to the expected profits of the business.

Unless otherwise agreed, partnership differences are settled by a majority vote of the partners. However, if the question involved is contrary to the provisions of the partnership agreement, it must have the consent of all of the partners. Some contracts as drawn may include a provision for arbitration of disputes before any court proceedings are taken. If such is required, then each of the disputing parties may choose an impartial person as an arbitrator. Both of these will then choose a third disinterested person, to create a board of three. Their determination will be final unless it can be shown that there was some irregularity or impropriety in the proceeding.

Each partner is an agent of the partnership in all transactions. He owes to the partnership and to his partners the highest degree of loyalty and good faith. He must account for all of his personal profits derived through or from any partnership transaction.

All partners must consent to any assignment of partnership property, any sale of the good will of their business, any interference of the operation of the business, any confession of judgment or submission of any dispute to arbitration. This requirement may be eliminated by a specific provision authorizing such action in the partnership agreement itself.

POWER AND AUTHORITY OF PARTNERS

Each partner, as an agent of the partnership, binds it by his acts within the scope of the business. Any person who knows that the authority of any partner is limited cannot, of course, bind the partnership by negotiating with him. These restrictions, however, are not binding upon anyone who has no knowledge of any limitation of power of any one partner.

An act of a partner not within the scope of the partnership business cannot bind the others unless it is specifically authorized by them. Knowledge of any facts by one partner binds the others when it is within the scope of the partnership business.

Illustration: Gorman, a partner in a stock brokerage firm, knew that the securities of one of their customers was not properly handled. The firm was charged with responsibility because the knowledge of one partner is considered as knowledge by all.

All partners are jointly and individually responsible for any wrongful act committed by one partner in the course of the firm's business which causes injury to others. Each partner is liable regardless of his personal participation in that wrongful act.

Illustration: Luke, a partner, made fraudulent representations in the sale of some partnership property to Keiser. Keiser sued all of the partners, despite the fact that only Luke committed the wrongful act, and recovered from them all.

The partnership, and that includes all of the partners, is responsible for any breach of trust by one of the partners, when it involves other people's property. A partner's personal assets are subject to the claim of partnership creditors if he is personally made a party defendant and the firm does not have sufficient assets. A partner's personal creditor may only reach his interest in the firm by a charging order or lien directing the partnership to hold and retain any moneys to be paid to the partner subject to the claim.

DISSOLUTION ACCOUNTING AND TERMINATION OF PARTNERSHIP

A partnership is dissolved when one of the partners withdraws or dies. The partnership is terminated on dissolution but continues until all of the affairs have been wound up.

Dissolution occurs at the end of the period for which the firm was organized. If no such period is specified, then it continues at the will of each of the partners. Any partner may withdraw at any time he desires; he need not continue against his wishes. Of course, his withdrawal is dependent upon the financial condition of the partnership. In winding up the affairs of the dissolved firm, he will be held accountable for his share of all of the obligations present and future.

A partner may compel a dissolution by applying to the court for such a decree. This may occur when the business becomes unlawful, in contravention of the agreement, or when he feels that the others are excluding him from partnership activities.

Dissolution does not discharge the obligation of the retiring partner. That can only be discharged by agreement between the creditors and the partners who will continue the business and assume the obligations of the firm.

LIMITED PARTNERSHIPS

A limited partnership is formed by authority of a specific law controlling its formation and its existence. This is necessary because a limited partnership introduces a new aspect in the law of partnership: limitation of liability. Primarily, it is composed of general partners, responsible for the operation of the partnership business and subject to the regular partnership liability.

However, it allows for the addition of limited partners as members of the firm. Unlike the obligations and responsibilities of general partners, the limited partner is only obligated to the firm and to creditors of the firm to the extent of his original promised investment. In formation of the company, a limited partner agrees to invest a definite sum of money. When he pays it, his liability for other payments terminates. If, however, he fails to make full payment, then he may be held responsible for the balance of the amount agreed upon. His share in the profits of the company is dependent upon the agreement at his admission to the partnership.

The creation of a company to include general and limited partners is governed by the limited partnership law which authorizes it. Generally, a certificate of limited partnership must include the name of the firm, the nature and address of the business, the name and home address of each general partner, the name, home address and amount of contribution of each limited partner and the share of the profits of each limited partner. This certificate must be filed in the office of the county clerk and its contents must be published in a newspaper in the county where its principal place of business is to be located. As in all of these requirements, the purpose is to make available to the public the information concerning the actual limit of liability of these special members of the firm.

The operation and management of the business of a limited partnership is carried on by the general partners. Their powers are, however, restricted by the rights and interests of the limited partners.

A limited partner may contribute money or property as agreed but he is not to render any services. The firm name must not contain the name of the limited partner. These precautions are necessary to avoid any impression by the public that he is a general instead of a limited partner.

His responsibility to creditors is limited to his investment in the company. However, if he participates in the control and management of the business, his liability may become that of a general partner as to those creditors who relied upon his apparent membership in the firm in that capacity.

He has the right to inspect the books of the company, obtain complete information about the state of its affairs and, if he can prove his right to it, he can have a dissolution decreed by the court.

Any addition or withdrawal of a limited partner may require the filing and publication of an amended certificate, in accordance with the law.

CORPORATIONS

A corporation is a form of business organization created by its members as prescribed by the corporation law of each state. Once created, it becomes a legal entity with rights, powers and privileges contained in the document by which it is created.

A corporation may be formed by a special law passed by the legislature, created for a special public purpose. Usually a business or stock corporation is formed by the execution of a certificate of incorporation in the name of its organizers and

under the authority of some specific existing law which authorizes its creation.

SOME DEFINITIONS AND DISTINCTIONS

A domestic corporation is one which is formed and created
by the laws within the state. All corporations formed outside of
the state, either in another state or in a foreign country, are
called "foreign corporations." By law a foreign corporation is
not permitted to carry on any business within the state; its contracts are not enforcible; it cannot sue or be sued, unless it obtains permission by filing a certificate with the proper state authority, usually the secretary of state.

A public corporation is formed to accomplish a public purpose, for a public benefit or to further some public need. Municipal corporations are formed to carry on local government in
cities and incorporated villages. Public benefit corporations are
created to construct or operate some public improvement,
such as the New York State Thruway Authority, The Port of
New York Authority, The New York City Housing Authority,
the Reconstruction Finance Corporation.

A professional corporation may be formed as authorized by
state law to practice, and its members or stockholders are entitled to the same protection as in other corporations, unless
they are personally obligated or are charged with malpractice.
It is possible that, as in a partnership, shareholders may be
liable for the malpractice of an associate.

Business or stock corporations are private corporations formed
for the express purpose of conducting business for profit under
corporate protection. Ownership, management and control
are in the stockholders, governed by the provisions of the law
under which they are organized. They are so named because
the members of the corporation receive shares of stock as an
indication of their ownership and their rights in the business.

Nonstock corporations are usually called membership corporations, formed to operate, manage and control some nonprofit activity. No shares of stock are issued. The organizers
and all subsequent members who join may receive certificates
of membership to indicate their participation, but these do not

create any rights to share in any financial benefits of the corporation.

Membership corporations are formed by a group of people, the organizers or incorporators, who prepare and execute a certificate of incorporation also called a "charter." This charter contains all of the life-creating facts of the corporation: its proposed name, its purposes, its principal place of business or office, and the powers that are to be granted to it in accomplishing its purpose. This is generally submitted to a court for approval and, if signed, it is then forwarded to the secretary of state for filing and payment of a fee.

Illustration: Religious, social, literary, benevolent, charitable and scientific organizations are formed in this manner.

THE FORMATION OF A BUSINESS CORPORATION

Persons planning to form a stock corporation to carry on a business for profit are usually called the incorporators. Since the formation of such an organization is a technical legal matter, they must have the proper legal advice to accomplish it. Failure to comply with the formalities will defeat the formation of the corporation.

Depending upon the type of business they plan to pursue, they will determine under what law they plan to incorporate. For example, a banking corporation must conform to the requirements of the banking law, an insurance corporation under the insurance law. Other specialized organizations are governed by specific laws in their formation.

They will then choose the corporate name they want to use. It may be necessary to consult the secretary of state to make certain that no existing corporation has that or a similar name. Since the name of a corporation is the only title used in all of its activities, it must not be the same as any other existing corporation. It must be distinguished from the name of any existing person. The use of the word "Corporation" in one form or another as a part of the name is generally the means by which that distinction is accomplished.

Illustration: The A.B.C. Corporation; The A.B.C. Corp.; The A.B.C. Co., Incorporated; The A.B.C. Company, Inc.

Qualifications of incorporators—those who will sign and execute the corporate charter—are determined by state law and vary. Some require a minimum of 3 who have reached majority. Some require that a certain percentage of them be citizens of the United States and residents of the state. The specific requisites must be determined prior to the formation. Each incorporator must subscribe and promise to buy at least one share of the company's stock. No corporation may be an incorporator of another corporation.

Prior to the formation of the corporation, if it is to be a large financial undertaking, there is usually initiated a promotional drive for financial backing. This is an effort on the part of the incorporators to obtain subscriptions on the stock issue.

This activity may be delegated to persons designated as "promoters." In their activities to bring all of the parties together to invest their money in this new enterprise, the promoters are considered as joint venturers. Their obligations to each other are in the nature of copartners. Since the corporation has as yet not been formed, these promoters are not in a position to bind the corporation legally by their acts or promises. They do however act in a fiduciary capacity for the corporation to be formed by their inducement of investors. As such, they are accountable to the corporation when it is formed.

The promoter is required to account to the corporation for any secret profits which he realizes in the same manner as an agent. In order to obtain the benefits of his activities, the corporation must ratify them when it is formed. Unless it does so, all of his commitments are his own personal obligation and liability.

The corporation is not responsible for any fraud or misrepresentation perpetrated by the promoter upon an investor. However, if his acts are ratified by the corporation, then responsibility for his actions is acquired by the adoption of the transactions which he executed.

"Blue Sky Laws" are enacted by the various states to limit any promotion schemes which may induce the unsuspecting investor to place his money in jeopardy.

When a stock issue is planned, an underwriting contract may be entered into between the corporation and a financial institution which will undertake to sell and dispose of the stock directly to the investing public.

THE CHARTER OR CERTIFICATE OF INCORPORATION

The certificate is prepared to include the name of the corporation, the location of its principal place of business, the purpose for which it is organized, the law or authority under which it is formed, the powers which the corporation is expressly granted in order to accomplish its purposes, the number and kinds of stock to be issued, the names of the incorporators, their home addresses and the number of shares of stock to which they have subscribed, and the names of the directors to act until the first annual meeting of the corporation. The certificate is then signed and sent to the state authority, usually the secretary of state, where it is to be filed and a fee paid. A copy of the certificate is filed in the office of the county clerk where the principal place of business is to be located.

CORPORATE STOCK

A share of stock is a proportionate interest in the financial structure of the corporation. The ownership of a share of stock then is the proof of ownership of such an interest.

Stock in a corporation may be purchased by subscription when it is formed, or thereafter by transaction either directly with the firm or through a broker on a stock exchange. Most corporations in this country are owned by the person managing and controlling the business of the corporation, or by his immediate family. The stock issued is not for sale to any outside investors. Actually, they refuse to sell the stock because it might wrest the control of the company from them. These are sometimes called "family" or "closed" corporations.

The large financial corporations we hear of, listed on the exchanges of the country, have, by the extension and growth of their financial and stock structure, long been removed from the control of its original owners and organizers. Their management and control is usually in the hands of those stockholders who own or control the greatest number of shares of stock.

A corporation may set up two basic types of stock, common stock and preferred stock.

Common stock, so called probably because it has no special benefits or preferences, is usually the greater in number of the stock issued by the corporation. This is the stock which is given the right to control the management and the operation of the corporation. The owner of such stock is entitled to vote in the annual elections for the board of directors and on all other questions presented to the stockholders. Holders of common stock are entitled to dividends from profits only after the preferred stockholders have been paid.

The other type of stock, the preferred, is so called because it is given the preference in the payment of dividends. No dividends can be paid by a corporation except out of profits. If there are profits, then dividends can be declared by the board of directors. First the dividends to the preferred stockholders are paid. If there are any profits left thereafter, there is a dividend declared to the holders of the common stock. The preferred stockholders do not have the right to vote and have no control or voice in the management and operation of the corporation. However, if for any reason there is any grievance as to the management of the corporation affecting their interest, they may seek the help of the court in a stockholders' action.

Preferred stock usually has a stated dividend rate so that the corporation must, if there is a profit, satisfy these stockholders by paying them their dividends at the established rate.

Some preferred stock when issued is made "cumulative." This in effect is a promise to the holder of the preferred stock that he will be paid a dividend every year, at the stated rate. If there is no profit one year, the dividend obligation will carry over to the next until such time as there is a profit and then all arrears must be paid up.

Bonds are an indebtedness of the corporation. A bond is a proportionate share of the entire debt, usually sold in $1,000 denominations. In order to facilitate the additional financing of a corporation by means of loans, bonds are sold by the corporation with a stated interest rate as an outstanding obligation. Bondholders are creditors of the corporation, while stockholders are members or owners.

The stockholders who are authorized to vote gather at the annual meeting of the corporation to determine who will constitute the board of directors for the next year and to decide any other matters presented to them.

With the tremendous increase in the number of stockholders in our nationally known corporations, it is impracticable and impossible to have all or even a fair percentage of the stockholders convene at the regular meeting. Because they are spread over the entire country, the number of stockholders actually attending these meetings is small in relation to the total. The "proxy" vote has therefore been developed, which gives the absentee stockholder an opportunity to have a limited voice in the management of the company. It is limited because it is usually sent out by the management of the corporation to have the voter affirm and approve the existing policies. In certain instances, where competing interests have been able to challenge the management, proxies have been sent out by these challengers to obtain the backing necessary to defeat the administration.

The board of directors is elected by the voting stockholders. The directors hold meetings regularly and thus control and supervise the operation of the business of the corporation. They declare dividends when the books show that there is a profit. They elect officers to carry out their policies. These officers are responsible only to the board for the proper execution of their duties. They are removable by the board if their services are not satisfactory.

Directors are in a fiduciary relationship to the corporation and its business. They may not acquire any special benefits or profits because of their position.

Directors are not usually paid for their services but act in their own interests as owners of the stock of the corporation. They are not personally responsible to the corporation or to the stockholders for the failure of their management policy unless it results from their unauthorized acts and conduct.

Officers of the corporation may be required to be members of the board of directors, by provision of the certificate of incorporation. As officers, they are paid for their services and are agents of the company. They are employed to carry out the instructions and the policies of the board in the operation of the corporate business.

An officer is not required to comply with the directions of an individual member of the board or of any stockholder. He is responsible only to the board as a whole and not to any individual member.

RIGHTS OF STOCKHOLDERS

The certificate of incorporation and the laws governing it determine the rights of the stockholder in his relationship to the corporation.

A stockholder may not interfere with the regular business and management policy of the corporation. He may submit requests and recommendations to the board. The only control the stockholder has over the board is through his vote and through his power to replace the members at elections.

He has the right to inspect the books of the company to determine the number of shares issued and the names of the stockholders.

He does not have the right to inspect any other corporate books and papers unless he can show a reasonable basis of suspicion that the management has been guilty of waste or other illegal acts. He may be able to show that some of the acts of the management were *ultra vires*. He may by recourse to the courts prove that such acts are unauthorized and ask for an injunction preventing the management from proceeding. He may also demand that the individuals responsible reimburse the corporation. Such acts are not considered illegal but merely subject to scrutiny.

Any stockholder may maintain a stockholder's action in his own name and on behalf of other stockholders to protect the corporation from the wrongful acts of its officers and directors. This is called a derivative action. He must bring in the corporation as a party defendant since it is under the control of those persons who he claims are abusing their authority.

Even though the corporation shows a profit, a stockholder
may not compel the board of directors to declare dividends.
Such function is within the discretion of the board entirely.
However, once a dividend has been declared, he may demand
that it be paid.

The basic importance of the corporate form of business organization is the limitation of liability which it allows. The
stockholder is not personally responsible for any of the debts of
the corporation; neither, of course, is the individual director or
the officer. The sole extent of liability is the money invested in
the acquisition of the stock. The money so invested is the limit
of his loss in the event of financial failure of the corporation.
The stockholder is only responsible for the obligation he incurred at the time of his subscription.

Since a corporation acts through its officers and board of
directors; they are its agents. As such agents, they are not personally liable for any commitments in the name of the corporation. However, they do bind the corporation in all of their acts
within the scope of their express and implied authority.

A corporation is responsible for the criminal, tortious and
negligent acts of its agents.

Corporations have been held liable in slander, malicious
prosecution, false arrest and even conspiracy, when such acts
were committed by their agents in the scope of their authority
and in furtherance of the corporation's business.

DISSOLUTION OF CORPORATION

A corporation created for a definite period of time automatically ceases to exist at the end of that time. The legislature,
having created a corporation, may by another enactment, terminate its existence. The corporation may, on consent of all
stockholders or after a judicial proceeding, surrender its charter.

The state attorney general may, by judicial proceedings, demand the dissolution of a corporation if it was insolvent, did
not pay its taxes or suspended business for at least one year.

A corporation may cease to exist when it is merged with another corporation. The effect of a merger is the acquisition of

all of the assets of the corporation by another corporation with the subsequent discontinuance of its business.

Consolidation is the joining of two corporations to form a new third corporation.

Reorganization is the change in the corporate structure when it is insolvent or in bankruptcy, to allow for an adjustment of the claims of its creditors and a continuation of its business.

Summation

Points to Remember about Forms of Business Organization

Our interest in the types of business organizations is motivated by many factors. Some may be anticipating the formation of a business and would naturally want to know the advantages and disadvantages of each. Some of us may want to invest in one and want to make certain that our interests will be protected.

The information, of course, is technical and requires legal guidance if it is to be used for the actual formation of a business. It is offered here so that sufficient information will be available to stimulate greater inquiry when legal advice is actually sought.

Things to be kept in mind are as follows:

The type chosen must conform with the personality of the individual. Individual ownership is best for those people who have the need to dominate and run things their way.

Partnership presents the advantage of sharing both the financial and the operating responsibility of the business. Both the individual and the partnership may do business under a firm name.

The limited partnership presents the added feature of having additional investors in the business who do not have the right to interfere. They are only responsible for the firm's reverses to the extent of their investment.

The corporation offers to the stockholder protection of his personal assets from the reach of the firm's creditors in the event of financial reverses.

CHAPTER 9

Marriage and Family Relations

The subject of marriage and family relations needs very little introduction or comment. Everyone knows about it. Yet exactly how much do we know?

Do we know just what obligations we undertake when we marry?

Do we have any rights? Can we expect certain benefits, as well as obligations?

What if things just don't work out? How can a marriage be dissolved?

Unfortunately, some of our friends have marital problems. We read of the more sensational ones in the newspapers. Other than the emotional differences, what are the legal causes that can affect a marriage?

The statutory law affecting marriage and divorce differs among the states in certain specific instances. Generally, however, the subject can be adequately covered by giving you the provisions of law which apply in the majority of the states and some unique individual exceptions. The general principles of marital obligations and their dissolution can be discussed because they apply universally.

MARRIAGE

Marriage is usually defined as a civil contract. By interpretation of the courts it is more than just a contract, it is a relationship in which the public and the state have a participating interest. It is the foundation of the family, the basis of our social structure. No change is permitted in this relationship without the approval of the state through its courts.

This attitude is indicated by the provision in one state that no uncontested divorce is permitted. The state has counsel assigned to defend the marriage and to preserve it. Another state requires that objections against a marriage be filed and heard by two justices of the peace.

The word "marriage" is used to denote the actual ceremony which solemnizes the contract. It is also the relationship which is created by that ceremony with all of its obligations and responsibilities.

The validity of the marriage is determined by the state where it takes place. Since some of the requirements for marriage vary in the different states, a marriage which is valid where it took place is recognized in all other states in the union. The rights under that marriage can therefore be enforced everywhere in the United States. This is established by the provision in the United States Constitution which requires all states to give full faith and credit to all enactments of the other states. Each state, however, has the right to control the activities of its own citizens. If a resident of one state goes to another state to get married because he wants to avoid certain restrictive provisions, limiting his right to marry within the state, his home state may refuse to recognize that marriage. Each state may by law make specific legal restrictions in its control of marriage. It may by law prohibit the marriage, within the state, of nonresidents who do not intend to live in the state.

CAPACITY TO MARRY

Persons legally qualified to enter into a civil contract are generally capable of entering into a marriage contract. There is some difference among the states as to the minimum age requirement for a valid marriage.

In most states the age of consent for males is 18 and 16 for females. But they may require the consent of their parents or guardian until the male is 21 and the female 18.

Several of the states have laws which prohibit intermarriage between the races, so-called miscegenation laws, making such marriages void and the issue illegitimate. However, such laws are in violation of the United States Constitution and have been declared to be in violation of the Fourteenth Amendment. Any such existing law of any state, not specifically repealed, is of no legal effect. Although the states have the right to determine requirements for a valid marriage or a valid divorce, there can be no violation of an individual's constitutional rights.

Marriages between blood relatives in any relationship closer than cousins are void because they are incestuous. Here again there is the possibility of criminal prosecution. Marriages between an uncle and niece or nephew and aunt are void. Children of such marriages are in some states considered illegitimate. In others, because the courts attempt to remove such stigma from the children, they are considered legitimate by legal enactment.

Many of the states specifically prohibit the marriage of epileptics, lunatics, idiots, imbeciles and people of weak and unsound mind. Some have included alcoholics, drug addicts, habitual criminals and poor persons in the list prohibited from marrying. These restrictions are based on the anticipation that they will not be able to properly care for and maintain their families and might create additional burdens for the state.

The marriage of a person who has a spouse living is void unless that marriage has been previously dissolved. A marriage may be dissolved by annulment or divorce. It may also be terminated by a proceeding instituted when one spouse has been absent for more than 5 years, or where the spouse has been finally sentenced to serve a term of life imprisonment.

All states require that an application to marry be made by the bride and groom giving some of their vital statistics. If they are underage, they also must present the consent of their parents. If there is any question concerning their age they may be required to furnish proof of age. Parental consent for underage applicants may be dispensed with if the marriage ceremony is performed by a judge.

At least three quarters of the states require a medical examination and certificate prior to the issuance of the license, to assure the absence in both of any communicable disease.

Each state requires that the marriage be solemnized by a religious leader, a public official or a judge. After such a ceremony some record must be made of the marriage by the filing of the marriage certificate with a designated office for the keeping of such public records.

About one third of the states also recognize common-law marriages, entered into within their borders. A common-law marriage is an agreement made by a man and a woman to live together as man and wife without any solemnization or official ceremony. No license is required, no certificate and no legal formality. It is entirely dependent upon their solemn intention to cohabit and live together in a decent and orderly manner, holding each other out to their neighbors and to the community as husband and wife.

A common-law marriage which is valid in the state where it was consummated is valid and recognized in all states. However, if a resident of a state which does not recognize the common-law marriage left the state to enter into such a marriage, the state has the right to refuse to recognize it.

Marriage by contract is another form of marriage without official ceremony and without a license. This form is only recognized in a few states. Both parties enter into a written contract of marriage. There may be a provision for filing or recording it officially. When that is done it becomes as valid and binding as though it were solemnized after the issuance of a license.

RIGHTS AND RESPONSIBILITIES OF HUSBAND AND WIFE

The husband is the head of the house. He chooses the domicile, the permanent location for the household. The wife and family must reside at the place chosen by him unless it is unreasonable and is detrimental to their health and welfare.

It is his duty to support and maintain his family out of his property or the result of his labor. He must maintain them in accordance with his financial ability. A husband who is prosperous may not keep his family in poverty. He may not limit them only to the bare necessities of existence.

Some states provide that if the husband is unable to support his family, it is the duty of the wife to help him in this responsibility.

The husband, when he acquires property during the marriage, is the owner unless it is taken in the name of both the husband and the wife or it is purchased by the earnings of both. Property which the wife owned before her marriage or which she has individually acquired since, continues to belong to her.

A husband who willfully abandons his wife and children or fails to furnish the necessary food, clothing, shelter and medical attention may be compelled to do so or be punished.

Desertion by the husband and failure to support his family may subject him to criminal prosecution. Uniform laws pertaining to desertion and the enforcement of support have been established and passed by various states. A person who deserted his family and is apprehended in another state may be compelled to contribute to their support by proceedings instituted in the state where he is located through the Family Court.

The wife has, in all states, been emancipated from the restrictions which existed in the common law relating to her individual rights to own and dispose of her property.

She has an independent right to enter into contracts in her own name. She may sue and be sued in her own name without being required to have her husband joined as a party.

Both husband and wife may, in most states, enter into contracts with each other concerning any subject matter, provided that they do not in any way impair their marital status or relieve the husband of his obligation to support his family.

The contracts of a married woman do not affect her husband's property and do not make him responsible unless they are for items necessary for the family and for the household. The wife is considered the agent of the husband in the purchase of necessaries for the home and he is held responsible for their payment.

Any property she acquires is her own. Any sum of money that she recovers in any lawsuit or as a result of any claim is entirely her own.

A wife may take out insurance on her husband's life and make herself the beneficiary since she has an insurable interest. This insurance continues in effect even though they are subsequently divorced.

Antenuptial agreements made between husband and wife are valid and enforcible provided they do not abrogate the husband's obligation to support her. Provisions in such agreements may include a waiver by each to inherit from the other, the participation in a religious marriage ceremony or the religious upbringing of their children. Questions of inheritance usually occur in second and later marriages when the interests of children of a prior marriage are involved.

A married woman has the right to sue a third person for injury to her person, her property or her character and reputation. In any of these actions, if the injury results in loss of consortium or loss of services of the wife, the husband is entitled to recover for such loss. A husband is entitled to the services and the charms of his wife, and anyone who interferes is liable to him. There is, however, no unanimity among the states concerning the right of the wife to the attentions and consortium of her husband.

A married woman is liable for her tortious acts. She can be sued for any damage which results from her wrongful acts. Her husband is not responsible for her actions unless they were instigated by him or done at his request.

Some states authorize a husband and wife to sue each other in tort, both as to personal injury and property damage.

In a few of the states, a married woman must petition the court to be permitted to act as a free dealer, in order that she may carry on her business activities without any restriction.

Some states permit a widow the right of dower. This gives her an interest in any real property owned by her husband at his death. The interest granted her varies. Some states give her a life estate, to be enjoyed only during her lifetime, while others only give her an actual percentage ownership.

The real property owned by a woman at her death is in some states subject to the right of "curtesy" in favor of her surviving husband. Similar to dower, it is intended to give the widower an interest in the property to keep him from being disinherited and left destitute at her death.

COMMUNITY PROPERTY

There are a few states which adhere to the principle that personal property acquired by a husband and wife during marriage is jointly owned. With certain exceptions, all property acquired by either spouse after the marriage is considered as community property. Each spouse owns an undivided one half in all such commonly owned property. Property previously owned or acquired after the marriage by personal gift or inheritance remains separately owned by the individual. In the event of divorce, each is entitled to his or her share of this community property. In the event of death, the survivor is entitled to his or her share while the share of the decedent is subject to disposition by will or intestacy.

CHILDREN

Generally, the relationship of parent and child is created by legitimate birth, by illegitimate birth or by adoption.

A birth is considered legitimate when a child is conceived or born after the marriage of its parents and in certain states when the parents marry after the birth of the child. Every effort is made to preserve legitimacy.

The duty of parents to give their children love, affection and kind treatment has been established by social usage and public opinion.

Both parents are entitled to the custody of their children unless there is a disruption of the family. The court will then award custody to one with reasonable visitation to the other. When deprived of custody or visitation, relief is obtained by means of a writ of habeas corpus.

The obligation to support the children rests primarily upon the father. If the father is incapacitated, dead or has deserted, this duty devolves upon the mother.

Most states do not hold the parents responsible for the torts of their children. However, there is a trend now developing to bring the parents into court to answer for the delinquent acts of their children. Some states actually hold the parents liable for the willful and malicious acts of the child. Damages which may be assessed against the parents in such states range from $250 to $500.

By special legislation, sometimes called the family-car law, the father, as the owner of the family car, is responsible for any damage resulting from its negligent operation by his child, with his permission.

The negligence of the parent will not prevent a child who has been injured and is suing through a legal representative, from recovering for those injuries. If the child is *non-sui juris,* his negligence does not make his parent responsible. The term *non-sui juris* means that he does not know the nature of his acts and that they are dangerous. If he is injured because his parents did not prevent him from committing that negligent act which resulted in his injury, he may still recover.

A parent is entitled to the services of his minor child. He may sue any person who has deprived him of those services.

Illustration: Reider sued Jalon for the loss of services of his son Richard, because Jalon, in negligently operating his car, struck and injured Richard. Reider was compelled to expend money for Richard's medical care and to hire help to substitute for the help that Richard gave him. Reider recovered for those damages independently of the recovery which Richard was awarded for his personal injury.

A parent is entitled to the earnings of his minor child if he notifies the employer and requests that those earnings be paid to him. If after such notice the employer pays the money to the infant, he may be compelled to pay it again to the parent.

A parent and child may not sue each other for personal torts in most jurisdictions. Under the common law it was not permitted because it affects the natural relationship of love, affection and respect within the family. However, an infant, in some states, is now permitted to sue his parent if the injury he sustained is due to the willful and wanton act of the parent.

Illustration: A father who drove a car while intoxicated was held to be wanton and reckless to a greater degree than mere negligence when by driving in that condition he had an accident which resulted in injury to his child.

ILLEGITIMATE CHILDREN

The natural mother of an illegitimate child is responsible for the care, support, medical and funeral expenses of the child.

The putative father is the one who is to be proved the father of the illegitimate infant. He can be compelled to support his child by a proceeding to establish paternity. These proceedings may be instituted by the mother or any public agency responsible for the child's care to prevent it from becoming a public charge. If the putative father acknowledges his paternity in writing, the illegitimate child may acquire certain rights against the father or against his estate.

The child may inherit from its mother. However, the mother can only inherit from her illegitimate child if he is not survived by a widow or children. If he has a widow or children surviving him, they inherit as though he were legitimate.

The courts of most states make every effort to avoid illegitimacy. They will, under most circumstances, determine the children to be legitimate if they are the issue of a void or voidable marriage.

A mother who gives an illegitimate child for adoption to an individual may change her mind and get the child back unless she has abandoned the child or consented to the formal adoption in court proceedings. However, if the adoption is carried out through a recognized adoption agency, the consent of the mother to the formal adoption may not be required. State legislation has been enacted to limit the time during which the natural mother may recant the adoption and demand the return of her child.

ADOPTED CHILDREN

Adoption is a legal proceeding brought in a court to have a child who is not the natural child of the petitioner declared to be his child by adoption. Such proceedings usually require the consent of the natural parents.

Each state has its own statutes and requirements for adoption proceedings. All require a court proceeding and a hearing to determine the qualifications and the rights of the adoptive parents as against the natural parents.

In an adoption, all parental obligations between the natural parents and the child are terminated. The reciprocal duty of support is ended.

There is a fair division of authority as to the right of the child to inherit from its natural parents after the adoption. Some permit an adopted child to continue its right to inherit from its natural parents while others consider this right terminated as well. The natural parents, however, lose their right to inherit from their child once the adoption proceeding is complete.

Most states agree that an adopted child acquires the right to inherit from his adoptive parents and they, in turn, acquire the right to inherit from him. If the statute is not specific, declaring that an adopted child shall inherit as if he were a natural child, the courts may be called upon to decide the question.

> Illustration: Statute in one case did not specifically give an adopted child the right to inherit as if he were a natural child. The will of Elias gave all of his property to his nephew, Jensen, if he died "without heirs." It made no specific mention of his adopted son, Edward, who claimed as an "heir." The court decided that the law which applied in this case did not make Edward an heir of Elias. The estate was given to Jensen, in accordance with the provisions of the will, because of an unfortunate choice of words.

Some states require that the foster and adoptive parents must be of the same religious faith as the natural parents of the child.

ANNULMENT, SEPARATION AND DIVORCE

Laws in all states declare certain marriages, though consummated, to be void for a variety of legal grounds.

Each state has the right to determine validity, so incestuous marriages and marriages of epileptics, drug addicts, alcoholics, habitual criminals, mental defectives and poor persons are some of the grounds for declaring a marriage void.

Legally, a marriage which is void never had legal existence and nothing need be done. However, in order to clear the record and to have proof available that the marriage which was performed is void, some proceeding should be had. Social Security, retirement and insurance records may require correction.

One means of doing this is to bring a proceeding in equity to declare the marriage void. However, other means may be used, depending upon the law of the state, so that in an applicable situation an annulment or even a divorce proceeding may be instituted, resulting in a decree or judgment to be used as authority for the change.

VOIDABLE MARRIAGE

A marriage which is induced by fraud or duress is voidable by a proceeding begun by the injured party. A marriage of a person under legal age or one who is mentally incompetent may be avoided by action of the infant or on behalf of the incompetent.

These marriages, however are valid and binding until they are avoided by an annulment proceeding instituted on behalf of the minor or the incompetent by his guardian or parent. The status of the marriage is declared to be avoided and the rights of the parties to community property or custody of children is determined. In those jurisdictions where the annulment is not authorized, the divorce may be used. Whichever proceeding is used, the effect is to leave the parties as though no marriage had ever taken place.

Children, the issue of such a marriage, are usually declared by the courts to be legitimate.

DISSOLUTION OF MARRIAGE

Certain of the states have by statutory enactment made relief available, by a special proceeding, where the marriage relationship has been affected after the consummation of a valid marriage.

If one of the parties becomes incurably insane after the marriage, the other may institute a proceeding to dissolve the marriage. If he can show by sufficient medical and psychiatric proof that such mental illness has continued for a designated period of years and that such illness is incurable, the court will issue a decree dissolving the marriage and leaving the petitioner free to remarry.

However, if it is the wife who is incurably insane, the husband will be granted such relief only if he obligates himself to support her as long as she lives, whether she remains in an institution or is subsequently released.

The subsequent sanity of the spouse does not affect this proceeding nor the status of the petitioner. Any marriage subsequently entered into by him is valid and not affected.

In those states where such a proceeding is not authorized, the courts may be permitted to grant such relief by divorce.

The other special proceeding to dissolve a marriage in some states is frequently called an Enoch Arden proceeding. This applies in cases where a spouse has disappeared without explanation and has not been heard from for a specified number of years. The remaining spouse may make an application to the court to be relieved of his marital obligation. He must show that the other spouse has been missing and has not been heard from for the required number of years. He must show that he made a sincere effort to locate the whereabouts of his missing spouse without success. He must claim that he therefore believes his missing spouse to be dead.

The court will then set a date for a hearing. A notice of such hearing must be published in a newspaper in the county where the couple resided. After hearing the testimony under oath, the court will then decree the marriage to be dissolved. Such a decree terminates the marital status; leaving the spouse free to remarry. It is not affected by a subsequent return of the missing spouse.

In such a proceeding it is not necessary to show that the absent spouse is dead. It is merely necessary to show diligent search and a conclusion that, since he has not been heard from, he is dead. Disappearance alone is not sufficient. A proceeding must be instituted for the marriage to be legally dissolved.

Those states which do not have such a proceeding usually provide for similar relief by an application for divorce.

Some states provide by law that any person whose spouse has been sentenced to a term of life imprisonment may apply to be relieved of his marital responsibility and given permission to remarry. This does not in any way affect the felon's property rights. He does not forfeit any of his property rights. He is merely declared legally dead as to his marriage and his marital rights. His subsequent pardon or release does not affect this determination or the remarriage of his spouse.

SEPARATION

A legal separation from "bed and board" is accomplished by agreement or court decree, and continues all existing marital obligations while giving the parties the right to live separate and apart.

SEPARATION BY AGREEMENT

A husband and wife may enter into an agreement by which they agree to live separate and apart from each other and determine between them the apportionment of their assets, the terms of support, alimony, custody, visitation and other relevant matters.

A few jurisdictions permit a separation agreement to be made in expectation of separation. Others contend that such agreements affect the marital status and are not legal until the parties by their acts have changed their status by separating.

The provisions of a separation agreement usually drawn with the aid of counsel, contain all of the terms agreed upon by the parties. They cover custody of the children, financial support of the wife and the children and rights of visitation with the children. There may be a provision that these terms are to be included and made a part of any subsequent decree of divorce.

The effect of a separation agreement, if it is fair and valid and not forced upon the other by fraud, duress or undue influence, is binding on both. Any subsequent change in circumstances or subsequent court adjudication will not affect the terms agreed upon by contract. The court does not have the power to interfere with the agreed terms except as to the support of the children or if the spouse may become a public charge.

A provision in a separation agreement for the support of the wife during her lifetime will not be terminated upon the death of the husband but will continue as a charge upon his estate.

In the event of a subsequent divorce and the wife's remarriage, the husband may have to continue to pay alimony unless the contract so states to the contrary.

When a husband and wife resume their marital relationship they automatically terminate their separation agreement.

Some states have by legislation made an existing separation agreement the basis for a divorce.

SEPARATION BY COURT PROCEEDINGS

In those jurisdictions where there is no provision for separation, all proceedings are for divorce. The grounds for such legal relief are set forth in the laws which authorize the proceeding.

If a wife does not want to sever her marital status, she may, in a court of equity, institute a suit for separate maintenance in all situations where she is entitled to an absolute divorce.

In those states where separation actions or actions for divorce from bed and board are recognized, they are usually based on cruel and inhuman treatment, desertion, abandonment, failure to support or such other grounds which indicate habitual intemperance, and such conduct which makes living together insufferable.

Illustration: Helen brought suit for a separation against her husband Eric on the ground of his adultery. She proved that he obtained an illegal divorce in another state, remarried and brought his new "wife" back to their hometown. She claimed that this action on his part was causing her mental agony and shame before her friends. The court found cruel and human treatment to warrant a decree of separation. She was entitled to but did not want a divorce.

Proof of the treatment which would entitle the plaintiff to a decree of separation is dependent upon the facts and the effect such conduct of the defendant has upon the plaintiff.

> Illustration: Hubert is suing his wife Claire for a separation on the ground that she was constantly taunting and tormenting him with her descriptions of her amorous affairs with other men. This was held sufficient basis for a separation decree because of cruelty.

The legal effect of a separation is to give each the right to establish his own household and to live separately and apart from the other. This is particularly important to the wife, since legally she is compelled to reside with her husband and cannot establish her own residence without being subject to the charge of abandonment. Both are relieved of their marital duty to cohabit. In some instances the guilty party may be ordered to refrain from communicating with the other. They are, however, not free to remarry since they are still married to each other.

In a separation action, the wife may be entitled to alimony *pendente lite,* during the litigation. Since she is no longer living with her husband and getting his support, she is entitled to that support until such time as the court will make its final determination. She will also be entitled to counsel fees, an amount adequate and sufficient to enable her to obtain an attorney to defend her. If the wife is the plaintiff, to obtain alimony and counsel fees she must show that she does not have the financial means to prosecute the suit and that she has a reasonable possibility of success.

After hearing the testimony at trial, the court will determine the issues and arrange for the support of the children. If the situation warrants it will allow the wife permanent alimony for her support.

In addition to separate domicile and support, the important issue of custody of children must be decided in a decree of separation. The court usually grants custody of children to the mother because of the belief that a child's place is with its mother. Even when the mother is responsible as the guilty party in a matrimonial action, the court may in the interest and welfare of the children award them to her. Usually, the court will grant generous rights of visitation to the other parent. It designates the periods when he may visit with them or take them out for entertainment or recreation. The court may also arrange for extended vacation trips.

However, when an offer is made by the spouse to return after an abandonment, it must be accepted. A failure to accept this return will expose the other spouse to a countercharge of abandonment.

DIVORCE

All states, within their legal jurisdictions, provide for the granting of an absolute divorce from the bonds of matrimony on various grounds. Adultery, extreme cruelty, abandonment, desertion, neglect, habitual intemperance, addiction to drugs, habitual drunkenness are some of those grounds.

In New York, until recently, the only basis for divorce was adultery. New legislation has introduced cruel and inhuman treatment, abandonment, imprisonment for more than three years and separation, either by decree or agreement, after one year, as additional grounds for divorce.

Extreme cruelty has been defined as the wrongful infliction of grievous bodily injury or grievous mental suffering.

Willful neglect is the neglect of the husband to provide his wife with the common necessities of life, when he is financially able to do so. It may also be the failure to do so because of idleness, profligacy or dissipation.

Incompatibility and a breakdown of the marriage have been added as grounds for divorce, thus tending toward no-fault. However, such grounds are not accepted by all states.

Divorce *a vinculo* from the bonds of matrimony is a termination of the marriage and all of its obligations. It does not usually relieve the husband of the obligation to support his wife and children. The court will provide for the custody of the children in its decree. Each spouse may then remarry depending upon the court's decree and the laws of the state.

An action for divorce then is brought by the person who claims to be affected by the conduct of his spouse. He sets forth the grounds on which he bases his claim and asks for a decree of the court to dissolve the marriage and give him custody of the children. If the plaintiff is a woman, she will also claim alimony *pendente lite* and counsel fees on the ground that she does not have the financial means to prosecute her action and that she has a reasonable possibility of success. She will also demand permanent alimony if she wins the divorce.

If the wife is the defendant she will, when she answers the complaint, make a request for alimony *pendente lite* and counsel fees to defend the action.

Defenses to a divorce action may show that the cause of action is outlawed by the statute of limitations, that the grounds for such action were procured by conspiracy, collusion and connivance or that the plaintiff condoned such act on the part of the defendant knowing of such behavior. As indicated above, the trend appears to be to eliminate the wrongdoing by one spouse as the basis for a divorce, although such a ground is always available. When the parties to a marriage realize and agree that it cannot continue, they are given an opportunity to terminate it.

A trial of the issues will be had. After an opportunity to hear all of the testimony and judge the demeanor of the parties the court will, by its decree, determine the outcome of the case.

Many states provide that such decree be temporary or interlocutory. It determines the rights of the parties as to marital status, alimony and custody of the children. However, the marriage is not terminated until the final decree is entered, depending upon the provision of the state law.

THE "FOREIGN" DIVORCE DECREE

The decree of divorce obtained in one state is recognized as a "foreign divorce" and enforceable in all other states. This is based on the clause in the United States Constitution which requires all states to give full faith and credit to all of the public acts, records, judicial proceedings and determinations of the sister states. Thus when a court obtains jurisdiction of the parties and the subject matter of a cause of action for divorce or separation, the judgment it renders is binding anywhere in the United States.

However, by judicial interpretation, each state has the right to determine for itself if the court of the sister state obtained jurisdiction of the action and the parties, before it can be required to recognize the decision.

The problem of enforcing a "foreign divorce" arises when a person who is resident of one state, seeking a divorce which is difficult to obtain, goes to another state and obtains a divorce there. He then returns to his home state and attempts to enforce the terms of that out-of-state divorce.

The basis of a court's jurisdiction of subject matter in a matrimonial action is usually whether the parties were married within the state or still reside there. Jurisdiction of the parties is based upon their appearing as participants in the case or being served with proper and legal process of the court. Under such circumstances the failure to appear or answer would constitute a default, if there is jurisdiction of the parties.

If the efforts to serve the legal process and obtain jurisdiction of the person are in compliance with the requirements of that state, then proper jurisdiction of the defendant has been obtained.

Illustration: The laws of one state require that the summons in an action for divorce be published in a certain newspaper within the state for a stated number of times and a copy of the summons and complaint be sent by registered mail to the last known address of the defendant. If the plaintiff, in attempting to obtain jurisdiction of the defendant, complies with that requirement, jurisdiction over the defendant has been obtained in accordance with the laws of that state sufficient to give that court's decision the constitutional right to full faith and credit.

However, if in the above situation the plaintiff failed to mail the copy of the summons and complaint as required, he failed to comply with the legal requirement. In failing to do so, the court did not under its laws acquire jurisdiction over the defendant. Its decision would not then be entitled to the recognition and enforcement by the courts of other states.

THE DIVORCE DECREE OF A FOREIGN COUNTRY

A divorce decree rendered in a foreign country will usually be recognized in all of our states on the basis of comity and friendly relations with that country.

However, the courts may determine for themselves whether the court of that country obtained jurisdiction of the parties and the subject matter. They may refuse to recognize such foreign decree if they find there was no jurisdiction.

ENFORCEMENT OF DECREE

A valid judgment obtained against the husband, which requires that he pay alimony, is enforcible against him in any state in which he resides or where he is apprehended. As in the enforcement and collection of any other judgment, any property belonging to the defendant may be reached and used to pay for the support of his children or the alimony to his divorced wife.

The proceeding to attach that property, also known as sequestration, entitles the property to be sold and the proceeds to be used to satisfy this obligation.

The failure or refusal of a defendant husband to pay alimony in accordance with a decree of the court may result in a fine or a jail term for contempt of court.

THE "QUASI-MARRIAGE"

The currently widespread practice of couples living together without the benefit of a legal marriage ceremony has brought to the fore the question of their legal obligations.

This "quasi-marriage," if it consists only in living together, does not in itself create any legal problem, since there is no legal commitment.

However, if this relationship is based on some agreement or mutual promise between the two persons, we have the elements of a contract and its consequent mutual obligations.

The matter then becomes merely a question of proof. If a

contract is established and the commitments under it are proved, then the courts will enforce it.

Of course, if a common-law marriage is established and such a marriage is legal in the state where litigation is instituted, then the regular marital responsibilities are in effect.

Summation
Points to Remember about Marriage and Family Relations

Marriage is the foundation of the family. The family is the basis of our social structure. The obligations and responsibilities in marriage and in the family form the core of communal existence.

Some of the basic concepts to keep in mind are:

Marriage is more than just a contract. It is a relationship vital to the public interest. It cannot be created or dissolved without permission or authority of the state.

The husband and the wife are responsible to each other and to the community. The children, although a primary obligation of their parents, are also considered the wards of the state, receiving the protection of the courts.

Each state by its laws authorizes the dissolution of a marriage. The grounds for such dissolution are specific and must be complied with. Annulment, separation and divorce are available depending upon the right to such relief.

The United States Constitution directs that a judgment of one state is entitled to full faith and credit in the courts of a sister state. However, the judgment must have been obtained in a court that had jurisdiction of the parties and the subject matter to be entitled to such recognition.

The "foreign" divorce is subject to the same scrutiny in the courts of the sister states.

Divorces obtained in a foreign country are recognized on the basis of comity between the countries. However, here again the state court is entitled to delve into the question of jurisdiction.

If these decrees and judgments are based upon the required jurisdiction then they are enforcible in all courts in the United States.

CHAPTER 10

Torts

Just what is a tort? How can we avoid committing one un-
intentionally? How can we protect ourselves against it? What
relief can we get?

SOME DEFINITIONS AND DISTINCTIONS

A tort has been defined generally as a civil wrong. It is an
invasion of any private and personal right which each of us has
by virtue of the federal and state laws and constitutions. It is
the duty of all to observe and respect these rights. A breach of
this duty, which is imposed by the law, is a tort.

Each one of us has the right to be secure in his personal
liberty and his personal safety. We have the right to enjoy a
good reputation if we deserve it. We have the right to enjoy
and use our property without any interference by others.

The subject of torts, then, includes a study of the rights of
the individual and the relief available to him if these rights
are violated.

The law attempts to provide relief wherever there is a
violation of a personal right. However, in addition to the tort,
there must also be a resulting damage or injury. Without damage there can be no recovery.

The personal right affected must be one which is created by
law and not by contract. Relief for a breach of a contract right
is available by an action on the contract. On occasion, one act
may, at the same time, be a tort and a breach of contract. The
relief then is at the election of the person who suffered the
damage.

Illustrations: Johansen rented a truck from Tomson to haul lumber. When he finished, he decided to haul some rocks he needed to fill the foundation of his new house. Driving the truckload of rocks over the rough road broke the springs. To recover his damage, Tomson had the choice of suing on the breach of contract or on the tort of conversion. Johansen had used the truck to carry rock without Tomson's authority.

Helen left her fur coat with Axel Furriers to have the sleeves repaired. During the week end, the owner's daughter went to a formal dance and was permitted by her father to use Helen's coat. The coat was stolen. Helen had the election of suing in conversion, which is a tort, or on breach of contract.

The person who commits a tort is responsible for all damage which flows directly from his act.

Illustration: Arbuckle attacked Bemis on the street, suddenly and without warning. In defending himself, Bemis raised his case, which struck Cole as he was passing by. Arbuckle was held responsible for the injury suffered by Cole.

A crime is a public wrong, an offense against the community, the government and public authority. By law, certain acts constitute crimes, although they may also violate personal rights. In addition to the criminal prosecution, the person injured may maintain a civil action in tort.

Illustration: Defamation of character is punishable as a crime and is the basis for an action in tort.

In the prosecution of a crime, the district attorney representing the state or the people must prove the defendant guilty of the crime "beyond a reasonable doubt."

In the civil action, the plaintiff must prove the defendant responsible for the tort and the damage "by a fair preponderance of the credible evidence."

Just as there can be no recovery on a tort without damage, there can be no recovery for damage by an act which is not wrongful.

Illustration: Lewis, excavating on his land, used dynamite. One explosion caused the windows of his neighbor's house to shatter, broke some glassware and chinaware. Terris, the neighbor, sued Lewis for the damage. At the trial Lewis proved that the blasting was necessary, that all precautions were taken and that no greater charge was used than was absolutely required. Since a person has the right to use his own property for legal and necessary purposes, Lewis was not responsible for the damage.

PARTIES RESPONSIBLE FOR TORTS

Generally, every person who violates the personal or property right of another is financially responsible for the damage directly caused by his act. However, persons who, because of their tender age or mental disability do not know the consequence of their acts, may be relieved of such responsibility.

Public officials or peace officers who, in their official capacity and in performance of their duty, violate a personal right of a private citizen may be absolved of liability because it was an act necessary for the public safety or the public welfare.

Illustration: Hooper, a policeman, arrested Benes without a warrant on the reasonable belief that he had committed a felony. Benes was found to be innocent. Hooper was not liable to Benes either in an action for false arrest or malicious prosecution.

Public security is paramount. A person's right to liberty is subordinate if there is a reasonable belief of guilt by the arresting officer.

The federal and state governments are sovereign and may not be sued unless they authorize it. The federal government and some of the states have established courts of claims to entertain all actions against them.

Illustration: Edon's car was rammed by a mail truck. He was compelled to institute suit to recover for his injury in the federal court of claims.

Any subdivision of the state, such as a city, a county or a board of education, may be sued. However, there may be a special requirement, such as the service of a notice of claim within 90 days as a condition precedent to the institution of the action.

Foreign governments cannot be sued unless they consent to be a party defendant.

Corporations are liable for the torts committed by their agents in the course of their duties to the same extent as natural persons.

Infants old enough to know the nature and consequences of their acts are liable for their torts.

Illustration: Culver, 17, operating his car with a junior license, was responsible for an accident which injured Panzer. Panzer sued Culver and recovered. However, a guardian had to be appointed for Culver to be his legal representative.

A husband is not responsible for the torts of his wife unless he instigated, coerced or ratified her acts. This, however, must be proved affirmatively if he is to be held liable.

He is entitled to the company and the services of his wife and infant children. If they are injured, he may join their suit for personal injuries and make a separate claim for any expenses he sustained because of those injuries and for the loss of their services.

Owners of animals as pets are generally not liable for the "first bite" unless they know of the pet's dangerous or vicious behavior. It then becomes their responsibility to control the pet.

Parents generally are not legally responsible for the torts of their children. Some states provide that the parent of a child responsible for a vicious, malicious or willful act may be liable in damages in a designated maximum amount.

An infant must have a "guardian *ad litem*," a legal representative, appointed if he is to sue or be sued. He may sue and be sued in torts, but may not be sued for a tort which is related to a breach of contract.

An employer is responsible for all acts of his employees performed in the scope of their employment. He is therefore responsible, with his employee, for damages resulting from the employee's torts. This rule is called *respondeat superior* and applies to the principal and agent relationship as well. Both parties are responsible, individually or together.

Joint tort-feasors are made responsible for their torts because of their relationship. They may be held liable individually or together. The release of one joint tort-feasor may release them all.

THE RIGHT OF PERSONAL LIBERTY

False arrest is a violation of the right to be secure of one's personal liberty. It is an unlawful detention committed by an official, in the name of a governmental authority, as an official function which is invalid or unauthorized.

It usually occurs when a private citizen is arrested by a peace officer without a warrant and without legal authority. A peace officer is any public official who is authorized to keep the peace, such as a policeman, a bailiff or a court officer.

If this unlawful detention by governmental authority continues, the tort of false imprisonment also results.

However, if after an illegal arrest there is a detention by legal process, such as a warrant, the tort is superseded and not actionable.

A false arrest may be accomplished by mere formal words of arrest as well as by force. A person who submits when told, "You are my prisoner," or, "You are under arrest," is a victim of the tort if such arrest is unlawful.

A legal arrest may be made without a warrant by a private citizen or a peace officer when a crime is committed in his presence. The crime may be a felony or a misdemeanor.

A peace officer may also make an arrest without a warrant when a felony has been committed, though not in his presence, if he has reason to believe that the person he is arresting is the one who committed the felony.

A private citizen making an arrest for a felony not committed in his presence exposes himself to an action for false arrest and false imprisonment if the person he arrested is subsequently released. He is not protected by the immunity which covers the peace officer.

Illustration: Grey, a private citizen, coming on the scene after a robbery, noticed the suspicious behavior of Earl at the scene of the robbery. He arrested Earl and held him in custody until the police arrived. The charge against Earl could not be sustained because of the lack of proof. Grey was liable in a civil action by Earl for false arrest and false imprisonment.

Neither a peace officer nor a private citizen may make an arrest without a warrant for a misdemeanor not committed or attempted in his presence.

Illustration: Zane, a policeman, arrested Stack without a warrant because he suspected him of selling fireworks, a misdemeanor. When the charge against him was dismissed, Stack sued for false arrest and recovered.

A person illegally arrested by an officer without a warrant may not be searched. Resistance to the arrest or to the search is not a crime. It cannot be considered as resisting arrest, resisting an officer in the performance of his duty, or escape from lawful custody.

To recover in an action for false arrest, a plaintiff must prove that he was detained or restrained, either forcibly or by verbal threat or order. He must show that the arrest was made without lawful process and under circumstances which did not authorize such action on the part of the defendant. He need not show any damages because the court or jury may consider such illegal restraint sufficient for a substantial amount in damages. However, if he did suffer special damages, such as a loss in business, a loss of pay, mental or physical anguish or illness, these will be considered by the jury in assessing the damages against the defendant.

A suit against a peace officer is usually brought against the governmental authority employing him on the basis of *respondeat superior.*

FALSE IMPRISONMENT

Another tort which affects a person's liberty is false imprisonment or unlawful detention. This tort may be committed by any citizen who without claim of public authority unlawfully restrains another. The tort consists of the detention of a person against his will without any justification.

The restraint or detention necessary in this tort must be complete. It must prevent the person from going about his business without interference and without hindrance. If he is compelled to make a detour or merely to take another route, it is not a detention, not a restraint. It must be such as to leave the person without any means of escape or retreat. It must be unlawful, without legal process and without justification. It can be accomplished by force, by threat or by command. The person must be aware of his detention.

Illustration: Olson, while asleep in his room, was locked in by a hotel manager who intended to charge him with the theft of some missing articles. The items were found and the door unlocked before Olson awoke. The manager was not charged with the tort since Olson was not aware of his restraint.

Damages here are inferred from the deprivation of a person's liberty. However, special damages will be considered in assessing the award of recovery.

MALICIOUS PROSECUTION

The tort of malicious prosecution results when a person, with malice and without reasonable grounds, institutes a criminal prosecution against another. By this act he will be held responsible for any resultant damages.

A plaintiff suing for malicious prosecution must show that a prior criminal proceeding in which he was the defendant was instigated and instituted by the person whom he is now suing. He must prove that the former criminal proceeding against him terminated in his favor. He must show that there was no reason for the criminal action against him and that it was prompted by malice on the part of this present defendant. Finally, he must show any additional or special damages he suffered.

Illustration: Planter, a carpenter, had a contract to do work for Denker. He received a cash advance to cover the cost of lumber. A subsequent change by Denker required more lumber, for which Planter did not get additional money. While the work was in progress, the lumber supplier made a demand on Denker for the balance. Denker became furious and instituted a criminal charge against Planter for misappropriation of funds. Before the trial, Denker was told that Planter had later paid for the lumber with his own money. Denker was not convinced and testified against Planter at the trial. The charges against Planter were dismissed. Planter then sued Denker for malicious prosecution. He was awarded damages for his imprisonment and for the injury to his reputation.

The distinction between malicious prosecution and false arrest is dependent upon the manner by which the tort is accomplished. The criminal proceeding which is the basis for the tort of malicious prosecution is begun by a valid legal process. On the other hand, neither false arrest nor false imprisonment is accompanied by a legal process.

MALICIOUS ABUSE OF PROCESS

The tort of malicious abuse of process is committed when a legal and valid process, issued by the proper authority, is used for an unauthorized purpose. The malice which is a part of the tort is presumed from the illegal use to which the legal process has been applied.

Illustration: Zeiger had a claim against Anton for $400. By means of a valid warrant of attachment, he levied an attachment on property belonging to Anton which was worth $4,000. The excessive amount of property which was attached renders the legal process, the warrant of attachment, void because it was maliciously misused.

In order to recover, the plaintiff, in such an action, must prove the issue of a valid process, the misuse of that process, and damages sustained by him as a result.

RIGHT TO PERSONAL SAFETY

An assault is a breach of the right to personal safety. It is a threat made by one person against another with an apparent intent to inflict bodily injury by force. It must appear to the person so threatened that it will be carried out and must put him in reasonable fear of bodily harm.

Illustration: The pointing of a gun at another is an assault. The effect is the same even though the gun is not loaded if that fact was unknown to the victim at the time.

If the means to commit the threatened injury are not apparent or available, the fear induced is unreasonable. However, when the threat and the apparent ability to carry it out are proved, general or compensatory damages are presumed.

Illustration: Aline was pursued by an unknown man at night. He did not catch up with her but was apprehended. It turned out to be Karger. She sued him for assault and recovered.

Special damages may be recovered if proved.

Illustration: Aline, pursued by Karger, fell, fractured a rib and was hospitalized. She recovered her hospital and medical expenses as well as the loss of her salary.

Punitive damages may be imposed if there is willful or malicious intent. They may be excessive in amount as a penalty for the malice involved in the tort.

Illustration: Pranksters decided they would teach Penner a lesson. They staged a framed holdup. Penner suffered a heart attack as a result of fright. There was sufficient willful and malicious intent proved to warrant an award of punitive damages in an action against them.

Provocation by abusive and threatening language is not sufficient as a defense for an assault. It may however, be considered in mitigation of damages.

A battery is an unjustified application of force to the person or body of another. It may be a completed assault. It may also be any contact with the body of another to cause him injury. Fear or anticipation of injury is not an element in this tort. All that is necessary is the application of force with a hostile intent and a resultant injury. Hostility need not be apparent; it can be inferred when the act is intentional and not accidental.

A battery may be consummated even though the force is applied indirectly or through the means of another agency.

Illustration: A slap given to a horse, causing it to bolt and throw its rider, has been held to be a battery.

Damages recoverable include all proximate and direct injuries and damages.

Illustration: A blow on the head, resulting in a concussion, disability and loss of employment for more than a year was included as part of the damages assessed against the defendant.

A battery may be justified if it is in defense of self or family. The use of force to defend oneself, one's family or property is justified. However, only such force may be used as is necessary to resist the attack.

THE RIGHT TO ENJOY A GOOD REPUTATION

Defamation is a violation of the right to enjoy a good reputation. This right continues and is available, however, only so long as the person, by his conduct, is entitled to enjoy a good reputation. A person who becomes involved in criminal or immoral activity may lose the right to enjoy a good reputation.

Slander is the defamation of a person's character which is made orally, by spoken word or gesture.

A libel is a defamation accomplished by printing, writing, pictures or effigies. It differs from slander, since it keeps the defamation alive for all in the community to see or to read.

To be actionable, a defamation must be communicated or published. There must be a malicious intent to do harm and there must be damages resulting from it. Communication is necessary, since reputation is based on a person's standing in the community. A person's character is reflected by his reputation in the community.

Malicious intent is necessary to show willfulness on the part of the defamer to cause damage to reputation. If the statement is proved to be false, then malice is presumed.

Finally, damage to that reputation must be proved before recovery can be had.

Defamation "per se" is any statement made about the reputation or character of another which imputes a crime of moral turpitude, a presently existing loathsome disease, unfitness for office or profession, or unchastity to a female. From the standpoint of legal interpretation, such statements have the effect of creating an immediate damaging opinion in the mind of the person who hears it. Such statements made orally are termed slander per se; in writing, libel per se.

A written statement which ridicules another person or holds him up to public contempt is actionable as libel per se.

In an action for defamation per se, damages need not be proved; they are inferred from the gravity of the charge. Proof of special damages may be considered for an additional award.

Truth is a complete defense in an action for defamation. However, the statement must be true in every respect before responsibility may be avoided.

Illustration: Erlihy called Roney a thief. Roney sued him for slander. Erlihy proved that Roney had cheated him in a deal. This defense of truth was not sustained. Technically a thief is a person who commits a larceny, while cheating or fraud may not always amount to a larceny. Roney recovered for the defamation.

Another defense is "privilege," a legal or justified excuse. Legislators, judges, lawyers and witnesses occasionally make statements which are defamatory. However, when they are made during a trial or in performance of a legal duty, they are legally excusable.

Another defense is called "fair comment." It applies to statements made about persons in public life—public officers, writers and public performers. The right to comment fairly about the conduct and motives of persons in the public limelight is one of the attributes of free speech in this country. However, the statement must be a fair reflection or opinion about the person in public life. When the statement clearly overreaches fairness and is directed at his personal life, there may be a violation of the privilege and a liability in defamation.

Illustration: A statement about a person seeking public office that he was a self-seeking opportunist, using his friends to obtain the nomination, was beyond the bounds of fair comment. The defense of fair comment was not available and the person making it was held liable for libel per se.

Not as a defense, but merely in mitigation of damages, a defendant in a defamation action may prove that he made the statements in good faith, without malice. He may show that there was provocation or that the reputation of the plaintiff was bad.

An action for defamation of the dead does not exist unless it is created by a special statute. Some states have such laws, which make a defamation of a dead person civilly and criminally actionable.

However, legal responsibility exists if a statement made about a deceased person is such as to cast aspersion and ridicule upon his living relatives. They may recover for the damages they sustain.

Illustration: A widow sued in defamation for statements made by the defendant that her deceased husband embezzled money from his business. When she proved those statements false and baseless, she recovered, because of the effect they had upon her reputation.

THE RIGHT OF PRIVACY

This is not a common-law right. Recovery for a breach of this right can only be based on an existing statute.

The right of privacy prohibits anyone from using the name, picture or likeness of any person for commercial or advertising purposes without his written consent. The purpose of such a law is to prevent unscrupulous persons from using the names and photographs of people in public life to increase the sale of their products without paying adequate compensation for such use.

The person whose name is so used without permission may maintain an action for money damages. He may also institute a suit in equity for an injunction to prevent the continued use of his name or his picture. He will then also demand incidental money damages. Some states also provide for criminal prosecution of any person who, without authority, uses the name or picture of another for his own commercial advantage.

TORTS AFFECTING POSSESSION AND OWNERSHIP OF PROPERTY

"Conversion" is an unauthorized assumption of ownership or control of property to the exclusion of the rights of its owner.

Illustration: Kenners borrowed Ewald's car to go to the store. He did not return it and later went to the beach. On his return, he had an accident and the car was demolished. The use of Ewald's car to go to the beach was a conversion, and Kenners was responsible.

A conversion may occur when the original possession is unlawful. If possession is lawful, a subsequent use, contrary to the rights of the owner is called "unlawful detention."

The relief for such a tort is a suit in conversion to obtain the money value of the property taken at the time of the conversion or the unlawful detention.

An action in replevin may be maintained if property is being withheld from its owner and he wants to regain possession.

Fraud and deceit is a tort for which recovery can be had if it induced the making of a contract. When fraud is used to induce a person to make a contract, he has the right to avoid all liability under it. He may also have it rescinded or reformed in a court of equity. If he sues in tort, he may recognize the contract, accept its benefits and still recover any losses he sustained, because of the fraud which induced him to make it.

Illustration: Rowan wanted to buy a house with a dry basement. Burroughs, the seller, guaranteed the basement was "bone dry." After he moved in, Rowan found there was seepage, and a new concrete floor had to be put in. Burroughs was held responsible and paid for the concrete floor.

REAL PROPERTY

Trespass is the violation of the right of a person to enjoy the possession and use of his real property without interference.

This tort is committed whenever the right to use or possess real property is interfered with and damage results.

Illustration: The telephone company put its poles across the land leased by Lester, without his permission. This was an interference with his right to the use of the property for which he could recover.

A trespass may be accomplished by an invasion or an unlawful entry upon the land. It can also be created by any act which affects the land or its use and enjoyment.

Illustration: The county was building a superhighway alongside Kaster's land and buildings. There were to be tunnels and overpasses in the vicinity. Underground water hindered the work of excavation, so pumps were installed to keep the water out. There was no shoring of the excavation up to Kaster's property line, with the result that one of the building walls developed cracks. Kaster sued to recover for the damage done to his building, and won.

"Nuisance" is the term applied to the tort which results when a person uses his property unreasonably and unlawfully, with threatened or actual damage to others. It depends entirely upon the damage or threat of damage which results from such acts whether relief is available. It is a violation of the right of every person to health, safety, comfort and morality.

Illustration: The chimneys from Kane's factory belch forth black smoke which is injurious to health, welfare and comfort of all of his neighbors. He may be compelled to stop using soft coal.

A public nuisance is one which affects the community and creates a condition which the community must control as part of its function of government.

Illustration: A certain house was suspected of being used for immoral purposes. This was enjoined as a nuisance which affected the welfare and morality of the community.

A private nuisance is one which causes damage and discomfort to a particular individual. It may also be a public nuisance, and may be actionable as both.

"Attractive nuisance" is the term used when there is an exist-

ing dangerous condition on land which attracts children at play
and may be the cause of injury. Generally, the responsibility is
placed upon the owner to make the property safe, despite the
fact that the children are trespassers. If it appears that the
dangerous condition, though necessary, is maintained without
proper safeguards, the owner will be held responsible. This is
particularly so when it is known that children come upon the
property to play, regardless of posted signs and high fences.

Illustration: Property adjacent to a school had a platform covered
by hinged doors. This chute was used to raise ashes and rubbish
from the boiler room 50 feet below. The doors were not properly
locked and a boy playing there fell to his death into it. The owner
was held responsible for failing to keep the chute locked.

RELIEF AVAILABLE IN TORTS

Money damages are one basis for relief from a tort. Recovery
is obtained by proving the right, the violation of that right, and
the damages which were incurred as a result of that violation.

General or compensatory damages are awarded to compensate the injured party for the loss he sustained. This may be
due to an assault, a battery, an arrest, a false imprisonment or
an injury resulting from the negligence of the defendant.

Nominal damages may be awarded to a plaintiff to indicate
that he sustained his lawsuit but that his damage did not warrant a substantial award. This may occur in an assault or a
battery when the injury sustained was minor. It may also occur
in a defamation per se where the proof was sustained but the
damage to reputation was not. Such a determination may result
in a "6¢ verdict."

Special damages are the by-products of the injury rather than
the direct damages caused by the injury itself.

Illustration: Ickerson was injured in an automobile accident due
to the negligent operation by Nelson. He recovered damages for
the pain and suffering of his injury and for the discomfort during
his stay in the hospital. These may be considered as his general or
compensatory damages. He also recovered for his hospital and
medical expenses, his loss of earnings, and for anticipated loss of
earnings during his disability. These are his special damages.

Punitive or exemplary damages are awarded when the tort is the result of malice and willful intent.

Injunction is available to a plaintiff in a court of equity to obtain relief from a continuing tort, where there is no other adequate remedy at law. When the plaintiff proves to the satisfaction of the court that the mere recovery of damages is not sufficient to give him adequate relief or that the tort has been resumed or is threatened, the defendant may be enjoined and directed to discontinue such activity.

Self-help, although available as a remedy against a tort, is to be used with care and caution and on rare occasions. Although it is recognized when used in defense of self, family or property, no greater force may be used than is actually necessary to resist the attack.

NEGLIGENCE

An action in negligence is an action in tort. It is based on an existing duty to use proper care and diligence in a certain situation, and on the breach of that duty, with resultant injury.

The intention of the defendant is not an element of the tort. Of course, if it was willful or malicious, then it may become another type of tort.

Negligence as we know it, then, is the failure of the defendant to use care and diligence as required under particular circumstances. The event which resulted in the damage or injury was due to this failure on his part.

Any person who fails to use that degree of care which is required of him under any particular circumstances is liable in negligence to the person who directly sustained damage or injury as a result of his failure.

Illustration: A bailee is required to use a degree of care with relation to the property in his custody dependent upon the type of bailment involved. A bailee for the benefit of the bailor owes a duty of slight care; a bailee for his own benefit owes a duty of great care, and a mutual-benefit bailee owes a duty of reasonable care.

The doctrine of contributory negligence relieves one party of liability in an accident due to his negligence if the other party, by his own negligence, contributed to its occurrence. In a jurisdiction where this doctrine of contributory negligence is applied and followed, a plaintiff, in order to recover, must plead and prove his own freedom from contributory negligence in addition to proving the negligence of the defendant.

> Illustration: John, driving his car, collided with Fred's car at an intersection controlled by a light. Fred was injured, and sues John. He shows that John was speeding across the intersection while the light was against him. John, however, proves that he was crossing when the light changed and Fred, anxious to get across, did not give him an opportunity to cross the intersection when he hit him. The proof of Fred's failure to give John the right of way after he began to cross the intersection may be considered as contributory negligence to defeat his claim. When both are negligent, no one can recover.

In those jurisdictions which do not recognize the doctrine of contributory negligence, the theory of comparative negligence is in effect. This, then, recognizes the possibility that in any given situation one party to an accident may be more negligent, more responsible for its happening, than the other. It will then allow the person less responsible to recover from the one who was primarily guilty of negligence. When there is a disparity of negligence and a disparity of responsibility, recovery is permitted to the one who is less culpable.

The "Last Clear Chance" theory is an apparent exception to the doctrine of contributory negligence. If it is shown that the defendant was aware of the plaintiff's position of danger, had an opportunity to avoid the accident, yet did nothing to prevent it, the contributory negligence of the plaintiff will not defeat his recovery.

> Illustration: The engineer of an oncoming train saw the plaintiff's truck across his track. He had sufficient opportunity to stop but did not, because he assumed that the truck was proceeding across. Recovery by plaintiff for injury to himself and damage to his truck was not defeated because he did not get off the track in sufficient time.

Res Ipsa Loquitur is a doctrine of recovery in negligence based on the fact that the instrumentality causing the accident was entirely within the control of the defendant. Under those circumstances, no inference can be drawn about the accident except that it resulted from the defendant's negligence.

Illustration: Defendant, under contract to demolish a building, failed to construct adequate protection against falling brick. Plaintiff, walking along the sidewalk, was struck by a brick falling from one of the walls. There was no other explanation for the occurrence but that one of the defendant's workmen on the wall was negligent in causing the brick to fall. The plaintiff recovered under the doctrine of *res ipsa loquitur*.

The *res ipsa loquitur* doctrine does not deprive the defendant of his opportunity to show that he was not negligent and not responsible but that the accident was caused by another intervening cause.

IMPUTED NEGLIGENCE DUE TO RELATIONSHIP

The negligence of an employee will be imputed to and binding upon his employer if the act which was negligently done was within the scope of the employment. This is also known as the principle of *respondeat superior*. The same principle of law applies to principals and agents.

A corporation acts through its agents. The negligent act of an agent will make the corporation responsible if the act was within the agent's authority.

The driver of an automobile, if he is negligent and causes damage, also makes the owner responsible, if his use of the car was authorized. The "family car" rule makes the father responsible for the negligence of any person in his family using the car with his express or implied permission.

Generally, the negligence of a minor who is "sui juris"—that is, he knows and understands that the consequences of his acts will not be imputed to his parents.

If the infant is *non sui juris* and does not know or understand the nature and consequences of his acts, then only such a degree of care is required of him as is required of an ordinary child of the same age, judgment, experience and intelligence under the same circumstances.

PERSONAL INJURY ON A PUBLIC STREET OR HIGHWAY

Usually the responsibility for the proper care and maintenance of a public street or highway rests on the subdivision of the state which controls that highway. It may be the county, the city or the town or village.

If an injury is sustained because of the negligent maintenance of that highway, the responsibility rests upon that agency.

To bring suit against that municipality, strict compliance with the existing rules is necessary. Permission to sue may be required if action is to be brought against the state, or the action may have to be brought in the court of claims, if there is one. There may be a special requirement to serve a "notice of claim" against an agency or subdivision of the state within 90 days to advise of the injury. In many cases this is a condition precedent to recovery. No recovery will be had and no lawsuit maintainable unless this requirement has been complied with.

In some instances the municipality may pass along the responsibility for the care of certain areas to the owners of the land abutting or contiguous to the public land. This is usually done in cities, towns and villages with the responsibility for sidewalks. If such an ordinance is in effect, the abutting owner is made responsible for the care and maintenance of the sidewalk in front of his property. He must keep it in repair, keep it clean and free of any obstruction. In the winter, under such an ordinance, he must keep the sidewalk free of snow and ice.

If the sidewalk fronting his property is used by the abutting owner for his particular benefit, then the proper care and maintenance of it becomes his responsibility.

The failure, then, of the abutting owner to keep the sidewalk free from any defect or obstruction which will cause injury to pedestrians is an act of negligence. He will then be held responsible to the person injured for any damage or injury which results.

Illustration: Bellows owned several trucks which he garaged in the yard behind his home. He built a runway from the garage to the street made of cobblestones. These were irregular and widely spaced, so that Talmadge, walking on the sidewalk, across the runway, fell and was injured. Bellows was held responsible for the cause of Talmadge's injury.

The basic responsibility as to snow and ice in the wintertime on sidewalks, street and highway is the responsibility of the municipality.

In areas which are for public use and not delegated in responsibility to any abutting owner, the liability rests with the municipality to keep the streets and sidewalks clear of snow and ice. However, there are several factors which affect that obligation.

A great deal depends upon the available facilities of the municipality to keep the areas cleaned. The volume of a snowfall, the weather conditions, the time elapsed since the last snow and the opportunity available to the municipality to clear it away are all to be considered. Generally, the basic requirement to establish liability is "notice." In order to be responsible, it must be shown that the municipality was aware of the existence of a dangerous condition and that it failed to remove it. This notice may be actual, by calling attention to the police or street-cleaning authority of the existence of the condition. This, of course, requires additional time and opportunity to have that condition removed, before liability attaches.

"Constructive notice" is established when a sufficient time has elapsed for the condition to have been discovered in the course of regular and normal inspection. When a dangerous condition is shown to exist in an area used by the public, the failure to remove that condition may constitute negligence on the part of the municipality, if a pedestrian is injured.

INJURY ON PRIVATE PROPERTY

The owner of private property owes a duty of care to all persons coming on his land. If he fails in that duty and a person is injured as a result, then he is financially responsible for the consequences of that injury.

The degree of care for which he is responsible depends upon the reason for which the person came upon the land.

The Business Invitee

A person who comes upon the land to do business with the owner or any member of his family is entitled to a reasonable degree of care on the part of the owner. He must see that the visitor is not exposed to dangers which will cause him harm. The existence of a condition caused by negligent maintenance or construction which results in injury to such a person will be his responsibility.

> Illustration: A milkman delivering milk was injured on the stairs when one of the wooden steps gave way under his weight. It was shown that the wood had become rotted and weatherworn. This condition was easily discoverable by inspection. The owner was held responsible for the milkman's injury.

The Social Guest

Most jurisdictions follow the old concept of the law that a person who comes on the land of another for a social visit, even at the invitation of the owner, is not entitled to the same degree of care as a business invitee. The principle underlying this rule of law is that the owner should not be more responsible to his social guests than he is responsible to members of his own family. By coming on the land, the guests assume the same risk as do the members of his household. The owner will only be held responsible if his guest is injured by affirmative acts of gross negligence on his part. Mere passive negligence which results in injury will not be his obligation.

> Illustration: A guest who went to the closet to get her coat, opened the wrong door and fell down the basement stairs could not recover because there was no affirmative gross negligence on the part of the owner.

Licensees are persons whom the owner allows to come upon his land for their own benefit or for their convenience. The owner is not required to take any undue precautions for their safety. The licensee must take the premises with all of their existing risks as he finds them. The owner is only responsible to him for any affirmative acts which result in his injury. Any known places of danger should be protected and signs so placed as to warn the licensee of their existence.

Illustration: Frank often gave Eli, his neighbor, permission to use his private road to get to the main county road on the other side of his property. He gave him permission on this particular day but forgot to tell Eli that a culvert over a dry creek bed was under repair. There were no warning signs on the road and Eli unsuspectingly damaged his car and was himself injured. Frank was held responsible.

Trespassers are persons who come on private property without permission of the owner. They are not entitled to any special duty of care by the owner. They are there without permission and at their own risk. The owner has no responsibility for their safety. However, he must not place any traps or other devices upon his land which are intended to injure them. He must not attack them or subject them to willful or malicious danger.

Illustration: Patton, annoyed and angered by boys cutting across his yard at night, placed a rope across the yard to trap them. Billie, running through, fell and broke his arm. Patton was responsible.

DEATH CLAIM ACTIONS

Under the common law, recovery could only be had for a personal injury. If the person died from those injuries he received, because of some one's negligence or responsibility, his claim for recovery was forfeited. Through changes in the laws effected by the state legislatures, a personal injury claim does not generally abate with the death of the person injured. In the event of death, the estate may recover.

The legislatures have established another cause of relief. This is the death-claim action. It did not exist under the common law, so that unless there is such a statute, in your state, such an action is not maintainable.

Particularly, it is a claim which is enforcible against a person who causes the death of another. Any person may bring such an action to recover any pecuniary loss which was brought about by the death. The action is not based on love, affection, grief, sorrow or loss of companionship of the individual. It is entirely dependent upon the loss of any financial or pecuniary benefit which the deceased contributed to the plaintiff. If the deceased supported the plaintiff, he may sue for the loss of this financial support.

The amount of the loss is determined by the age of both the plaintiff and the deceased and their respective life expectancy.

In such an action, the plaintiff does not have to plead and prove that the deceased was free of contributory negligence. The defendant, however, may defeat the recovery if he proves contributory negligence of the deceased in a jurisdiction where this is applicable.

MALPRACTICE

An action may be brought in malpractice against any person who holds himself out to the public as a member of a profession, qualified to render services as required in a skillful and competent manner.

The plaintiff in such an action will be required to prove that he retained the defendant to perform these professional services and that this employment was accepted.

He will also be required to prove that he suffered damage or injury through the acts of the defendant, either because he did not use reasonable care in exercising his skill and learning or because he did not possess the necessary experience, skill and learning. He may also show that the injury was due to a practice and procedure used by this defendant which is not recognized by his profession.

Such a claim is usually very difficult to prove.

Illustration: Action against dentist or doctor.

Summation

Points to Remember about Torts

Each one of us is endowed by state and federal law with the right to enjoy personal liberty, personal safety, a good reputation and the ownership of property undisturbed and unmolested.

The person who invades and violates these rights is financially responsible for any damage he causes.

The knowledge of these rights and the relief available, in the event of the invasion, of these rights, requires that we keep the following in mind:

A tort is a civil wrong.

What are some of these torts, and what relief is available to us?

Who is responsible for a tort?

Why is negligence considered a tort?

What is the basis for recovery in negligence?

What is the responsibility of a property owner?

What is a death claim action?

What is malpractice?

CHAPTER 11

Wills and Estates

Without doubt, the most important subject of law which relates to the layman and his property is the subject of wills.

The reason for such a categorical statement is that a living person usually makes certain that his wishes are carried out when his personal and property rights are affected. He will personally see to it that these rights are protected.

Unfortunately, this is not possible where the estate of a deceased person is concerned. His property is left for others to administer, others to care for and distribute. The money, the property, the estate that he spent his lifetime amassing is no longer within his personal control.

The only way in which he can continue his dominion over his property after death is to make certain that his wishes are clearly and definitely expressed in a valid and enforcible will. When he is no longer around to take care of his affairs, his appointed executor, with the help of the courts, will handle his affairs for him.

However, unless he obtains competent legal advice, he may yet fail in this purpose. His will may not be valid and enforcible because it did not comply with the legal requirements. Even if it is valid, it may not express his last wishes.

DEFINITIONS AND DISTINCTIONS

A will contains the instructions of a person, recognized by law, which direct the distribution of his property at his death.

When created according to the requirements of the state law, a will becomes a directive which must be followed by the person appointed in it to administer the estate.

A will does not become effective until the death of the maker. Until that time he may make any changes he wants, provided he complies with the legal requirements. He may revoke it or he may amend it by a subsequent will.

The "testator" is the person who makes and executes a valid will. If it is a woman she is called the "testatrix."

An "executor" is the person appointed in the will to administer and distribute the estate. A woman is an "executrix."

The "estate" includes all of the property that was owned or controlled by the testator at the time of his death. This includes both real and personal property. The executor, when he is qualified by the court, will gather all property into the control of the estate and then distribute in accordance with the directions under the will and the laws of the state which regulate it.

A "bequest" or a "legacy" is a provision in the will which gives to a named person certain personal property owned by the testator. This person is called a "legatee."

A "devise" is a provision to grant real property owned by the testator to a person named in the will. He is called a "devisee."

If the executor, named in the will, fails or refuses to act, another person will be named to replace him. He is called an "administrator with the will annexed."

TYPES OF WILLS

The "holographic" will is written entirely in the handwriting of the testator. Usually, it does not comply with the legal requirements for execution, though signed by the maker.

Most states do not recognize and will not enforce a holographic will unless it complies with the other legal requirements of a valid will. The effect, then, is the same as though the decedent died "intestate"—without a will.

Of those states where a holographic will is recognized, some require the signatures of witnesses as a part of the will itself, while others merely require that the handwriting and signature of the decedent be authenticated by witnesses.

A person who executes a will which is not recognized by the courts of his state loses the benefit of testamentation. He loses the right to dispose of his property at his death to those persons he wants to inherit from him.

A "nuncupative" will is an oral will. It is a statement made orally by the deceased to two or more persons in which he indicated his desire to dispose of his property in the event of his death and told them how he wanted it to be distributed. To prove and enforce such a will, it becomes necessary after his death to have this oral will reduced to writing and signed by the witnesses to whom it was made.

An oral will is recognized in about two thirds of the states. However, there are certain specific provisions. It may only dispose of personal property and the amount is limited. It must be made during the last illness of the deceased, from which he did not recover. In this respect it is similar to a "gift *causa mortis*" discussed at the end of this chapter.

A nuncupative will may also be made by any person in military service, regardless of his rank, and by a mariner including a merchant seaman of any rank. The only requirement is that the soldier be in actual military service in some anticipation of combat or other risk, as going over seas. A mariner must be on a vessel in waters which are subject to the ebb and flow of the tide. Under these circumstances, all states recognize an oral will.

Illustration: Kiely, a soldier at Camp Dix, about to go overseas, told two of his buddies that he wanted his girl friend, instead of his parents, to have all of his property. He never went overseas. He stayed at Camp Dix until the end of the war. Several weeks after his discharge he was killed in an automobile accident. He had made no other will and had not revoked his oral will. The two friends established the will and his girl friend, and not his parents, inherited his personal property.

The will of a soldier or a mariner, once made, is valid unless it is revoked. It is not terminated when the military tour of duty or the sea voyage is over. If it is not revoked, it remains in effect as his last will.

A "conditional" or "contingent" will is one which specifically states that it is only to take effect upon the happening of death in a certain way, or under certain conditions. Unless the conditions are fulfilled, the will does not take effect as the last will of the decedent.

> Illustration: Testator left a will which stated, "To My Beloved Mary, I am going on a trip to India. If I do not return, I leave all my property to you. John (signed)" He returned from his trip to India and died some time later. Mary claimed under the will. She did not inherit because the will was held to be conditioned upon his failure to return from India.

A "conditional legacy" is a provision in a valid will which is based on some stated contingency. The legacy will lapse and fail if the contingency occurs, but it will not affect the will.

"Multiple wills" are several individual documents, each properly executed. Together they constitute the will of the testator. This may occur when a testator draws his will in duplicate and executes each in accordance with the legal requirements. Usually, this is done for fear that the will may be lost. If multiple wills have been executed, they must all be produced at the death of the testator. The absence of one of the original duplicates may create a presumption that it had been revoked by the testator. In view of this possibility, the formal execution of duplicate copies of the same will is not recommended. A will which is subsequently amended by one or more "codicils" may also be considered a multiple will. The codicils and the original will must be presented for probate together. They constitute the last will of the decedent.

"Mutual" or "reciprocal" wills are separate instruments, each executed by individual testators, containing reciprocal provisions for the disposition of their property in accordance with an agreement between them.

A "joint will" is one instrument with provisions agreed upon and executed by two or more persons. This constitutes the last will of each of the persons who executed it. When the first dies, the will is probated to dispose of his property as provided for. The will, by prior agreement between them, specifically covers each eventuality. When the survivor dies, the will is probated as to his property, to take into consideration the disposition of all property as previously contemplated.

THE RIGHT OF TESTAMENTATION

The right to make a will and to leave property by will is not a natural or inherent right. It is not guaranteed by the fundamental or common law of the land.

It is a privilege granted by the legislature to the citizens of the state. As in contracts, the value and importance of the will is its enforcibility. A will which is not enforcible, because it does not comply with the legal requirements, is of no value.

Most states require a person to be of sound mind and at least 18 years of age before he can execute a valid will. Only one state permits a person of 14 to make a valid will. A minor can only dispose of personal property by will. He may not dispose of real property until he attains maturity.

All states have given the married woman the right to dispose of her own property. Certain restrictions are provided, however, to prevent disinheritance, or where community property, curtesy and dower are involved.

Persons who suffer from a physical disability have the same right to execute a will as normal persons. However, it must be shown that a person who is blind, deaf, dumb or illiterate knew and understood the contents of the document he executed to be his will.

A person who has been finally sentenced to imprisonment for life does not forfeit his property, nor does he lose his right to dispose of his property by will. However, at least one state requires that he make provision for testamentary disposition within 6 months after the date of his sentence.

MENTAL CAPACITY

A person making a will must be of sound mind. However, there is no particular degree of mental capacity necessary. A person who knows the extent of his property, the names of all related persons who are to inherit from him, and the nature of the act when making and executing a will. has sufficient capacity to execute a valid will.

Any person suffering from a form of mental disturbance may, nevertheless, execute a valid will if it is done during a lucid interval.

A person who uses alcohol or drugs, even excessively, is not for that reason alone incapable of making a valid will. To defeat his will, it must be shown that his natural intelligence, memory and judgment have been paralyzed and his mental capacity affected.

Old age and senility is not in itself a bar to testamentation. The test is his awareness of the important elements previously discussed.

Illustration: Brandon was 78 and ill. He had inherited a large estate of personal and real property which he managed himself. He directed his attorney to draw his will and made corrections so that three drafts and revisions were required until it was acceptable to him. The will contained all of the names of his legatees and the amounts of their legacies at his direction. At his death, an attempt to prevent the probate of the will was made on the grounds of incapacity. This was overruled by the evidence. The will was admitted to probate.

The will must be the act of the testator expressing his wishes and his instructions. It must be freely made by him without domination, fraud or undue influence.

Illustration: Quade was a widower who lived alone. His children were all married and living away. Five years before his death he made a will leaving his entire estate to his children. One year before his death, he made a new will giving all of his property to his young housekeeper. When this will was put in for probate, it was shown that during the last year and one half, Quade was ill, that his friends were not permitted to see him, and that the housekeeper appeared to dominate him in every respect. The will was not admitted because from the evidence it appeared that it was not an indication of his will. The previous will was then admitted.

THE FORM AND CONTENTS OF A WILL

No particular form of will is required by any of the states, with the possible exception of Louisiana. All that is necessary to have a valid will is a statement in writing which expresses the instructions of the decedent concerning the distribution of his property. This statement must be signed by him and attested to by two or more witnesses as required by the particular state.

However, a will generally begins with a statement such as "I, John Jones, being of full age, of sound mind and memory, do hereby declare and publish this to be my last will and testament." These words need not be used. Any opening statement which properly describes the document will suffice. The testator may include a sentence to the effect that this will revokes all prior wills made by him.

The first clause or paragraph usually arranges for the payment of his just debts and funeral expenses. He may here provide for his funeral in any way he desires: for a special ceremony, for burial, cemetery, headstone, vault and care of his grave.

Another provision names his executor, to gather, manage and distribute his property as provided for in the will. He may provide for more than one executor if he wishes. He may name an individual or a bank or trust company to act as such.

A bond is required to assure the proper handling of the estate by the executor. However, the will may provide that such a bond be dispensed with, if that is authorized by law.

All subsequent provisions will then specifically apply to his distribution of his estate, with the designation of legatees and devisees as his beneficiaries. Generally, a legacy must be paid as designated even if the estate is drastically diminished, the reduction being passed along to the residuary legatee. If there is no residue, then all legacies will abate, and be reduced proportionately.

Usually the last dispositive clause is the "residuary clause" and provides for a "residuary legatee." This person will inherit the remainder of his property, not otherwise distributed. This includes all legacies and devises which, though previously provided for, fail and remain with the estate.

SAMPLE OF A SIMPLE FORM OF WILL

I, John Smith Brown, being of sound and disposing mind and memory, do make, publish and declare the following to be my Last Will and Testament, hereby revoking all wills by me at any time heretofore made.

First—I direct my executor hereinafter named to pay my just debts and funeral expenses as soon after my decease as may be practicable.

Second—I direct that my remains be buried in the Old Barnhope Cemetery in Cantwell, Tennessee, as near to my parents as is possible.

Third—I give to my granddaughter, Alice Day, the sum of $5,000 as her own, to do with as she sees fit. I direct that all estate and transfer taxes on this legacy be paid out of the residue of my estate, and I hereby charge my estate with the payment of all such taxes.

Fourth—I give to my sister, Jane Worth, the sum of $15,000 to her own absolute use forever. I direct that all taxes, both estate and transfer, upon this legacy be paid from the residue of my estate so that my sister Jane may receive the full amount of the legacy without any deductions. I also charge my estate with the payment of these taxes.

Fifth—All the rest, residue and remainder of my estate, real, personal and mixed, and wheresoever it is located, I give, devise and bequeath to my wife, Elisa Brown, to her absolute use forever. This provision for my wife is to be in lieu and instead of all dower right in my estate.

Sixth—I give to my brother, Joshua Brown, the sum of $100, for reasons which to me are good and sufficient, particularly because he refused to help me when I needed him.

Seventh—I hereby nominate, constitute and appoint my wife, Elisa Brown, to be executrix under this my Last Will and Testament, with the same full power to sell, lease, transfer or convey any real property of which I may die seized or possessed, as I might exercise were I alive and personally acting.

Eighth—It is my wish and will that my executrix should not be required to furnish any bond or other security for the faithful performance of her duties.

IN WITNESS WHEREOF, I have hereunto set my hand and affixed my seal this   day of January, 1975.

JOHN SMITH BROWN (signed)

SIGNED, SEALED, PUBLISHED AND DECLARED by John Smith Brown, the testator, as and for his Last Will and Testament in the presence of us, who at his request and in his presence and in the presence of each other, have hereunto subscribed our names as witnesses.

Samuel Strong   1973 Owens Road, Parkhurst, California
Thomas Case   182 Broad Street, Cedar Rapids, Michigan
Philip Kane   93 Stone Street, Oceanside, New Jersey.

N.B.—It is important to keep in mind that the wording of the will need not be formal as long as it is clear and unambiguous. Also, and most important, it must be remembered that unless the will is properly executed in accordance with the necessary formalities, it may not be admitted to probate. The testator must tell the witnesses that he is about to sign and execute his will. He must ask them to be his witnesses. He must sign in their presence, and they in turn must sign in his presence and in the presence of each other. These facts are actually included in the attestation clause. He need not, however, disclose its contents to the witnesses.

There are certain rules which apply to the disposition of property by will. These are generally the same in all of the states. If they do vary, it is in the technicalities of a strictly legal nature which do not concern us here.

All states provide for the widow, to make certain that she is not disinherited and left a public charge. The exact provisions vary from state to state. She is, however, allowed to inherit in certain instances in spite of contrary provisions in the will.

Almost half of the states still have the right of dower to protect the widow. This right consists of an interest in the real property owned by her husband at his death. The exact interest varies according to the law of the state. One may give her a life interest as to one half of the real property while another may give her outright ownership. In most states, a widow may disregard the will and elect to take her intestate share, if she is not satisfied with its provisions. She may choose that provision of the law or of the will which is more beneficial to her.

The husband, the widower, is not treated as well, and some states make no provision for the husband in the event of disinheritance. Only about one fourth of the states still give him the right of curtesy. This, similar to dower for the widow, is an interest in the real property owned by the wife at her death. Several of the states, having discontinued the right of curtesy, grant him the right of dower.

In states where the community-property system still applies, because the husband and the wife own their property jointly neither spouse may dispose of more than half of their community property since the other half belongs to the survivor. All property which comes into the possession of either or both during their married life, except by gift or inheritance, is community property and belongs to both of them jointly.

Some states restrict the proportion of the estate which may be left to charity when there are immediate relatives of the deceased surviving. California restricts it to one third and New York to one half. Ohio provides that all bequests to charity included in wills made within one year from the date of death are void.

These examples are an indication of the specific provisions of law that apply to wills and estates in the various states. It further emphasizes the need for the technical legal knowledge required to draw a valid will.

Some states provide that an attesting witness to a will is not to be allowed to take a legacy, through the will, if his testimony is required to establish it. This is a caution to persons who leave a legacy to anyone in appreciation for being an attesting witness. However, if the attesting witness is also a close relative who would also share in the estate under intestacy, then, if he is needed to testify, he will be given the share he would have received under intestacy. In no case will an attesting witness get more than the amount provided in the will.

Illustration: John is the brother of the decedent. He had been the attesting witness to the will and his testimony was necessary to establish the proper execution of the will. It provided that John was to get $5,000. There was a widow and two brothers surviving. If there were no will, John would have been entitled to one fourth of the estate. As an attesting witness, he was limited to the $5,000 specified in the will.

EXECUTION OF A WILL

When the will has been drawn, with all of the provisions to the complete satisfaction of the testator, it is ready for its formal execution. The validity of a will is dependent upon its proper execution, in accordance with the requirements of the state in which it is accomplished. The failure to comply with them may result in the refusal of the court to admit the will to probate.

Generally, all states, with the exception of Louisiana, have the same requirements. The testator must request the witnesses to attest to its execution. He must advise them that it is his will, although he does not have to disclose its contents. He will then sign his name at the very end of the will. He should also sign at the bottom of each page of the will, if it contains several pages. The witnesses will then sign the attestation clause which is below the signature of the testator. It is essential that the testator sign in the presence of all the witnesses and that they sign in the presence of each other.

It may be admissible to have the testator sign the will prior to the gathering of the witnesses, but he must then acknowledge to all of the witnesses that this document is his will and this his signature. The witnesses will then sign in the presence of each other. If the testator acknowledges his signature then the attestation clause must include the statement that he acknowledged it. The number of witnesses required varies from two to three, depending upon the state. They should include their home address when they sign.

The attestation clause is not an integral part of the will but is used to prove the will. Without such a clause all of the required witnesses must be present to testify as to the execution. With such a clause, only one may be sufficient, if available. In the event of death or absence of all of the attesting witnesses, the mere proof of the handwriting of the testator and the witnesses may be sufficient to indicate to the court that the will was properly executed.

After the last provision in the will, a statement may be included, sometimes called "the testimonium clause," followed by the attestation clause.

Illustration: "In Witness Whereof, I have hereunto set my hand and affixed my seal this (15th) day of August, 1975.

John Smith (signed)
Signed, Sealed, Published and Declared by John Smith, the testator, as and for his Last Will and Testament in the presence of us, who, at his request and in his presence and in the presence of each other, have hereunto subscribed our names as witnesses.

Elias Truehorn   97 Hoe Road, Pitcairn, Ohio
Selam Goodhue   1897 Delaware Boulevard, Omaha, Nebraska
Caleb Hart   321 Shore Road, Los Angeles, California."

You will note that the contents of the attestation clause actually set forth the required steps of the formal execution of a will. The witnesses merely acknowledge that those requirements were complied with.

As mentioned, Louisiana has its own particular provisions as to wills. A nuncupative will in that state is to be dictated by the testator to a notary public in the presence of three witnesses, or it must be written by him, or for him, and then read to five witnesses. A holographic will is written, signed and dated by the testator without any further formality. "Statutory testaments" are executed by having the testator signify before a notary public and two witnesses that the instrument is his will. The "sealed and mystic testament" is written by or for the testator, placed by him in an envelope and then sealed before a notary public and three witnesses with the declaration that the envelope contains his will.

REVOCATION

All states agree that to revoke a will the testator must have the same mental capacity as is required in making one. It must be accomplished with the same free will and lack of domination, fraud or duress.

An attempted revocation by a testator who does not have mental capacity or who is subject to domination, fraud or duress is not effective. The will is still valid and in existence. If it was destroyed by the testator while mentally incapacitated, its contents and execution may be proved by other evidence since it is still in effect.

A will may be revoked by the execution of a new will or a codicil which may amend, replace or make ineffective all prior wills. A codicil is a document which is executed with all the formality of a will and which amends or changes the provisions of a prior existing will. The codicil and the prior will constitute the entire will of the testator. A codicil is practical when the original will is long and contains many provisions or when the mental capacity or physical condition of the testator may create a doubt as to his testamentary capacity. If the codicil is not probated because of lack of capacity, the previously executed will may still be valid, so that at least that portion of his testamentary wishes will be carried out.

Revocation takes place when the testator or someone at his specific instructions burns, tears, cancels, obliterates or destroys his will with the intention that it be revoked. There is no need for a complete destruction. Any act which indicates such an intention of the testator has been found sufficient.

Illustration: Frank, in going through his papers, came across a will. He showed it to his secretary saying, "Here's an old will. It no longer suits my needs. I'm going to draw another." He then made a tear into the paper but not completely across. He did not throw it away. When he died some months later, without having made a new will, the beneficiaries attempted to have it probated. This was defeated because he had effectively revoked this one.

Any writing to constitute a revocation of the will must be executed with the formality of a will. However, if this writing is on the will itself, it may be only considered a revocation if it is also a cancellation or obliteration of the will. This writing on the will must show an intention to revoke by cancellation.

Illustrations: Harold wrote across the face of his will the words, "Will Revoked," then signed his name and dated it. This has been considered effective.

Struel wrote at the bottom of his will: "I hereby cancel this will," and signed his name. This was not sufficient for a revocation because it was not a cancellation nor was it a formal revocation.

A will known to be in the possession of the testator before his death is presumed to have been revoked by him with intent to revoke if it is not found among his possessions.

A will shown to have been in existence at the death of the testator and subsequently lost or destroyed can be proved by two witnesses who can show the provisions of the will clearly and distinctly. If a correct duplicate copy is available, it may be used instead of a witness.

Alterations made by a testator before execution must be initialed, or some comment made about them in the attestation clause, if they are to be effective.

If made after the execution, an alteration will not be effective nor will it destroy the will, no matter who made it. It may be established and proved according to its original contents.

Some states have provision for the deposit of a will with the probate court in the testator's county of residence.

Wills may be kept in a bank vault for reasons of security, to prevent their destruction. However, in the event of death, a judicial proceeding may be necessary to obtain access to them, usually in the presence of a representative of the state tax department.

Proceedings to admit a will to probate vary according to state practice. Basically, they consist of an application to the probate or surrogate's court by the person named in the will as executor, requesting that the will be admitted to probate.

A hearing is usually required to establish the will as having been properly executed. Notice of this hearing is given to all persons named in the will and to those who might share in the estate if the will is not established. This notice is a process of the probate court and is called a "citation."

Any person who has reason for contesting the admission of

the will must file documents to signify his opposition. If there is such a contest, the surrogate's court will proceed with the formality of a trial to determine the validity of the will. The person proposing a will has the burden of proving that the testator had the necessary testamentary capacity and that he properly executed it.

If there is no contest, the witnesses will testify as to the execution of the will. If the court is satisfied both as to execution and capacity, it will authorize the issue of "letters testamentary" to the executor. This gives him the authority to gather the assets of the estate and then distribute them in accordance with the provisions of the will. After all of the legacies are distributed and the expenses paid, he will account to the court, include all of the expenses of the estate, the fees for his attorney and the fees which he is allowed. He will then, at the court's direction, make payment of all of these obligations of the estate and then pay over the balance to the residuary legatee, the person named in the will to get all of the estate not otherwise distributed. When he has accomplished all of this, he will be relieved by the court of his obligations to the estate. His bond will be discharged and the estate will be closed.

INTESTACY

If the decedent died leaving no valid will, his estate will be administered by an intestacy proceeding. Some state laws permit small estates to be administered with less formality.

All states provide for the appointment of an administrator. He is the person who will be authorized by the court to gather all of the assets left by the deceased. He will keep them in his name as such administrator and, after paying all debts, obligations and expenses, distribute according to the state law. The law provides for the relationship of persons who may apply to be an administrator.

Letters of administration will be granted to the nearest kin entitled to share in the estate if competent and willing to accept. Usually, it is given to the person entitled to the greater share, including the surviving spouse, children, grandchildren, parents, brothers or sisters and other next of kin. If these are not available, the provision is made for a "public administrator" who will handle the administration of the estate and distribute according to the law of the state.

An application is made to the surrogate or probate court by the person claiming letters of administration. A hearing on this petition must be had. Process in the form of citations are issued and served upon all persons related to the deceased. On the return day, the date set for the hearing, all objections are heard. If the court is convinced that the person who applied is entitled to them, he will direct that letters of administration be issued. This authorizes the administrator to act in behalf of the estate. He will then gather all of the assets and property belonging to the decedent. He will pay all expenses and obligations. He will, with the supervision of the court, distribute the estate according to the laws of descent and distribution of the state, pay his attorney and his own commissions. On filing of a final accounting, in which he lists all of the disbursements, the court will relieve him of his responsibility and discharge his bond.

The laws of descent and distribution of property of an intestate are determined by the legislative enactments in the state.

Essentially, they give the wife the entire estate if there are no children, parents or brothers and sisters of the decedent. If there are children, then the wife may receive one third in some states and one half in others, and the children get the balance, to be shared equally.

If any of the children are deceased, then the grandchildren take the share that their parent would have received and share that equally.

Some states give the surviving spouse the entire estate whether there are parents or brothers and sisters alive, as long as there are no surviving children or grandchildren. Other states give the spouse one half and divide the other half among the parents or, if there are no parents, then among the brothers and sisters.

If there are no close relatives, then the one in closest relation to the decedent will inherit. If there is a contest to determine relationship, the person nearest of kin will inherit all.

Real property is subject to the rights of curtesy and dower in those states which provide for it.

Illegitimate children inherit from their mother. She may inherit from her illegitimate child if there is no spouse or children surviving the illegitimate. Some states permit an illegitimate child to inherit from a person who acknowledged in writing that he was his father.

Small estates of personal property may be settled and distributed without formal administration proceedings if probate or surrogates court is so authorized by state law.

Property left by a person who has no relatives or next of kin, escheats to the state.

State laws may permit adopted children to inherit from their natural parents and their adoptive parents. They are then included as heirs or descendants.

OTHER TRANSFERS OF PROPERTY WITHOUT A WILL

A gift *causa mortis,* in anticipation of death, may be accomplished when personal property is given by the owner to another as a gift with an expressed intention that it is to take effect in the event of his death. Usually, it is done by a person in apprehension of death. If that fear is not realized and the owner recovers, he has the right to demand the return of his property. In order that the gift shall become effective, the cause of death must be the same as anticipated by the decedent.

Illustration: Jameson and Manson, both soldiers, were severely wounded and were sure that they were going to die. Both were treated by a medic on the battlefield. In appreciation, Jameson gave the medic his watch, because he believed he "was going to die anyway." Manson gave him a gold ring. "If I die, I want you to have it." Jameson recovered, Manson did not. The medic kept the ring but had to return the watch.

A "Totten trust" is created by means of a bank account. It occurs when one person opens a bank account in his own name "in trust for another." If the account is not closed before the death of the "trustee," it becomes effective as the property of the beneficiary named in the account. However, if the beneficiary dies before the trustee, the trust is terminated.

Illustration: Harmon opened an account in his name "in trust for his daughter, Elaine." Upon his death, the money on deposit in the bank became the property of Elaine. It was not even considered a part of Harmon's estate.

Joint bank accounts in the names of two or more people, "payable to either or survivor," creates a presumption of a joint tenancy and a right of survivorship. If there is no proof of fraud or undue influence at the time the account was opened, it will be conclusive.

Illustration: Klausman opened an account jointly with his niece, "payable to either or survivor." When Klausman died, his niece was entitled to the money on deposit.

Summation
Points to Remember about Wills

It is unpleasant to think about death and we try not to think about it. But it has a nasty way of coming on suddenly and unexpectedly. We must be prepared at least to make certain that such property as we have gathered during our lifetime will be given to those who are deserving and entitled to it. That can only be done by leaving a valid will.

To know some of the basic legal requirements for proper testamentation, we ought to keep some things clearly in mind.

A will should be in writing and properly executed. The manner of execution is dependent upon the requirements within the state.

The will must express the desires and wishes of the testator. He must be legally capable to execute a valid will.

To be enforced, a will must be probated in the courts having such jurisdiction. The property is then to be distributed in accordance with the provisions of the will.

In the event of death without a will, a proceeding in intestacy will be instituted.

CHAPTER 12

Real Property and Trusts

The subject of real property is presented for your general information. It is not likely that you will be confronted with problems concerning this subject without having an opportunity to get specific and competent advice from your attorney.

However, in keeping with the purposes of this book, all of the principles of law will be explained to make it easier for you to understand them when you meet them again.

DEFINITIONS AND DISTINCTIONS

Real property or real estate can best be defined as land or any property which is closely and permanently affixed to the land.

Illustration: A building, growing trees, minerals.

"Fixtures," although usually considered personal property, may become real property if they are affixed to the property with the intention that they become a part of the realty.

Illustration: A large statue, placed upon a lawn in a permanent foundation as an adornment, was considered a part of the realty because of the owner's obvious intention.

Unless so intended, articles which are attached and do not require any destruction of the building to be removed retain their character as chattels and are personal property.

Illustration: Gas ranges, although attached to the realty by means of gas pipes, do not become fixtures.

Chattels which are attached by a tenant retain their characteristics as personal property. However, if they are not removed by the tenant at the expiration of his term or his lease, or if he does not reserve his ownership in them, they will be considered as abandoned by him and will become the property of the landlord.

Illustration: Capitol China Co., a decorator of chinaware, installed a large kiln, operated by gas, on rented premises. When lease was terminated the company stayed on as a holdover tenant. It lost its right to the kiln on failing to remove it before the term of the lease expired.

An "easement" is the right or privilege to the use of land belonging to another. It is any use or benefit from the use of land by a person not the owner.

Illustration: A telephone company obtains an easement when it is permitted to place its poles and wires across the land or property it does not own.

An easement may be created by a written agreement between the parties or by operation of law. As an interest in real property, it must be in writing signed by the party to be charged because it is within the Statute of Frauds. By operation of law known as "prescription" it is also created when a person uses the property of another openly, continuously and under conditions which are inconsistent with the owner's rights. When this use continues for a definite number of years, as required by the particular state, the owner cannot contest this use.

A "freehold estate" is either an interest in land which is permanent and can be inherited or it is a "life estate," a right to enjoy the use of it during the lifetime of the person in possession. This is a technical distinction from a "leasehold" or a "tenancy for years."

Freehold estates then are divided into estates of inheritance and estates for life.

An "estate of inheritance" gives the owner title, complete ownership and the right to possession. The owner is said to have an "estate in fee." When the ownership right is absolute and not subject to any condition or limitation, it is known as an estate "in fee simple" or "fee simple absolute."

"Seizin" is the possession and ownership of real property by a person who has or claims an estate of inheritance.

"Dower" is the interest which a widow has in the real property owned by her husband at his death. "Curtesy" is the interest which a widower has in the real estate owned by his wife at her death. These rights are not recognized in all states.

When two or more people own real estate together, their interest may be as "tenants in common," "joint tenants" or, if they are husband and wife, they may be "tenants by the entirety." The difference is not merely technical but determines the rights of the parties as to ownership and survival.

A tenancy in common is created by a grant or devise of land by deed or by will made to two or more persons in any proportion. Each of these persons is the owner of his undivided proportionate interest. He may sell it or he may devise it in his will. He may use it as security for a loan or he may use it in any way which is not inconsistent with the rights of his co-tenants. The use of the term "tenant" is to be distinguished from a tenancy under a leasehold. These tenants in common own a proportionate share in the land. The other tenants in a leasehold rent and use the property of the landlord under a lease or agreement. A tenant in common has the right to have the property partitioned to determine and sell his particular share. In the event of death of one, his heirs inherit his share and interest. His co-tenants are not affected by his death in their share of the property.

A joint tenancy is created when an interest in land is devised to two or more persons in equal shares, giving each the same title and equal possession. The intention to create a joint tenancy must be clear and unmistakable. The primary distinction from a tenancy in common is that here a right of survivorship is created so that upon the death of one of the joint tenants the survivors take the interest of the decedent. The heirs of the deceased joint tenant get nothing. In the event of sale of his share by one of the joint tenants, the relationship of the others with the purchaser becomes a tenancy in common.

Illustration: A mother devised her land to her two daughters. One of the daughters died. The other claimed title to the entire property to the exclusion of her niece, because of a joint tenancy. The court held that unless it appears that a joint tenancy was clearly and unequivocally intended, only a tenancy in common is created. There was no right of survivorship here and the niece took the share that her mother had.

A tenancy by the entirety is created when land is devised to two people who are husband and wife. Each owns the whole estate subject to the right of the other. There is a right of survivorship and on the death of one the other gets the entire estate. Neither has the right to sell or mortgage without the consent of the other. If the grant to a married couple specifically creates a tenancy other than by the entirety it is effective. It is only when there is no other specification that the tenancy by the entirety is created.

Illustration: Louis and Christina bought land, each contributing money from his individual property. The deed specified a joint tenancy. Christina sold her share and Alex, the buyer, sued for partition of the property to determine his share. Louis claimed the property was owned by the entirety and Christina had no right to sell. The court held that by their grant they held jointly and the sale was valid. Alex was entitled to maintain his action since, after the sale, Alex and Louis were both tenants in common.

"Adverse possession" is a means of obtaining ownership to property by operation of law other than by purchase or by devise. A person who holds and uses land by actual, open, continuous and hostile possession under some claim of authority inconsistent with the rights of the owner, has an interest which may ripen into ownership. Such possession for a number of years, ranging from 5 to 20 in the various states, gives the person in possession the right to resist any efforts at repossession by the original owner.

Illustration: Ponter bought his land from Dorlan, who did not have full title to it. Ponter moved onto the property and lived there openly, continuously and with possession hostile to the interests of the true owner. After the period required for adverse possession, the true owner will not be able to proceed against Ponter to repossess his land.

A squatter is a person who enters upon land not his own without any legal authority and uses it. The rights of the owner are always dominant as against him, since he has no claim or color of title.

A REAL ESTATE TRANSACTION

The seller of land will usually put his property up for sale at a definite price and under definite terms. He may advertise it directly in a newspaper or by placing a "For Sale" sign on it. He may not want to become involved in such a transaction and may instead list it with a broker whose business it is to obtain buyers. He may give the broker an "exclusive" right to sell. This means that he will not place this property for sale with anyone else for a given period. However, he may thereby become obligated to the broker for his commissions, if during that period he sells it directly. If he does not give an exclusive right, he may list the property with several brokers. The first broker to produce a buyer who is ready, willing and able to buy will earn his commissions. He may also obtain a buyer by having his attorney recommend one to him. Although attorneys are not usually authorized to act as real estate brokers, unless they are also licensed as such, they may, because of their confidential relationship to their client, be permitted to act in occasional transactions.

The commission of the broker according to custom is earned when he obtains a buyer who is "ready willing and able" to buy on the seller's terms. The seller is usually responsible for the payment of the commissions. The fees, as set by custom, are about 5% of the selling price. However, the seller may make any other agreement with the broker he wants at the time he lists the property. Some sellers agree to a stipulated figure rather than a percentage. Others will agree to pay commissions only after contract or after title to the property has actually been closed.

THE BINDER

The binder is a memorandum between the buyer and the seller, which usually contains all of the terms of the agreement between them. It may include the terms of broker's commission, since he is the person who usually negotiates with the buyer at this stage. The binder may be prepared by the seller or by the broker. It may include certain provisions not acceptable to the buyer if he were properly advised. For that reason, it is suggested that a person buying real estate avoid signing a binder, if it is at all possible. The payment of a deposit by the buyer and the receipt of the broker as agent for the seller in which the purchase price is stated, should suffice until such time as the attorney for the buyer and the attorney for the seller can negotiate a contract.

THE CONTRACT OF SALE

The contract of sale is the formal agreement between the buyer and the seller. It includes all of the terms and provisions agreed upon by them. All items agreed upon must be included or the right to enforce them will be lost.

An agreement for the sale of real property is within the Statute of Frauds. It must be in writing and signed by the party to be charged to be enforcible. Any items agreed upon by the parties and not included in the written contract will not be admitted in the event of a lawsuit. This is called the "parol evidence rule." A written agreement is presumed to contain all of the agreed provisions. No proof will be accepted which is intended to vary the terms of the agreement.

The contract should contain the names of the buyer and seller, their addresses and the description of the property sold. This description usually includes the street address, the block and lot number, if it is in an area that has been subdivided, and a description "by metes and bounds." Metes and bounds is an accurate surveyor's description of the property, both in measurement and in geographical direction.

Illustration: ". . . the land and building known as 105 Grand

Street, in the City of Nashville, Tennessee, also known as Lots
#12, 13 and 14 in Block 4573, more particularly bounded and
described as follows: BEGINNING at the northeast point of intersection between Grand Street and 15th Avenue running due
north 106 feet along the easterly side of Grand Street, thence 100
feet due east, thence 106 feet due south and thence 100 feet due
west along the northerly side of 15th Avenue to the point and
place of beginning."

The contract will include the purchase price of the property,
the amount to be paid by the buyer at signing of contract, the
amount of the existing mortgage, if any, and the balance to be
paid at closing of title.

If there is an existing mortgage, the contract will state
whether the buyer is assuming its obligation or taking subject
to it. By assuming it, he undertakes to become personally liable
for its full payment. By taking subject to the mortgage, he
merely undertakes to continue making the payments as they
fall due. If the payments of principal and interest are not made,
the mortgagee will foreclose on the mortgage. He may then sell
the property to satisfy his claim. If the buyer took the property
subject to the mortgage, he undertook no personal liability as to
the balance due on the mortgage. By assuming it, he may become personally liable for any deficiency judgment, if the sale
does not satisfy the amount due on the mortgage.

If a new mortgage is to be obtained, the contract will specify
the type of mortgage the buyer is to obtain, the length it is
to run and the rate of interest. If a mortgage in that amount is
not available under the terms stated, then the sale need not be
consummated. The buyer is to be given a certain length of
time to obtain a commitment from a lending institution. If the
buyer is unable to obtain a loan, then the seller may under the
contract be given an opportunity to obtain a loan secured by a
mortgage. Time may be important to the buyer or to the seller
and they may specify that it is "of the essence." If the loan is
not obtainable with the mortgage terms as agreed within a
stated time, the contract may be considered terminated, since
the condition precedent, the getting of the required mortgage
loan, has not been met.

All existing encumbrances which are recorded against the property should be listed. The buyer may refuse to accept the property with easements or restrictions on it. However, if it is included in the contract which has been signed, then he is bound to accept it.

Illustration: The gas or electric company may have some of its pipes or wires running underground through the land. The buyer may refuse to have this interference with his enjoyment and use of his land. However, if it is listed in the contract and he has signed, then he must accept it.

All existing restrictions on the land should be described in the contract, since the subsequent use of the land may be affected. Prior owners may have entered into restrictive covenants which run with the land and are binding on subsequent purchasers.

Illustration: By agreement, the owners of a tract of land agreed that no parcel of that tract was to be used for anything but residential construction. They further stipulated that all homes built would be of a certain type and would be of brick or fieldstone. Since this agreement was held to be binding on all subsequent purchasers, the failure to include this restriction in a contract was held sufficient basis for refusing to accept title.

The contract will state the type of deed that is to be given to the buyer on the date of closing. These may be a full covenant and warranty or a bargain and sale deed. These are described later in this chapter.

Any personal property, appliances or equipment which are to be transferred with the property must be listed, since it is a part of the sale.

Also listed are the adjustments to be made as to taxes, water charges, interest on existing mortgage, fuel on hand and similar items. This proportionate adjustment covers the responsibility of the seller up to the date when title passes from the seller to the buyer. These adjustments apply to those houses which are resold. New homes will not have any of these items for adjustment except real estate taxes. All taxes, in any event, should be paid up to date and all assessments included in the contract.

Most contracts include a statement that the title, acceptable to a named title company, will be considered satisfactory to the buyer. If there is any item on the record which makes the title to the property unacceptable to the title company, then it will not be acceptable to the buyer. It does not necessarily imply that a title policy must be taken out with that company.

A tentative date for the closing of title will be decided depending upon the time generally required to search title and get the necessary commitment from a lending institution. If the buyer is to obtain benefits under the Veterans Administration, a longer period of time may be required for clearance and the other administrative details that are essential before title may be closed.

Although not always expressly included in a contract, there is an implied warranty that the seller has good title to the property and that it will continue until law day, when the deed is to be delivered.

The broker's commissions may be referred to in the contract. However, the seller and broker may have a separate agreement as to that.

REMEDIES FOR BREACH OF CONTRACT

The remedies of the parties for breach of contract are essentially the same as those discussed under the subject of contracts.

If the buyer breaches his contract, the seller may sue for the breach of contract and damages incurred as a result of the breach. If he paid the broker's commissions, had expenses for advertising and, in reselling the house, suffered a loss and had to sell for less, he may charge these expenses to the buyer.

In the event of a breach by the seller, the buyer is entitled to the recovery of any money paid by him under the contract and any loss he sustained as a result of the breach.

In addition, both the buyer and the seller may obtain relief in a court of equity to enforce a contract for the purchase and sale of land. This is available to each of them when they cannot obtain adequate relief at law by the mere payment of money damages. Each may obtain the aid of the court to compel the other to go through with the contract. This is called "specific performance."

PREPARATION FOR CLOSING OF TITLE

The buyer, either through his attorney or through a title company, will examine the record title of the property to see that it is marketable. If the seller has an abstract of title, that is, a listing of all encumbrances of record against the property, he may be required to have it brought up to date for the use of the buyer.

A search of the records, usually located in the office of the county clerk, will reveal the chain of title in the property, a listing of all transfers of the property and all mortgages, liens and other existing encumbrances.

If any encumbrance is found against the property which is not listed in the contract, the seller should be advised so that he will have an opportunity to clear it before the date of closing. If he fails to do so and it is substantial in nature it may be the basis for the refusal of title by the buyer because the property is not marketable.

All tax offices should be checked to determine the amount due on city tax, town tax, village tax, school tax. If there are any special assessments, they should be determined and, unless listed in the contract, notice that they are unpaid should be sent to the seller.

A survey of the property made by an engineer is important, and if not furnished by the seller then one should be made by the buyer. Mere visual inspection may not reveal an irregularity.

Illustration: Bradford moved into his house after the transfer of title. All parts of the transaction had been completed. He did not have a survey made of the land he bought. The day after, he found an obstruction across a portion of his driveway preventing him from using his garage. A hurried visit to his neighbor revealed that a portion of the driveway was not within the property he had bought. This was confirmed by a subsequent survey. Bradford had to buy a small, wedge-shaped piece of land at a price much greater per foot than the cost of the land on which his house stood. Had he checked it by survey and refused to take title, seller would have been required to pay instead.

It is often practical to have a title policy on property purchased. It includes an abstract of title. It assures the buyer of getting a marketable title and insures him against all claims as to title for which he personally is not responsible.

LAW DAY—CLOSING TITLE

At the time agreed upon for the closing of title, the buyer and the seller or their authorized representatives must be present.

The seller or his attorney will have the deed ready for delivery.

The buyer will have the money as required.

The bank will have its representative if a new mortgage loan is to be made.

The title company will have its representative if a title policy has been obtained by the buyer.

Of course, the attorneys for the buyer and the seller will be present.

The steps in the title closing proceedings need not be specifically itemized here. The important features which concern us are as follows: The buyer is to be assured that he is getting a marketable title in accordance with the contract. The title is acceptable to the title company. There are no encumbrances or restrictions which have not been agreed upon. Any objections made to the seller have been cleared up or adequate adjustment is to be made. Finally, the deed and the new mortgage, if there is to be one, are acceptable to the buyer.

Both sides will then make arithmetic computations of the adjustments to be made. Some will be in favor of the seller. This will consist of such items as fuel and insurance for which he has made payment and which must be proportionately charged to the buyer for the period that he will occupy the premises from the date of closing. The others may be in favor of the buyer and will consist of those items, such as water or taxes, for which the seller did not pay prior to law day. The items listed in the contract will be adjusted from the records presented by the seller.

The closing statement is actually a balance sheet which indicates the account between the buyer and the seller. The purchase price due the seller less the payments made by the buyer, less the amount of the existing mortgage, is the balance due on the contract from the buyer. To this balance is added the difference between the adjustment totals. Usually, it is in favor of the seller so that it is added to the balance due him. This final sum is to be paid by the buyer to the seller in exchange for which he will receive the deed which must be recorded.

United States excise stamps are no longer required to be attached to the deed or to any mortgage involved in a real estate transaction. However, some of the states, as a means of additional revenue, may require a tax to be paid for recording, in addition to the regular recording fee. The deed is then filed in the office of the register or clerk of the county where the property is located.

BASIC FACTS ABOUT THE DEED

The deed is the document which conveys or transfers title from one person to another. The successive recording of deeds from seller to buyer, grantor to grantee, creates the chain of title which determines the rightful last owner of the property. Title usually begins with some original grant from the King of England, from the United States Land Office or from the state in which it is located. The record will then show the transfer from the original grantee to the person who acquired it from him. In this subsequent transaction, he, the seller, now becomes the grantor and his purchaser now becomes the grantee.

Each grantee gets no better title to the land, no better right, than his grantor had before him. Of course, the grantee may improve his title by clearing away an incumbrance, a lien, a mortgage or a restriction by some subsequent transaction.

In the event of death of the owner, the transfer of the property may be accomplished through the probate or surrogate's court. Any gap in the chain of title will then be completed by the records of that court in the transfer of title from the estate of the decedent to the person entitled to the land, by will or by descent.

TYPES OF DEEDS

The "bargain and sale deed" is the most common deed in use generally in communities where there has been a constant transfer of property through the years. In New York City, for example, the bargain and sale deed is generally acceptable in most real estate transactions.

The grantor in such a deed makes no express covenants as to the title he is conveying. By implication, he warrants that he has a marketable title and that he is transferring a marketable title to his grantee.

The "bargain and sale deed with covenant against the grantor's act" is similar to the regular bargain and sale deed except that it will include the statement that he, the grantor, "has not done or suffered anything to be done whereby the premises have been encumbered in any way except" as mentioned in the deed. By this statement, he obligates himself for any claims against the title which are the results of his own act and which have not been made known to the buyer. If, after the passing of title, any claim should mature which affects the grantee's title and which is the result of any act of the grantor, the covenant may be enforced and any loss sustained by the grantee recovered from the grantor.

The "full covenant and warranty deed" expressly states that the grantor is seized of the premises in fee simple. That means that he owns the property and has the right to possession without any condition. He further warrants that he has the right to sell it.

The grantor promises and warrants that the grantee will enjoy the ownership and use of the property and that no one will interfere with or dispute that right, by claim of title. The grantor will be financially responsible for any damage or loss sustained by the grantee for any such claim. This is known as the covenant of "quiet enjoyment."

He warrants also that the premises, conveyed, are free from encumbrances except as listed in the contract and in the deed.

The grantor will execute or procure any further assurances of title should they become necessary. If anyone claims title or interest in the property, he will obtain such documents as will be necessary to satisfy that claim. The grantor, under this warranty, obligates himself to clear away any claims that may thus arise.

The final covenant is that the grantor will forever warrant the title to the premises.

The "quitclaim deed" is used primarily to release any claims which anyone may have against the property. Although it may be used to transfer title to property, it is generally used to release from claimants any interest or title to the property which they may have or claim to have. Such a deed, when recorded, will quiet and remove any claim against the property which may exist on the record.

THE BOND AND THE MORTGAGE

The bond is a document usually given in a loan transaction which indicates that the person who executed it is indebted to the lender according to its terms. In some transactions, the same purpose may be accomplished by a promissory note. It is an indication of an existing indebtedness.

The mortgage is given to secure the payment of the bond or the promissory note. The security is the land on which the mortgage is given. The effect of a mortgage varies in the various jurisdictions. In some, as in New York, a mortgage does not transfer title to the property, it is merely an indication of an existing encumbrance which is extinguished when paid. In other jurisdictions, notably Maryland, the mortgagee gets legal title while the mortgagor retains possession of the land. However, all the mortgagor has is an equity of redemption, a right to redeem his land. The title remains in the mortgagee, the lender of the money, as long as the debt is still outstanding. A third method of handling such a situation is to give the lender of the money a "deed of trust" to the property and give him the right to sell the property in the event that the debt evidenced by promissory notes is not paid as agreed.

Actually, the effect is the same, although technically and legally there is a difference in these three methods discussed.

The effect is to give the person who is lending the money, the mortgagee, the right to proceed against the land in the event that there is a default in the payments as agreed between the parties.

In states where the mortgagee does not get legal title, he has to proceed against the mortgagor, the owner of the land, to foreclose his mortgage. He proves the debt, the mortgage, the default and asks the court for permission to proceed against the property in order to be paid. He will then ask for, and obtain, the court's permission to have the property sold at auction, and to apply the proceeds against the expenses of the proceedings and the original indebtedness. If the proceeds are not sufficient to satisfy the indebtedness, he may obtain a deficiency judgment which will enable him to proceed personally against the mortgagor to recover the balance. Any buyer of real property who assumes an existing mortgage as part of the transaction similarly becomes liable on any deficiency judgment if he is made a party to the foreclosure proceeding.

The owner of property may obtain more than one loan, using his land as security. It all depends, of course, upon the willingness of the person lending the money. The mortgage which is first recorded against the property obtains prior rights. A mortgage subsequently recorded becomes a "second" mortgage and is subject to the rights of the first. If the first mortgage is foreclosed, all rights of the second mortgage are wiped out. If the second mortgage is foreclosed, all proceedings are subject to the first mortgage which continues to exist as an encumbrance against the property.

In the jurisdiction where the mortgage constitutes a transfer of legal title subject to the right by the owner to redeem, the mortgagee has the right to sell the property in accordance with the terms of the mortgage or, if the terms require a foreclosure, he may then be compelled to proceed through the courts.

A deed of trust with the right to sell usually includes the requirement of advertisement and sale according to the terms of the deed of trust or the law which applies within the state.

THE LEASE

The owner of real property may by a contract called a lease, give the use of his land to another for a consideration called rent. The lease can be "at will" or for a stated period.

The owner becomes the "lessor," or landlord, and the person who leases the property is the "lessee," or the tenant.

The lease is, of course, subject to all the requirements of a contract. It must also include any terms and conditions to which both have agreed.

As it concerns real property, it is subject to the Statute of Frauds and is usually required to be in writing. Most states agree, however, that a lease for less than a year is not required to be in writing.

The contents of a lease usually include a description of the property which is leased and the term or duration for which it is to be effective. It contains the rental, either annually or monthly, and the manner in which it is to be paid.

Unless otherwise agreed, repairs are usually to be made by the landlord if the property is residential, or by the tenant if it is business property under exclusive control of the tenant. Ordinary repairs of business property are generally the responsibility of the tenant and special or unusual repairs the responsibility of the landlord. Those parts of the building for the common use of all tenants are the landlord's obligation. This would include the roof, the stairs, the vestibule and similar areas.

The tenant may transfer or "assign" all of his interest in the leased premises, or he may transfer or "sublet" a portion, if this is not restricted by the lease. The lease may require that an assignment or a sublet must be on written permission of the landlord only.

"Eviction" is the legal term which means that the tenant is deprived of the use of the premises.

If the tenant fails or refuses to pay his rent, or in some other way breaches the terms of the lease, the landlord may institute legal proceedings to have the tenant evicted. This is known as "dispossess" or "distress" proceedings. Each jurisdiction has its own rules, but the main feature of it is that it is summary, swift and without delay. The landlord must be given his property back immediately, if he is entitled to it.

A tenant is considered to be technically evicted when the landlord disturbs his peaceful possession of the premises. This is called "constructive eviction." It may result when there is a fire and the landlord fails to repair within a reasonable time. It may also occur when there are other factors which disturb the tenant's enjoyment of the leased premises. The failure to supply heat, or the presence of rodents or vermin, may be the basis of a constructive eviction. In such a situation, the tenant may be justified in refusing to pay the rent until such time as the landlord makes the leased premises tenantable, even though he continues in possession.

A lease may contain some provision for renewal. The tenant may be required to give notice to the landlord of his desire to renew under the lease. Some leases contain an automatic renewal clause. In some jurisdictions, to protect the tenant from the effect of this clause, the landlord is required to give notice to the tenant of the existence of such a clause, advising him that unless he gives notice of his refusal to renew, the clause will become effective. If such notice is given by the landlord and the tenant fails to comply, then the renewal clause becomes binding.

"Holdover" is the term used for tenants who stay over on leased premises after the expiration of their lease. Possession must be surrendered on the last day of the term. The failure to do so creates a holdover tenant. Depending upon the jurisdiction, the landlord may have him dispossessed as a trespasser or he may hold him on a month to month or year to year basis.

Because of emergency housing regulations, some states require that no dispossess proceedings may be instituted unless the landlord proves to some authority on housing that he has a right to institute such proceedings. He will then obtain a "certificate of eviction" authorizing him to institute such proceedings.

In the event of fire, the rent usually continues unless the premises are made uninhabitable. Then the rent ceases until repairs are made and they are tenantable again.

If a fire causes total destruction of the property, the landlord may reserve an option in the lease to demolish the building and rebuild. If he does, the lease may be deemed terminated on notice.

Security paid by the tenant to the landlord to assure future rent payments or the return of the premises in good condition, is in some states made a trust fund to be held by the landlord for return to the tenant. This is to protect the tenant's money in the event of the landlord's insolvency.

The lease may provide that in the event of any disputes which are brought to court, both parties waive their right to a jury trial.

Fixtures, particularly in business property, not removed by the tenant at the end of the lease become the property of the landlord, if not controlled by lease or state law.

The landlord is given the right by the lease to enter the premises only to demand the rent, to show the premises to prospective tenants at or near termination of the lease or when the premises are abandoned by the tenant.

The rules and regulations in small print on the back of a lease become a part of it. Failure to comply with its provisions, such as one prohibiting pets, may expose the tenant to an action for breach of the lease.

A lease is terminated at the expiration of the term, by subsequent agreement of the parties, by certain conditions in the lease and by operation of law. Condemnation of property by a public authority for public use or the unlawful use of the premises by the tenant are examples of termination by operation of law.

Death of the tenant or the landlord does not terminate the

lease because it is a contractual obligation binding upon their estates.

A "tenancy at will," as distinguished from a tenancy for a stated period, can be terminated at any time and by either party on notice to the other side.

HOMESTEAD PROVISIONS

Some of the states give the head of the household an exemption to prevent a judgment creditor from foreclosing on his homestead. The law generally describes what a homestead constitutes. It includes the dwelling and the land used by the family. The value of the property exempt varies from $500 in one state to $12,500 in another.

This exemption continues on the property even after the death of the head of the house and as long as it is used as a home for the family. The homestead is inheritable by the widow and minor children.

Both husband and wife are required to join in the deed selling their homestead. The proceeds of such a sale are also exempt from the claims of creditors for a reasonable time until they can be invested in another property.

"Eminent domain" is the taking of private property for public use by condemnation. Any government agency may, after deliberation, determine that certain private property is necessary to be acquired for a public purpose. It may be for a park, a school, a reservoir or to build new houses that replace slums.

There is usually some federal, state or local law which authorizes this plan. Such a law is passed by the legislature and transfers title in this private property to the agency requesting it.

The agency will then proceed by court process to compensate the private owners for that property. Negotiations are at first carried on privately in an effort to come to terms as to the value of the property condemned. If there is no agreement, then proof is submitted in court by both the agency and the private owner to have the value determined. Testimony is produced by real estate experts who testify as to their opinion

of the value of the property. The court will then, after all of
the testimony is in, decide the value which the governmental
agency is to pay for that property.

PROCEEDINGS TO REDUCE ASSESSED VALUATION ON REAL ESTATE FOR TAX PURPOSES

In those states where real estate taxes are paid to municipalities or counties by owners of real property, an assessed valuation of the property is determined on each parcel by a board
of assessors. This total assessed valuation of all real property
is then used as the basis for determining the tax rate by divid-
ing it into the estimated budget for the next fiscal year. Each
parcel is then taxed by multiplying the assessed valuation by
the tax rate. In some instances the owners may feel that their
property is overassessed. They will then institute a proceeding
"in certiorari" to review the tax assessment of the board of
assessors. Testimony is introduced by the taxing authority and
the individual to prove their respective contentions. The court
will then, on the basis of the proof, determine if the assessed
valuation is correct or place another valuation on it in accordance with the proof.

TRUSTS

A trust is created when legal title and ownership to property
is given to a person called a "trustee" to apply the proceeds
from such property for the benefit and use of another. Trusts
are often created to provide for the care and maintenance of
dependents.

The person who grants the property or creates the trust is
called the "settlor"; he may accomplish this by an *inter vivos*
trust, effective during his lifetime or by will.

The beneficiary is the person for whose benefit the trust is
created. He may also be called the "cestui que trust."

Unless the trustee is given the power to sell the property as
well as the right to hold it, the power of alienation of the property is thus suspended. It cannot be sold until the trust is termi-

nated by the provisions of the original agreement or by operation of law.

> Illustration: Felix wanted to provide for his crippled son. He created a trust by granting a parcel of his real estate to a bank as trustee. The agreement of trust provided that the proceeds from the property were to be paid to his son. The trust provided that it was to terminate upon the son's death when it was to return and be a part of Felix's estate again. This property cannot be sold as long as the son lives and the trust exists.

A trust agreement relating to real property is within the Statute of Frauds and must be in writing.

THE RULE AGAINST PERPETUITIES

This rule is based on a well-recognized principle that the right of sale or alienation of property should not be suspended for an unreasonable length of time. When a person owns real property he may sell it whenever he wants to. When it is the subject of a trust, it cannot be sold until the trust is terminated. When the trust is for the benefit of several persons, then it will naturally not terminate until all of the beneficiaries are dead. The right of alienation of this real property is then subject to the lives of the beneficiaries.

All states have regulations limiting an unreasonable suspension of the saleability of real property. Some states consider suspension for two lives, that is, during the lifetime of two existing beneficiaries, as reasonable. Others make no limitation as to the number of beneficiaries, provided that they are in existence when the trust is created.

> Illustration: Francis is wealthy and has four children. He creates a trust for the benefit of all of his children by setting aside a sum of money with a bank as the trustee. This trust is based on the lives of all four children. Since they are all alive and "in being," the trust is valid in that particular state.
>
> Jules, a friend of Francis, also creates a trust. However, he makes it for the benefit of his two children and his grandchildren. He does not name the grandchildren but includes them in the general term so that any born after the trust is created will be

protected. This trust is not valid since not all of the beneficiaries are "in being."

Trusts may be created for any lawful purpose which the settlor or cestui que trust requires. They may also be created by operation of law. Generally, this situation is implied when a person who has been entrusted with property or funds uses them for his own personal gain. The law enables this profit to be considered as a trust fund for the benefit of the original owner of the property.

Illustration: Horton, the guardian for a minor, has property and money left in his charge for that minor. He used some of these funds to make personal investments and made a personal profit. These gains, which he made at the expense of the estate in his possession, were considered as a part of the trust fund and he will be compelled to account for them.

Summation

Points to Remember about Real Property

Real property is concerned with land and those items which are a permanent part of the land, such as buildings, mineral deposits and timber.

Property may be owned individually or by two or more persons. If it is acquired by two or more, then the nature of their ownership will determine their respective rights.

Transactions concerning real property are more formal and require legal advice and preparation to a greater degree than those concerned with personal property.

Here are some specific questions you should be able to answer:

If you are buying a house, does the binder which the seller wants you to sign deprive you of any rights before you even sign the contract?

Is there an existing mortgage? Do you have to assume it, or can you take the property subject to the mortgage?

Are there any restrictions which may deprive you of the proper enjoyment or use of the property?

What kind of a deed are you to get?

If you are leasing property, what restrictions are imposed in the lease which may prevent you from carrying on your business? Is there any zoning or other restriction established by the town or village which may prevent you from carrying on your business?

Are there any rules and regulations in small print on the back of your lease which may limit you in the use and enjoyment of your premises?

Do you want a jury trial in the event that there is any dispute with your landlord?

Is there an automatic renewal clause in your lease? Is there an option to renew? What about any property which you attach to the realty; is it reserved as your property when the lease is terminated?

| CHAPTER 13 |

Criminal Law and Procedure

The criminal law is a portion of our laws, both administrative and substantive, which control the behavior of our citizens as members of the community.

Since the purpose of these laws is to protect the community from the wrongful and harmful acts of individuals, the basic principles are generally similar throughout the country, although the specific rules and their applications may vary among the states.

Criminal law is a very technical part of our law because it concerns the liberty of the individual. Because of our basic doctrine that a person is presumed innocent until he is proved guilty, every safeguard is made available to the person charged with any crime. This does not mean, however, that a person charged with a crime may safely sit back and feel secure in the thought that the law is on his side. It is up to him through proper legal counsel to make use of every defense that the law provides for him.

A crime may be defined as an act which is forbidden by law. If such an act is committed and the person responsible is caught, tried and convicted, then his punishment is determined by the law which he has violated.

Punishments as prescribed in the law are dependent upon the gravity of the crime. A capital offense is one which the state recognizes as punishable by the death sentence. In other crimes the punishment may be imprisonment in a state prison, in a county or a city jail.

The punishment may be a fine or imprisonment or both. The

severity of punishment is also dependent upon the criminal record of the defendant.

Conviction of a crime may disqualify a person from holding public office and may cause him to be deprived of the right to practice his profession, particularly if that profession is based on trust and confidence.

The convicted person may receive such other penal discipline which the court considers adequate in that particular situation.

A "felony" is generally defined as a crime which is punishable by death or confinement in a state prison. The statute which establishes the crime and its punishment usually indicates whether it is a felony.

"Misdemeanors" are all other crimes not considered felonies. The punishment for misdemeanors is less severe since the crime itself is less serious in nature.

The third category of criminal or antisocial behavior is called an "offense." It is not considered a crime, but is serious enough to warrant punishment according to the direction of the law which creates it. An offense is usually a violation of local laws or of rules of accepted public conduct and behavior.

Illustrations: An assault with a weapon would be considered a felony by the law which defines it and which prescribes the punishment on conviction.

A simple assault without any weapon would be considered a misdemeanor.

Disorderly conduct, vagrancy or public intoxication are considered offenses and as such would probably call for a short sentence in the county jail or the workhouse.

As we have mentioned, a crime is an offense against the state and the people of the state. The action against the offender is prosecuted by the district attorney or any public officer charged with such a duty. The criminal action is brought in a special criminal court or in a special division of criminal actions in a state court.

The title of the action would be "The State against John Jones" or "The People of the State of ———— against John

Jones." In some states it will be "The Commonwealth of _____ against John Jones."

The individual who was injured as a result of the crime is not a party to the criminal action. However, he will be an important witness and is called the complainant or the complaining witness. When called, he must appear and testify at the trial relative to the crime. The purposes of the criminal proceeding are to punish the offender and to act as a deterrent to others who may contemplate such action in the future.

Each state is sovereign in its power to determine those acts which are defined as crimes and to prescribe adequate punishments. This power is, however, restricted since the states are prohibited from passing laws which are contrary to the Bill of Rights of the federal Constitution and to those limitations in their own constitutions which are intended to protect the liberty of its citizens.

"Bills of attainder" are prohibited. No state legislature may pass any law which, in effect, will cause a person convicted of a felony to forfeit his property.

A person finally sentenced to a term of life imprisonment, though deprived of all his civil rights and considered legally and civilly dead, has the right to own property, make a will and devise his property.

"Ex post facto" laws are prohibited. No state may pass a law which will, in effect, make an act, which was legal and permissible when committed, punishable as a crime. This includes those laws which increase the penalty of crimes committed prior to their enactment.

Illustrations: A law which prohibits the sale of liquor cannot affect those sales which were legal before the law was passed.

A law which increases the punishment of a crime from 5 years to 10 years in a state prison cannot affect a crime which was committed before the penalty was raised. The punishment for the crime previously committed must be 5 years.

No law shall be passed which violates the right of the people against unreasonable searches and seizures.

No person shall twice be put in jeopardy of his life for the same offense. This is commonly known as double jeopardy. In effect, it means that once a person has been tried for a crime and found not guilty, he cannot again be tried for the same crime.

No person shall be compelled to be a witness against himself in a criminal prosecution. This is the well-known Fifth Amendment. Actually, it is only one portion of the Fifth Amendment of the United States Constitution, a part of the Bill of Rights. It guarantees a person protection from testifying in any proceeding which may tend to expose him as guilty of a crime. This testimony may not be used against him. However, this claim of self incrimination may not protect a person from testifying if he has been given immunity and a guaranty that he will not be prosecuted for any crime revealed by his testimony.

No person may be deprived of life, liberty or property without due process of law. This guarantees to all the right to a hearing, the right to submit a defense, the right to cross examine and to be confronted by all witnesses. No law shall be passed by any state which will abridge and violate these constitutional safeguards.

Crimes are either "malum in se," inherently vicious and harmful in nature, and so declared by law, or they are "malum prohibitum," created by law because they are contrary to the public welfare, safety, health or morals.

The vicious crime, malum in se, requires a criminal intent. This must be proved before a conviction can be had. No intent need be proved to convict for a crime which is malum prohibitum, since none is necessary. The only proof required here is that there is a law which prohibits such an act and that such an act was committed by the person who is charged with it.

A mistake of fact may excuse the commission of a vicious crime but will not excuse a crime created and prohibited by statute.

Illustrations: Sitrux shot and killed a man he mistook to be a burglar. If proof of these facts is presented, he may be absolved of the crime.

Russell is charged with violating the law which prohibits the sale of liquor to a minor. The mistake of fact based on the minor's statement that he was over the required age is not sufficient to relieve him of his criminal act.

"Intent" in the commission of a crime is the state of mind of the individual which is consistent with criminality. The intent may be actual and specific to commit the crime.

Illustration: Jones set fire to a building owned by Sohmer to get even with him for a fancied insult.

This intent may be "constructive"; that is, implied by the law from the nature of his activities. A person who intends to commit one crime is responsible for any other crimes which result. The intent for the other crimes is constructive and presumed from his criminal intent and activity.

Illustration: Doe bought a gun to commit a "stick-up." In attempting it, he killed an innocent bystander. He is presumed to have intended to commit the murder; the intent here is constructive. This is an example of a felony murder. When a person commits a felony and a person is killed, he may be charged with murder.

Malice is an ill will or an evil disposition from which an unlawful act may result without any legal justification.

The term "malice aforethought," sometimes used in relation to murder, implies premeditation to indicate a cunning mind and evil deliberation.

"Motive" is the element which may induce and create the intent to commit a crime. Motive is not essential in proving a person guilty of a crime. However, intent is necessary. The presence of a motive will help to establish the intent.

Illustration: To convict Alfred of shooting Roberts, intent must be proved. If it is shown that Roberts had run away with Alfred's wife, the motive is present from which the intent may be inferred.

CAPACITY TO COMMIT A CRIME

All persons are held responsible for their acts. This is a presumption of law. Based on this presumption, the prosecution need only establish those elements which prove that the defendant committed the crime. The defendant then has the opportunity to prove as his defense that when he committed the crime he was not legally responsible. The prosecution must then establish that the defendant was legally responsible.

The burden of proof in a criminal case is always on the prosecution. This is another of the safeguards based on the legal presumption of innocence. The matter of incompetency is a defense which the defendant must establish by legally sufficient evidence. Once he does, it then continues to be the burden of the prosecution to show that the defendant was legally competent to commit the crime with which he is charged.

Generally, infants below 7 years of age are conclusively presumed to be incapable of committing a crime. Usually, even proof that a crime was committed by a child under 7 is not sufficient to charge him with a crime. Such a child is by law not considered mentally capable of committing a crime.

A child between the age of 7 and 12 is still considered incapable of committing a crime. However, if it is proved that the child had the mental capacity to know the nature of the act he committed and to know that his act was wrong, then he may be held chargeable with the crime.

Under special laws relating to criminal activity of children under 16, an act which, if committed by an adult, would be a crime, can only be charged as "juvenile delinquency" if committed by a child under 16. However, if the act is such as to expose an adult who committed it with death or life imprisonment, the child may also be charged with the same crime. Thus a juvenile may be charged with treason, kidnapping and murder.

> Illustration: A boy of 15, arrested and charged with holding a man up with a gun to get some money, will only be charged with juvenile delinquency. He may, however, be charged with murder if it is shown that he committed a deliberate and premeditated murder.

A person is not excused from punishment for the commission of a crime unless it is proved that at the time he committed the crime he did not know the nature and quality of the act and did not know that it was wrong. There is a new trend to accept medical evidence proving mental illness.

A person who is actually insane when he commits a crime will not be held accountable for it and will probably be sent to a mental institution.

A person who is sane when he commits the act but becomes insane while awaiting trial, cannot be tried and must be kept in a mental institution until such times as he regains his sanity so that he can be tried. A person who is insane is not deemed capable of properly defending himself in a criminal prosecution.

A tendency or propensity to commit crime is not a defense as mental incompetency. It is the duty of every citizen to resist those temptations and to avoid criminal activity or to be punished for the crimes he commits.

Voluntary intoxication is never an excuse, sufficient to avoid punishment, for committing a crime. However, if the crime requires the necessary elements of intent and deliberation, and these cannot be shown because of the inebriated condition of the individual, the crime cannot be proved.

Persons whose will is imposed upon and who commit a crime while under the domination, duress or threat of another may be excused if such domination is proved.

CRIMES AGAINST THE PERSON

Homicide is the killing of one human being by the act of another human being.

There are certain homicides which are considered legal, others justifiable. An executioner carrying out the legal direction of a court commits a legal homicide. A police officer who kills a prisoner escaping from custody or a person suspected of committing a felony fleeing arrest may be excused for a justifiable homicide.

A person who killed in self-defense to protect his own life and safety may be excused if it is shown that he did all in his power to avoid killing but was compelled to do so in order to save his own life.

Accidental or excusable homicide occurs when it is the result of an unforeseen and unexpected accident. It must be the result of a lawful act done in a lawful manner with ordinary care and without criminal intent.

> Illustration: Anthony, Jim and Clancy all stood by watching Joe chop wood. Suddenly, the axhead flew off and killed Jim. Joe had no warning that the axhead was loose. This is an accidental and excusable homicide.

Felonious homicide is the charge for intentionally causing the death of another.

Murder is the killing of a human being by a deliberate and premeditated design to effect his death. It is also the killing of a person by any act which is so imminently dangerous as to indicate a depraved disregard for the value of human life.

> Illustrations: A person who deliberately causes a railroad or airplane accident would be charged with murder if anyone is killed. The planting of a bomb in a place of public gathering which causes death is chargeable as murder.
>
> When death results from the commission of the crime of arson, the charge is murder.

When the killing is the result of deliberation and premeditation, it will be considered as murder in the first degree. This has also been classified as "murder with malice aforethought." Where there is no such premeditation, the charge will be murder in the second degree.

The charge of manslaughter is a lesser charge in a felonious homicide. The statute of each state will list the crimes which are chargeable as manslaughter. Here, a design to effect a person's death is not necessary. Manslaughter is usually the charge when a person is killed by another in the heat of anger and passion. If the death is accomplished with a dangerous weapon or by unusual means it may be manslaughter in the first degree, otherwise it may be in the second degree. The distinctions of degree are important because the punishments vary according to the gravity of the charge.

The term "corpus delicti" is often used in connection with homicide. The general impression, though in error, is that it means the "corpse" or body of the person murdered. Since the corpus delicti is necessary to prove a murder or manslaughter, the erroneous impression has been created that the body must be produced. That is not the meaning at all. This term actually means proof of the crime. In a homicide, there must be proof of the death of the person who is claimed to have been killed. This must be so direct and tangible that his absence can be explained by no other reason than by a violent death.

Illustration: In addition to other proof, the dentures of the deceased were found in a furnace. This was the corpus delicti, the proof that his death was due to violence.

Kidnapping is the crime of taking a person against his will, without authority and with a criminal intent for the purpose of collecting a ransom for his safe return. This has been established as a capital offense in most states. If the person is transported across state lines, it becomes a federal offense and the penalty is death.

A criminal assault or an assault and battery is an unjustified attack upon a person with or without a deadly weapon with an intent to injure or kill him.

Robbery is the forceful and unlawful taking of money or property from the person of another, by first putting him in fear of his life or his personal safety.

Extortion is the crime of taking or obtaining money or property induced by the wrongful use of force or fear.

Blackmail is the use of letters, containing threats and producing fear, to obtain money.

Conspiracy is the combination of two or more persons with intent to commit a crime.

Perjury is the making of a statement under oath which is false. It is usually made with a corrupt purpose and intent and is known to be false by the person making it.

Subornation of perjury is the crime of willfully inducing a person to commit perjury.

CRIMES AGAINST PROPERTY

Arson is the willful and malicious burning or setting fire to a dwelling, a building, a car or a vessel.

Larceny is the crime of taking property from the possession of any person with intent to defraud and deprive him of it.

Burglary is the crime of breaking into and entering a building or other enclosure with intent to commit a crime.

Malicious mischief is intentional injury to the property of another.

Possession of burglar tools is usually a misdemeanor. However, if there has been a previous conviction of any crime then it may be charged as a felony.

Criminally receiving stolen goods, knowing them to be stolen, is a felony.

Forgery is the making or altering of a writing with intent to deceive or defraud. Uttering is the publication or the putting into circulation of a document with knowledge that it is a forgery.

AN ATTEMPT TO COMMIT A CRIME

Some statutes stipulate that an attempt to commit a crime is a crime in itself. It is punishable according to the particular law which was violated. Legally, it is an act which is directly connected with an intent to commit a complete crime but fails to complete its commission. To prove an attempt to commit a crime, the prosecution must show that there was a criminal intent and a wrongful overt act.

CRIMINAL COURT PROCEDURE

Generally, persons charged with minor offenses are brought into court by means of a summons. The officer who sees the offense committed gives the offender a summons, which is a notice to appear in court at a designated date.

On the return day, the date set in the summons, the name of the person summoned, now known as a defendant, is called from a calendar or list of all similar cases. When his name is called the person may plead "guilty" or "not guilty," to the charge.

If the plea is guilty, he may ask the court for an opportunity to explain the commission of the offense merely in mitigation or reduction of punishment. The court may then pronounce sentence or may adjourn the case for sentence at a later date.

If the person objects to the charge and disputes his responsibility, he should plead "innocent" or "not guilty." This creates an issue for which a hearing or a trial is necessary. The officer may or may not be in court. Since proof must be presented to convince the judge beyond a reasonable doubt that the defendant is guilty, the matter may be adjourned or postponed to some later date. Witnesses may be necessary and the defendant may then want to get a lawyer to represent him.

On the adjourned date, the case is called again and, if both sides are ready, it will be set down for trial.

A trial is a hearing before a judge, magistrate or justice of the peace. Evidence concerning the charge is then presented by the prosecutor and contradictory evidence is presented by the defendant. The evidence consists of the testimony of witnesses and documents or other material submitted by each side intended to convince the judge. The hearing may or may not be taken down by a reporter or a person on the court staff to retain a permanent record of the proceedings.

Although in a hearing on a minor offense the proceedings are informal, the purpose is to prove the defendant guilty of the offense as charged beyond a reasonable doubt. If the judge is convinced that the defendant is guilty, he will render such a decision. The defendant will then be sentenced in accordance with the specific punishment set forth in the particular law under which he was charged. The punishment may be a fine, a jail sentence or both in certain instances.

If a person served with a summons fails to answer it on the return day, the court may order a warrant to be issued. A warrant is a written order of the court directing that a person named in it be apprehended and brought before the court.

A person apprehended and arrested under the authority of a warrant must be brought before the court as soon as possible. He is given an opportunity to plead to the original charge and to the charge of failing to answer the summons. A hearing may be held then and the matter may be disposed of immediately or it may be adjourned to a later date for trial.

If the case is adjourned to a later date, the defendant may be held in custody, released on his own recognizance or on the promise of his attorney that he will appear on the date of trial. If held in custody, he may make application to be released on bail.

"Bail" is the security that a defendant or a person charged with a crime must give to assure the court that he will not leave the jurisdiction of the court and will be available when necessary for the trial of the case or for sentence after trial. In the event the amount of money required by the court as such bail is not available to the defendant, he may get someone to post bail for him. If he can't do that, then he may obtain a bond either from a private individual or a bonding company in the required amount. A bonding company charges a premium for such a bond and will usually not issue one unless the person obtaining it leaves some adequate assurance that there will be no default.

In situations where bail is not set or is excessive, the defendant may institute a proceeding by means of a writ of habeas corpus to have the question determined in a superior or supreme court.

MISDEMEANORS

A prosecution for a misdemeanor is usually begun by an information. It is a written statement made and sworn to before a judge which charges that a person named in it is believed guilty of a designated crime.

The judge or magistrate will then examine and question the person making the charge to determine that the crime has been committed and further that the grounds are reasonable for believing that the person named committed that crime. When he is satisfied, he may issue a summons or a bench warrant, depending upon the gravity of the crime. A bench warrant will direct that the person named therein be apprehended and immediately brought before the court.

When a peace officer or a private citizen sees a crime committed he may arrest the offender and bring him into a police station. He or the person against whom the crime was committed will then be the complaining witness to prefer charges.

The person arrested will be brought before the court and

arraigned. That is, he will be informed of the charge against him. He will also be told that anything he may say will be held against him and that he is entitled to an adjournment to get a lawyer. These statements must be made by the court and must be recorded so that there will be no doubt that they were made to the defendant and that he responded. These are special constitutional safeguards which must be complied with. Failure by the court to follow this procedure has resulted in having a conviction set aside.

Illustration: Johnson was convicted of a crime and sentenced to serve a term in the state prison for 10 years. After having served 5 years, he realized that when he was arraigned he was not asked these questions and was not given an opportunity to get a lawyer. He made an application to the court, the records of the arraignment were found and they indicated that he was right. The conviction was vacated and Johnson was released. This legal proceeding is known as a "writ of error *coram nobis.*"

If the defendant agrees to proceed on the adjourned date, the court will ask him to plead to the charges against him.

If he pleads guilty he will be sentenced. Usually the date of sentence is adjourned so that the court will have an opportunity to investigate the defendant, the crime he committed and his background, to determine the sentence to be imposed. Although the sentence is specified in the statute which governs the crime with which he is charged, it is the maximum which is allowable. The court may in his discretion and in extenuating circumstances, make his sentence more lenient.

The sentence may consist of a term in the county jail or it may be the same term with execution of the sentence suspended during the good behavior of the defendant. Thus, the defendant may not be required to serve his sentence if he does not get into any further difficulty with the law during the period for which he was sentenced. If he does, however, he may be sent to the institution to complete his term.

The court may place the defendant on probation. This type of sentence, the same as the suspended sentence, is only pronounced when the defendant appears to have a good chance of rehabilitation at home, so that incarceration is not indicated. The court will indicate the term of probation. The defendant will then be supervised by a probation officer during that period to assure compliance with the terms of probation such as regular employment and residence at home with a satisfactory social environment. If the defendant complies with these requirements, he will not be incarcerated and will complete his term of probation to be free from further punishment. However, if he violates his probation by not complying, he may be brought back before the court and sentenced to serve his time in an institution.

If the person arrested pleads not guilty, the court will hear witnesses to determine if there is enough evidence to hold the defendant to stand trial on the charge.

He will have an opportunity to cross-examine the witnesses who testify against him. He may even be permitted to present his own witnesses to prove that he should not be held.

After the examination, the court may discharge him if there does not appear to be sufficient evidence to hold him for trial.

If the evidence is sufficient, the court will hold him for trial in a court of special sessions or a similar court with jurisdiction to try misdemeanors. If it is found that the crime for which he is to be held is a felony, the court may hold him for the grand jury to be indicted. In either case the defendant has the right to demand a jury trial.

The discharge after a preliminary hearing is not an acquittal or a vindication of the crime. It cannot be the basis for a claim of double jeopardy.

THE GRAND JURY

Although the indictment by a grand jury is provided for in all states, some rarely use it and proceed by information only.

The grand jury is a group of citizens of the county where they reside. They are picked and empowered to inquire into all crimes which are committed and triable within their county.

The grand jury originated with the provisions of the Magna Carta. It is intended to prevent a citizen from being imposed upon by a despotic government and charged with a crime based on insufficient evidence. The provision that a person must be tried by a "jury of his peers" applies to the grand jury. If they find the evidence against him sufficient, they will indict him and hold him for trial on the charge. If they find the evidence insufficient, they must discharge him.

The construction of the grand jury varies with each state. In New York State, 30 grand jurors are drawn by lottery from a large panel to appear on the first day. They are usually designated to serve for a month, or as long as it is necessary to accomplish their particular task. Only 23 of the 30 serve, the others are then excused. Of the 23, 16 must be present to act as a quorum so that the acts and deliberations of the grand jury will be valid. Twelve grand jurors are necessary to indict a defendant if they agree that the evidence is sufficient.

WHAT IS AN INDICTMENT?

The indictment is an accusation in writing which states that a certain person is charged with a designated crime. The indictment is usually prepared by the prosecutor or the district attorney. The case of the defendant is then placed on a calendar of other cases to be presented to the grand jury. When its turn comes, the district attorney will present his proof by means of witnesses and other evidence to show that this named defendant is responsible for the crime which was committed and with which he is charged. If 12 or more of the members of the grand jury agree that the evidence is enough to hold him for trial, the foreman of the grand jury will write the words "a true bill" across the face of the indictment and sign his name as foreman. It will then be presented by the grand jury in open court. The indictment then becomes the record of the charge against the defendant on which he is to stand trial.

If the defendant is in custody or on bail he will be arraigned to plead to the indictment. If he pleads guilty, he will be held for sentence while the pre-sentence investigation is completed. On the adjourned date, he will be sentenced in accordance with the law and with the discretion of the court based on the pre-sentence report. If he pleads "not guilty" he will be held for trial. He may then make application again for bail.

If the person who has been charged with the crime and indicted is not in custody or has not been apprehended, a warrant will be issued for his immediate arrest. When apprehended, he will be taken before a magistrate and arraigned for pleading to the indictment.

On arraignment he must again be advised of his constitutional safeguards as to an adjournment to get a lawyer and the charge must be read to him. He may plead guilty, not guilty or former jeopardy.

When the punishment of the charge is death, a defendant may not be permitted to plead guilty in some states. An automatic plea of not guilty is entered for him. The prosecution must prove the guilt of the defendant beyond a reasonable doubt.

The defendant may plead "not guilty by way of insanity." The import of such a plea is that when he committed the crime, he suffered from such a mental defect that he did not know the nature of his act or that it was wrong.

The plea of "not guilty" or of "former jeopardy," creates an issue of fact which must be tried before a jury and places the burden upon the prosecution to prove that the defendant is guilty of the crime as charged beyond a reasonable doubt. This issue of fact in a felony must be tried before a jury of 12 citizens, residents of the county where the case is to be tried.

The jury trying a felony must agree unanimously on a verdict in order to convict the defendant. Under the law, the defendant is presumed innocent until he is found guilty by a unanimous verdict of the jury.

The trial of a misdemeanor may be held before a magistrate sitting as a Court of Special Sessions or by three judges who constitute the court. Two of the three judges sitting as a Court of Special Sessions must agree to convict a defendant of a misdemeanor.

Among additional constitutional rights and protective devices favoring the defendant is his right to a speedy trial. If that is denied to him, he may, by an appropriate proceeding, have the indictment or information dismissed.

He also is entitled to a public trial. However, in the interest of good morals and common decency the court may, in certain cases, exclude the general public where the testimony is particularly salacious and indecent.

The defendant must be given an opportunity to be represented by an attorney and may have such adjournments as are reasonably necessary to obtain such legal representation.

A defendant is entitled to be confronted by the witnesses who are testifying against him. He must be given an opportunity to cross-examine them under oath to test the truth of their testimony and their credibility.

When charged with a felony, the defendant must be present during all proceedings, or the subsequent conviction will not be sustained.

PLEA BARGAINING

Before the trial is held, there may be a conference of the prosecuting attorney, the defense attorney and the judge, to determine if, by consent of both sides, the case can be disposed of by a plea of guilty to a lesser charge, to avoid the expense and the delay of a trial.

PRE-TRIAL DIVERSION PROGRAM

Some jurisdictions have established a procedure for first offenders in less serious crimes. If accepted for such a program, the defendant will be assigned to drug or alcohol treatment, psychological counseling, training or volunteer work, as may be appropriate for his rehabilitation. Upon the successful completion of such assignment, the criminal charge is usually dismissed. If the assignment is not successfully completed, the criminal case is then continued with disposition by trial or by a guilty plea.

THE YOUTHFUL OFFENDER

Special attention is paid to youthful offenders, and most states have statutes which attempt, by rehabilitating and educating them, to direct their activities, and their interests into more constructive channels. Special schools and penal institutions, with less stress on punishment and more stress on understanding their problems, have been created. Sentence of a youthful offender is based on his ability to adjust. If his behavior at the institution reveals an ability to adjust in the community, he may be given that opportunity. He will then be paroled and permitted to reside at home under the supervi-

sion and guidance of a qualified parole officer to help him keep
out of trouble.

THE INDETERMINATE SENTENCE

Most states have developed a type of sentence which permits
the person convicted of a crime to benefit by his experience.
In this case, he is released before the end of his term if his
attitude and behavior merit such action.

The sentence as included in the penal statutes sets a minimum and a maximum for each crime. When the person has
served his minimum term he is then eligible for parole consideration. He also is given the benefit of earning time off for
good behavior. This accumulated time off also will reduce the
actual time spent in the institution.

THE DETERMINATE SENTENCE

In order to assure uniform punishment for all defendants
convicted of the same crime, some states have enacted a uniform determinate sentencing act which removes discretion from
the judge. The Act mandates the length of the prison term
based upon the gravity of the crime, the prior criminal record
of the defendant and other factors which may mitigate or ag-
gravate the punishment.

PAROLE

When the prisoner becomes eligible for consideration by the
parole authority it investigates the possibility of releasing him
to some planned program outside of the institution. If his
friends or relatives offer to provide a home and employment,
they will be investigated. If found satisfactory, they will help
influence the board of parole, assuming that the record in the
institution is satisfactory.

The prisoner is then released for parole supervision. Parole
is an agreement between the prisoner and the state. His release
is conditional upon his behavior in accordance with the agreed
terms. If he fails to live up to them, the parole authority has
the power to return him to the institution without any trial.
Until a prisoner completes his proper sentence, he is under the
control of the correctional and parole authorities.

During his release, the parolee must live at home, keep regular hours and have regular employment. He must associate with acceptable companions—persons who have no previous record of delinquency. He must show an improvement of personal and moral habits.

In the event of violation of parole, a report of such violation is usually submitted to the parole authority. After a hearing, the parolee may be returned to the institution or, if the violation is not of sufficient gravity, he may be given another opportunity. He is entitled to an attorney and his constitutional rights.

A parolee who does not violate may complete his maximum sentence while on parole and be discharged from any further obligation for his transgressions against society. After a certain number of years, he may make application for the return of some of his civil privileges and rights which he lost when convicted of a felony.

Summation

Points to Remember about Criminal Law and Procedure

The criminal law is intended to protect the community from the criminal acts of its citizens. However, it is also intended to protect the person charged with the commission of a crime. It assures him a fair trial in accordance with all the rules of criminal procedure.

A person charged with a crime is entitled to certain constitutional safeguards. The criminal laws and procedures are technical and formal to grant him the benefit of every doubt. It is intended to punish the guilty but also to protect the innocent. This is in keeping with our legal concept that a person is innocent until he is proven guilty.

The law which creates the basis for a criminal prosecution also sets forth the punishment to be imposed.

It is the responsibility of the state then to prove a person charged with a crime to be guilty beyond a reasonable doubt. When convicted, that is, found guilty by a court or a jury of the crime charged, he will be sentenced in accordance with the provisions of law which apply in the particular case.

CHAPTER 14

Civil Rights and Limitations

The subject of civil rights and civil liberties is concerned with the interrelation between the individual and government, be it federal, state or local.

By authority of the United States Constitution and the constitutions of the states, provisions have been made to protect the individual from the laws and the actions of government which deprive him of life, liberty and property without due process of law or which deny him the equal protection of the laws.

Without reducing the power or authority of government, these Bill of Rights provisions assure the individual that the laws enacted by the federal or state governments and the acts of their representatives, pursuant to these laws, will be necessary, reasonable and proper.

Thus any state, federal or local law which infringes upon these individual rights, or any act of a government representative which violates them, is subject to challenge by the person aggrieved. Such proceedings are begun in the state or federal courts and may be brought up on appeal as high as the United States Supreme Court for final determination, since they deal with constitutional interpretation.

Civil liberty has never been exactly defined, but it denotes the right to worship God according to the dictates of an individual's conscience, the right to marry, establish a home, bring up children, acquire useful knowledge, engage in business, make contracts and be free from physical restraint, without unreasonable government interference.

RELIGIOUS FREEDOM

The people are assured by constitutional guarantee that neither a state nor the nation shall establish a state church or support or prefer one church or one religion over another.

Illustration: A State Board of Regents recommended that a certain prayer be recited in the public schools daily in the presence of a teacher as part of a program of moral and spiritual training. The Supreme Court decided that such a prayer promulgated by a state agency was in violation of the "establishment of religion clause" in that "it is no part of the business of government to compose official prayers for any group of American people to recite as a part of a religious program carried on by government."

Every person has the right to his religious beliefs and opinions as dictated by his conscience and his judgment. He has the further right to profess those beliefs in any form and by means of any prayer he may think proper.

Illustration: A state law required each school day to begin with the salute to the flag and the pledge of allegiance. Any child who refused to comply was subject to expulsion and, during this unlawful absence from school, would be treated as a delinquent. The child's parents were liable to prosecution and if convicted were subject to a fine or imprisonment. Readmission to school would be possible only on compliance with the law.

This law was challenged by a member of a religious sect which considered the flag an image proscribed by the Bible. He believed that the obligation imposed by the law of God is superior to those laws enacted by a temporal power. His child was expelled when he refused to salute the flag. The Supreme Court, in deciding this case, found this law to be unconstitutional and in violation of the "free exercise clause."

"Free public education, faithful to the ideal of secular instruction and political neutrality, must not be partisan or inimical to any class, creed or faction. . . .

"The purpose of the First Amendment was to limit the power of government to act in religious matters and not to limit the freedom of religious men to act religiously, nor to restrict the freedom of all men, religionists, atheists and agnostics."

LIMITATIONS ON RELIGIOUS FREEDOM

Religious practices, as distinguished from religious beliefs, may be subject to control if they contravene the morals, peace and public order of the community. The free exercise of religious worship is allowed all men provided that the liberty of conscience is not to be construed to justify practices inconsistent with the peace and safety of the community.

Illustration: Reynolds was arrested and convicted on a charge of polygamy for which he received a sentence of two years in prison and a fine of $200. He appealed, claiming that his religion, as he understood and practiced it, accepted the doctrine that it was the duty of male members of his church to practice polygamy.

Failure to do so would expose him to punishment by damnation in the life to come. The Supreme Court sustained his conviction. A law against polygamy is within the legislative power of government. Although the laws may not interfere with religious belief, they may control religious practices. To prohibit such control would make the professed doctrines of religious belief superior to the law of the land. It would permit every citizen to become a law unto himself under the guise of the constitutional guarantee of religious freedom.

SUNDAY CLOSING LAWS

One area of constitutional concern is the enforcement of Sunday closing laws against persons whose religious practice it is to keep holy another day of the week. Most communities have laws which, with certain exceptions, prohibit the sale of merchandise on Sunday. Those religionists who are compelled by law to close their businesses on Sunday and by their religion on another day of the week claim a violation of both the "establishment" and the "free exercise" clauses. They are forced to lose a day's business because of government interference. The Supreme Court has held Sunday closing laws valid and enforcible under the legislative power to promote order, peace and welfare of the community.

PRIVATE RELIGIOUS SCHOOLS

Every person has the right to send his child to a private school where he can be taught the principles of his religion as well as secular subjects. However, the private school must comply with the requirements of the state education department with regard to the secular subjects. Unless the school maintains an acceptable standard of instruction, the private school will not be qualified and the child may be compelled to attend the compulsory public school.

FREEDOM OF THOUGHT

A person's right to his thoughts cannot be challenged by government. It is a corollary to his constitutional right to express them. This applies to those beliefs and thoughts which are unpopular and inimical as well as those which are accepted in the community. Any law which interferes with a person's beliefs and penalizes him for them will not be sustained, and its enforcement will be vacated.

Illustration: Speiser was an honorably discharged veteran who filed for a tax exemption in the amount of the veteran's benefits he had received, pursuant to a state law. He was required to sign an oath that he did not advocate the overthrow of the state and federal governments by force or violence.

When he refused to sign, the tax exemption was denied to him. The Supreme Court concluded that the action of the tax assessor and the law which authorized this action violated Speiser's rights to his beliefs and that he was not compelled to divulge those beliefs if he did not choose to do so.

FREEDOM OF EXPRESSION

Everyone has the undoubted right to express his ideas, his opinions and his sentiments. The content of those expressions is within the personal discretion and judgment of the individual, though it is not free from control.

If the expressions are dangerous, illegal or offensive when they are made, then the person is subject to the consequences and the penalties imposed. Although the will of the individual to express himself is free from restraint, it is the abuse of that free will which is the object of the punishment.

Every citizen has the right at any time to bring the government or any person in public authority before the bar of public opinion for any just criticism of the exercise of that authority.

Illustration: Wood, after a close contest, was elected sheriff of his county. Thereafter, one of the state judges called a grand jury to investigate corruption of public office-holders. Wood declared in a printed leaflet that judicial officers threatened political intimidation and persecution of voters under the guise of law enforcement. He was held in contempt of court and fined. On appeal it was found that the proceeding had been used to punish him for his expression of opinion and, since there was no record of the reasons for his conviction, it was reversed.

LIMITATION OF FREEDOM OF EXPRESSION

This guarantee, too, is not without limitation. Although it gives a person the right to speak out against government, the extent of such criticism is limited by the danger that these expressions may result in a threat to the very existence of the government.

Illustration: Gitlow wrote an article in which he proposed the take-over of state power by the proletariat starting with strikes of protest, developing into political strikes and then into revolutionary mass action. He was charged under a state law with advocating criminal anarchy, and was tried by a jury and convicted. His conviction was sustained by the Supreme Court on the ground that freedom of speech and freedom of the press do not protect disturbances to public peace or attempts to subvert the government.

Freedom of speech and freedom of the press are both cornerstones of democratic institutions. They are distinguished only in the forms of publication and expression. These freedoms are not confined to books, newspapers and periodicals but embrace every medium of communication such as radio, television, motion pictures and theatrical productions. They are free from unreasonable censure or control unless they violate a law which specifically and clearly sets forth certain standards and criteria for the protection of the public peace, morals and welfare.

Recent litigation has established that freedom of the press does not excuse a reporter from complying with the authority of a court subpoena to testify about the source of his information.

FREEDOM OF ASSOCIATION AND ASSEMBLY

The people have the right to meet in public places and to discuss in an open and public manner subjects which affect the public welfare. They have the right to vent their grievances, to protest oppression and to petition government to improve conditions.

A person may not be prosecuted for the mere participation in peaceful assembly and lawful discussion unless in so doing he engages in conspiracy against public peace.

Illustration: De Jung participated as a speaker at a meeting called by the Communist Party to protest illegal police raids on workers' homes and meeting halls. The meeting was interrupted by the police and he was arrested, charged with violating a state law against advocating revolution, found guilty and sentenced to seven years in prison. On appeal, it appeared that the actual charge on which he was convicted was for conducting a meeting sponsored by the Communist Party. The conviction was reversed by the Supreme Court on the ground that peaceful assembly for lawful discussion cannot be made a crime.

LABOR UNIONS AND COLLECTIVE BARGAINING

Based upon the right of assembly and association, labor unions were organized to improve conditions of the working-man in industry. The importance of the labor union in stabilizing labor relations and reducing the disruptive effects of strikes and lockouts was recognized by government in the enactment of legislation to encourage collective bargaining between labor and management. The resulting labor contracts between employers and unions have, on the whole, brought greater stability to labor relations, industrial productivity and the national welfare.

In recent years, however, many state legislatures, in an effort to control the abuse of power by unions and to protect the individual worker's "right to work," have passed laws which assure the non-union worker of freedom from discrimination in getting and holding a job because he is not a union member. Laws have also been enacted which forbid a union to deny any person membership by reason of race, color or creed.

PICKETING

Picketing in a labor dispute is permissible, and no state law may interfere with the right of employees to demonstrate and make known their grievances against their employers. However, if there is a threat of a breach of the peace, police action may be used with reason to control and prevent such a possibility.

Picketing not related to a labor dispute cannot be prohibited by law since it is the right of any individual or group to express opinions by signs or other means of communication. However, as an expression of belief, it is subject to control in the event of danger to the public peace. The individual participants of course are subjected to the penalties which result from the abuse of this right.

The distribution of pamphlets, handbills and circulars may not generally be forbidden by law without exception. Under the authority of police power and the responsibility of government for the safety and welfare of the community, the distribution of such material may be controlled by reasonable restrictions. However, a state law which required that persons sponsoring or distributing any pamphlet or circular must have their name and address on it was found to be unenforcible by the Supreme Court.

PERSONAL FREEDOMS

Based upon the constitutionally declared principle that a citizen's militia is necessary, the people are given the right to bear arms, and this right is not to be infringed. However, again under the state police power for the protection of the community, laws have been passed and enforced which control the ownership, possession and procurement of certain firearms. State laws require the licensing of pistols and revolvers; they make the possession of concealed weapons without a license a criminal offense and require that certain weapons obtained as war souvenirs be turned in to the police.

A person may not be compelled to do any work against his will as a violation of the peonage and slave-labor laws. He may, however, be compelled to do certain work as punishment for a crime after conviction or to render services which are due the state, such as jury duty, military service, assignment of conscientious objectors to work of national importance in time of war and assignment of certain work as a condition to receiving public welfare assistance.

Any person born or naturalized in the United States is a citizen of the United States and of the state in which he resides. He is thus entitled to such privileges and immunities of citizenship as assurance that he will not be deprived of his right to vote because of race, color, sex or his inability to pay a poll tax. He is not to be excluded from service on a grand jury or a petit jury because of his race, color or sex.

No state may, by its laws, sanction or support any discrimination as to the use of any public or private facility because of race, color or religion. There is some question about the government's right to compel an individual to open his private facilities to the public without restriction or discrimination, but there is no doubt at all that anyone who offers facilities or accommodations to the general public does not have the right to discriminate because of race, color or creed.

POLICE POWER, LIMITATION ON PERSONAL RIGHTS

In addition to the previously mentioned authorized limitations on civil rights, the states and the federal government have the power to control certain activities in carrying out their sovereign responsibility to promote the health, morals, safety and welfare of the state or community. Thus state laws have been enacted requiring compulsory vaccination to protect the other inhabitants against the spread of smallpox. In certain cases, the sexual sterilization of inmates of state-supported institutions has been authorized when the inmates were found to be afflicted with a hereditary form of insanity or imbecility. Statutes providing for the commitment of a psychopathic personality, defined to include persons who by habitual course of sexual behavior have shown an utter lack of power to control sexual impulses and who are likely to commit injury, have been held to be enforcible. Some states have passed laws which forbid the intermarriage of epileptics.

In the matter of taking property in an emergency, the government may destroy animals which have been found to be dangerous, destroy woodland to fight forest fires, confiscate farm products or animals in interstate commerce if there is a danger of spreading disease.

SEARCHES AND SEIZURES

Everyone is protected against the unreasonable search of his person, his house or his premises and the seizure of his papers and personal property by any law-enforcement officer or representative of the government.

A search and subsequent seizure of property is only valid if it is authorized by a warrant which was duly issued or if the search and the seizure are incidental to a valid arrest.

Illustration: Preston was convicted with two others of conspiring to rob a bank. The three had first been arrested and charged with vagrancy when they were seen acting suspiciously in a car at three o'clock in the morning. Sometime after the arrest, some of the police officers searched the car and found two revolvers and other equipment which indicated that they had planned to rob a bank. This evidence and the confession of one of the defendants was the basis of this conviction. The Supreme Court held that the evidence obtained in the search of the car without a warrant was inadmissible since it was too remote to be treated as incidental to the arrest and the conviction was reversed.

Unless evidence is legally obtained after a legal search with a warrant or as incidental to a legal arrest, it cannot be validly received in a criminal proceeding against the owner.

A warrant authorizing a search must be based upon a statement under oath by a law-enforcement officer which describes the place to be searched and the person or thing to be seized. It must also set forth sufficient reason and probable cause to show the need for the search. This requirement makes general searches impossible and prevents the seizure of items not described in the warrant.

Illustration: Federal officers, armed with a warrant to arrest one man, found two other men with him and arrested all three; the officers seized documents found on their persons and in the cabin in which they were hiding. This evidence was held to have been illegally obtained and not admissible at their trial.

RIGHTS OF AN ACCUSED IN A CRIMINAL PROCEEDING

A person accused of a crime in violating a specific law has the right to challenge the law and the arrest if it is so vague and indefinite that it does not set up definite and ascertainable standards of guilt.

Illustration: A law which provided that any person not engaged in lawful occupation, who is known to be a member of a gang, who has been convicted as a disorderly person at least three times or who has been convicted of a crime in any state, is a gangster and is subject to a fine or imprisonment, is invalid and unenforcible since it violates the requirements of due process.

As a general rule, a person who is arrested has the right, with certain exceptions, to make application to be released on bail, which guarantees his appearance at the trial. The amount of the bail should not be excessive and should be commensurate with the circumstances of the crime. In the event that bail is refused or is too excessive, he has the right to make another application to the court by means of a writ of *habeas corpus*.

Under constitutional guarantee, no person shall be held to answer for a capital crime unless he has been indicted by a grand jury. However, by court interpretation this requirement of due process is met where a state law authorizes criminal proceedings to be instituted by "information." This is a sworn statement made by the person bringing the criminal charge. Based upon the "information," a warrant may be issued and a hearing held before a magistrate to determine if the accused is to stand trial. At this hearing the accused has the right to be represented by counsel and to cross-examine witnesses testifying against him.

However, in those states requiring a grand jury indictment, the grand jury must be fairly and legally selected.

> Illustration: An indictment by a grand jury in a county in which no member of a considerable Negro population had ever been called for jury service was held void when the defendant was a Negro.

The right of an accused to have the assistance of counsel to defend him is essential and fundamental to a fair trial. When arrested, the accused must be given an opportunity to obtain counsel. The failure to grant him that opportunity is to deprive him of his constitutional right of due process of law. Furthermore, when the defendant is indigent and does not have the funds to retain counsel, then at his request the court must appoint counsel to defend him properly.

The accused is entitled to a speedy and a public trial of the charges against him not inconsistent with those delays necessary and proper for the prosecution to prepare the case for trial and to have the witnesses against the accused available to testify.

A person may not be prosecuted twice for the same offense, whether it is a felony or a misdemeanor. However, the plea of "former jeopardy" will only be entertained by the court if the current prosecution is for the same identical offense as the prior one.

The actual presence of the accused at a trial for a felony, involving life or liberty, from arraignment to final judgment, is vital to the proper conduct of his defense and cannot be dispensed with.

A witness in any proceeding which legally requires his

testimony may refuse to answer any question on the ground that the answer may incriminate him and be used in a future proceeding against him or that it might uncover evidence against him. This claim of self-incrimination must be explicitly and specifically stated or it will be deemed to have been waived.

A person accused of a felony is entitled to be tried by a jury which must be not only impartial, but drawn from a cross-section of the community without systematic or intentional exclusion of any group. When such requirement has not been met, a conviction will be reversed. By state legislation and court interpretation, jury trials are not deemed essential to due process and may under some state laws be dispensed with as long as the accused is given a fair and impartial trial.

If the defendant believes after conviction that he did not receive a fair trial or that there was an error of law committed, he has the right to appeal that conviction to a higher court, within a reasonable time thereafter.

However, if, at any time after conviction, the defendant can show that he was deprived of a fair trial by a violation of due process or the equal protection of the laws, he may bring the matter up for reconsideration by means of a writ of *coram nobis*.

A person convicted of a crime, after a trial, must be sentenced pursuant to the provisions of the law under which he was charged, indicted and tried. He is not to be exposed to any cruel or inhuman punishment.

WOMEN'S RIGHTS

Women have equal legal rights with men as guaranteed them by the United States and the state constitutions.

The 14th Amendment of the United States Constitution states: "All persons born or naturalized in the United States, and subject to the jurisdiction thereof, are citizens of the United States and of the State wherein they reside. No State shall make or enforce any law which shall abridge the privileges or immunities of citizens of the United States; nor shall any State deprive any person of life, liberty, or property, without due process of law; nor deny to any person within its jurisdiction the equal protection of the laws."

The 19th Amendment states: "The right of citizens of the United States to vote shall not be denied or abridged by the United States or by any State on account of sex."

The proposed 27th Amendment awaiting ratification states: "Equality of rights under the law shall not be denied or abridged by the United States or by any State on account of sex."

Generally, unmarried women and those who under certain state laws have been qualified as "feme sole" are not limited or restricted in any way as to their legal rights. Certain states require a married woman to declare herself as a "feme sole" independent of her marital status to enable her to carry on a business on her own.

Legal limitations and restrictions are only applicable as to the rights of married women by reason of their marital obligations and the rights of their husbands. Under common law, a surviving husband, in the event of the death of his wife, is entitled to an interest in the property and the land she owned. Thus her right to sell or convey her property requires that her husband join and agree to any sale.

Despite the fact that the laws which were responsible for this limitation have been repealed, the practice has continued requiring her husband to join in the sale, and, in some instances, to join in the purchase of property, to avoid any possible future claim as to his curtesy rights to her estate.

Otherwise, a married woman has the same right and power as a married man to acquire, own, possess, control, use, convey, lease, or mortgage any property she owns.

She has the right to make contracts, become an accommodation maker, endorser, guarantor or surety for another person. She may become an incorporator, director or officer of a corporation. She may pledge her separate property without consent or joinder of her husband, and may carry on a business or profession. She has the right to, and should establish, her own independent credit status.

Her separate earnings belong to her, except in the states where community property laws are in effect.

She may sue and be sued in all respects as if she were unmarried, and is liable for her torts.

In her marital status, she has an equal right to have custody of minor children of the marriage and to receive their earnings. She may join in any lawsuit to recover for any injury they sustain and for any medical expenses she advanced.

She has the right to bear children, and the refusal on the part of her husband to have children may be the basis for a claim of abandonment by him of his marital obligations. She has the right to support in accordance with the financial capacity of her husband, and his failure to do so may also subject him to court action.

Abortions

A woman's fundamental right to privacy under the Constitution includes the qualified right to terminate a pregnancy by undergoing a voluntary medical abortion.

Pursuant to recent legislation and a determination of the United States Supreme Court, the decision to effectuate an abortion during the period before the end of the first trimester of pregnancy is dependent upon the medical judgment of the physician in concurrence with his patient.

After the first trimester, abortions may be regulated by state legislation to protect the woman's health during the second trimester and to preserve the life of the fetus after six months of pregnancy.

Discrimination

It is illegal for an employer to discriminate against women with respect to compensation, terms and privileges of employment, pregnancy, childbirth or related medical conditions.

The refusal of credit or of the extension of credit on the basis of sex is also a violation of the laws relating to consumer credit.

Generally, therefore, discrimination against women is not
based on law but rather on practice. As in all instances where
people's rights are withheld and restricted by prejudice, there is
always the right of access to law for the correction of such
violations.

Summation

Points to Remember about Civil Rights

Our right to life, liberty and property was granted to us
by the provisions of the United States Constitution and the
constitution of the state in which we reside. If we are citizens
of the United States, then we are automatically citizens of
the state in which we reside. Such citizens, and even aliens
living in this country, are protected from any law passed by
the federal government or our state governments which
deprives us of life, liberty or property without due process of
law or which, without legal reason, deprives us of our right
to be protected by the law. We are also protected from any
act by a representative of these governments which interferes
with or deprives us of these rights without due process.

Specifically, we have the right of freedom of religion, which
means that we may be religious or not, depending upon the
dictates of our consciences. We may be limited in the practices
of our religions, however, if, by such practices, we affect the
peace, safety, morals or welfare of the community. We have
the right to think as we please, and we have the further right
to express our thoughts without restriction. However, if our
expression violates the rights of others or if it threatens the
peace, safety and welfare of our community, we may be
subject to punishment or penalty after a fair trial under due
process of law.

Since a criminal prosecution against a person accused of
the commission of a crime is instituted and prosecuted by a
government agency, usually in the name of the people or the
state, state and federal constitutional safeguards are particularly applicable. The rights of the defendant are therefore
assiduously guarded to see that he is given a fair trial. His

rights include a speedy, public trial by an impartial court, based upon testimony presented by the prosecution and subject to cross-examination by counsel representing him. This is based on the principle that a person is innocent until he is proven guilty, and this proof of guilt must be "beyond a reasonable doubt" in the mind of the judge or jury authorized to decide.

Every person has the right to protect any one of his rights which he feels has been violated. In defending himself against the tyranny of government, no matter how slight, he is preserving the rights of all of us, usually at great cost in money, effort and time.

How do we defend these rights?

The first step is to know what those rights are.

CHAPTER 15

Financial Aid and Security Laws

A country is only as strong as the economic condition of its people, its industry and its commerce. The United States government has made great progress through legislation to promote business productivity and to achieve financial stability. By means of similar legislation, it has also been instrumental in stabilizing the economic security of its people, its workers and those less fortunate who are not able to support themselves.

Because of the experiences of the depression years in the 1930s, the federal government created and established programs to give financial aid and security to its citizens through active cooperation with state and local governments. This was achieved with significant success in Social Security, Unemployment Insurance, Workmen's Compensation, and Aid to the Blind, the Totally and Permanently Disabled, the Aged and Dependent Children. The only area still within the complete control of the states is public assistance to the needy.

PUBLIC ASSISTANCE

Each state and local community has the duty to provide some financial aid to those of its people who are not able to support themselves and their families. It is also important to the welfare of the community that these people be helped and restored to a position of self-support to prevent them from continuing as a charge on the community.

Any person, therefore, under 65 years of age or the head

of a family who is unable to support himself and his family is eligible for such financial help. Each state bears this burden individually and establishes such standards and requirements of eligibility it deems necessary and proper. The amount of this aid is of course dependent upon the financial condition of the state treasury, the number of people requiring such help and the various factors affecting the state fiscal policies.

PUBLIC ASSISTANCE TO THE AGED, THE BLIND, THE DISABLED

The federal government has established a program accepted by the states to assist them in offering financial and other services to the needy aged, the blind, and those who are totally and permanently disabled. The actual program is set up in each state in accordance with its facilities and standards and subject to the conditions of the federal government which must be met in order to qualify for a grant of federal funds.

A person is considered "needy" and eligible for public assistance in the community in which he resides through the old age assistance program if he is over 65; if his income and his financial resources are not sufficient to provide him with the necessities of life compatible with decency and health; and if he has no one who will bear the burden of supporting him.

Any person who is blind or totally and permanently disabled will be eligible for public assistance in accordance with the requirements of the state and the federal program if investigation reveals that he has no other means of support.

AID TO DEPENDENT CHILDREN

Another program in which the federal government participates gives financial aid to any child in any state who lives with a close relative in need himself, not having the income or the resources to provide the care and subsistence for that child compatible with decency and health. The maximum age in most states is 18, while some states set the maximum at 14 and others at 21.

SOCIAL SECURITY

The basic concept of Social Security is that an employee contributes a percentage of his earnings during his productive years into a fund which is matched by an equal amount by his employer. This is the federal government's method of providing an income to a worker and his dependents when his earnings are affected by retirement, disability or his death.

These contributions are computed on the basis of his gross earnings and are withheld by his employer. At the end of each quarter year, the employer is required to forward both contributions to the Internal Revenue Service, to be credited to the account of the employee to determine his eligibility and his entitlement.

In order to qualify for benefits, it is necessary to accumulate a requisite number of work-credit years. An employee is credited with a quarter year coverage if he earns wages of $260 or more for a three-month period. Self-employed persons are also eligible under this program. They contribute on a percentage basis and are credited with four quarters of coverage if they earn a net profit of $400 or more during the year.

Information and brochures are available at the local Social Security office indicating the number of credit years required and the benefits available.

Each worker is required to obtain a permanent Social Security number used to identify him in the program and in federal and state tax returns.

Social Security provides the following benefits: retirement, disability, burial payments and medicare.

RETIREMENT INSURANCE

Any person, eligible for benefits, on reaching retirement age, must make application and will receive payments in accordance with the work-credit years and the amount of his contributions, for the rest of his life.

These payments may be affected if the retiree decides to work in addition to receiving his payments. Earnings in excess of a stated amount may proportionately reduce his payments. However, after the age of 72, there is no limit to earnings.

The program also makes available benefits to dependents of a retiree who are unmarried children and under 18, unmarried disabled children, dependent husband or wife, and a wife who is caring for unmarried dependent children.

MEDICARE

As a part of the Social Security program, Medicare provides hospital insurance to help pay for hospital care and related services and medical insurance to help pay doctor bills and other medical services.

The plan does not provide hospital or medical care directly. The patient selects his physician, who then determines what hospital and medical services are required and arranges that they are provided.

The patient, as a member of this plan, is identified by a personal health insurance claim number, and all services are charged to his account. As required, the patient may be asked to pay a certain basic minimum charge and a balance over and above the insurance coverage. Due to the constant increase in the cost of services, annual review may require that the dollar amount to be paid by the patient be increased. It is suggested that the member communicate with the local Social Security office to determine the status of his account.

HOSPITAL INSURANCE COVERAGE

All employees covered by Social Security or the Railroad Retirement Plan and all persons who are self-employed and within the plan are entitled to the benefits of hospital insurance. One per cent of their Social Security contributions is allocated for this coverage. Persons who are over 65 and not covered may enroll and pay premiums directly to the Hospital Insurance Trust Fund.

HOSPITALIZATION AND RELATED SERVICES

Any person who qualifies pursuant to the provisions of the

program is entitled during each benefit period to admission to a hospital for a period of up to 60 days and is responsible only for the payment of the minimum deductible amount—at present $72. If any additional hospitalization is required, the patient will be required to pay at the rate of $18 per day from the first to the 90th day.

If the patient requires further hospitalization, he has available to him a lifetime reserve of 60 days, which he can use when necessary throughout his life. However, he will then be required to pay $36 per day, while insurance will cover the balance of the cost.

BENEFIT PERIOD OR SPELL OF ILLNESS

In order to measure and limit the use of this insurance coverage, a benefit period or spell of illness begins when a person is first admitted to a hospital. Any number of subsequent admissions for treatment of the same or another illness is still considered as a part of the same benefit period. The benefits are limited only as to the number of days used. He is then entitled to 90 days of hospitalization as set forth above. After his discharge, if he has not been a patient in a hospital or in a nursing home for a period of 60 days, he may begin a new benefit period and is entitled to another 90-day hospitalization period on paying the required minimum and balance.

EXTENDED CARE BENEFITS

After discharge from the hospital, it may be necessary for the patient to have nursing care at a nursing home. This is still a continuation of the benefit period. If he was hospitalized for at least three days, he is entitled to 20 days of services at a nursing facility, without any additional cost. If, however, additional care is required, he may have another 80 days for which he will have to pay at the rate of $9 a day, while the insurance will cover the balance.

HOME HEALTH CARE AND SERVICES

After hospitalization and extended care in a nursing home, if it is necessary for the patient to have home care such as a visiting nurse, physical, speech or occupational therapy, he is entitled to up to 100 visits without cost to him.

MEDICAL INSURANCE AND COVERAGE

All persons who are members of the hospital insurance program may apply for medical insurance. This is voluntary and requires the payment of a premium, payable monthly or deductible from the monthly benefits received from Social Security or the Railroad Retirement Plan.

Medical Services

A member of this plan who has received the services of a physician is entitled to a refund of the reasonable charges paid of 80 per cent after he has paid the first $60, the deductible minimum, during each calendar year. This means that he must pay the first $60 of his medical bills for the year. Thereafter he will be entitled to a refund of 80 per cent of all subsequent bills, so that he will only be paying 20 per cent.

Outpatient Hospital Services

When a patient is rendered outpatient services in a hospital, either for diagnosis or treatment, though not previously admitted, he will be covered. If he has already expended $60 for the year under the medical insurance plan, he will only be responsible for 20 per cent of the reasonable charges and the insurance will cover the balance of the cost.

Home Health Care and Services

Where there has been no hospitalization and home health care is required, medical insurance will pay for up to 100 visits, provided that the patient has paid $60 for the calendar year as required above.

Other Medical Services and Supplies

If the member has met the $60 requisite, he will only be responsible for 20 per cent of the cost of radiation therapy,

diagnostic tests, pathology services, medical equipment and
devices, ambulance service and other such medical requirements, while his medical insurance covers the balance.

STATE PARTICIPATION OR MEDICAID

Each state has been authorized by federal law to supplement this program as it applies to persons who are now receiving public assistance or those whose incomes and financial
resources are marginal. State legislation may relieve the financial burden of those in financial need and absorb the actual
cost of services such as the basic cost in the medical coverage,
the basic cost in hospital coverage and any additional cost
involved.

UNEMPLOYMENT INSURANCE

Each state has established an unemployment insurance
program with federal financial participation. The states comply
with certain minimum requirements and the federal government contributes a portion of the necessary funds.

Each state has the right to determine qualifications for the
payment of benefits, the acceptability of reasons for the unemployment, the conditions under which an unemployed person is "able to work" or is "available for work." However no
state may withhold benefits to an individual who refuses to
accept employment when the job is available due to an existing strike or lockout.

An employer of four or more workers is required to pay
a tax for the calendar year of their employment. These contributions together with state and federal financial participation constitute a fund from which payment is made to those
workers who have lost their employment through no fault of
their own and are unable to find work. The purpose is to give
them financial aid until such time as they become re-employed
and to assist them in finding work. Payments are generally
available for a period up to twenty-six weeks, after a waiting
period of one week from the time of application, and they bear

a proportionate relation to the prior weekly earnings of the individual.

The benefits are paid through the state employment office, and the applicant is required to report personally each week available for work and certify that he has not worked. He may then be sent out to a job and must accept employment when offered. Refusal to accept employment may disqualify him from further benefits.

In certain emergencies, many of the states have enacted legislation which increases the period of unemployment benefits another thirteen weeks to assist in the efforts to find employment.

WORKMEN'S COMPENSATION

Any employee who is disabled as a result of injury or disease causally related to his employment may be reimbursed for his medical and hospital expenses and may receive disability payments for the duration of such disability. In each state, employers in certain occupations and industries are required by means of insurance or other security to assure these benefits to their employees.

When injured on the job, the employee must notify his employer and file a claim with the appropriate department in his state. Based upon the medical proof, a hearing will be held to determine the extent of permanent disability, if there is any, and benefits will be computed to be paid to the person injured.

VETERAN'S BENEFITS

A veteran of the United States armed forces with a discharge other than dishonorable is entitled to job protection, job preference, education and training, home and farm loans, tax exemptions, Social Security and unemployment insurance benefits, disability compensation and pension.

The counseling and other services of the Veterans Administration and the state employment offices are available to the veteran to assist him in his readjustment to civilian life and to enable him to become self-supporting, including GI Bill training and vocational rehabilitation. Veterans' preference laws are not considered discriminatory.

PRIVATE PENSION FUNDS

Those employees who are members of private pension funds established by their employers are protected and have a vested interest by federal legislation if they transfer to another job.

EMPLOYEE RETIREMENT INCOME SECURITY ACT

The Congress of the United States has declared that there has been a substantial increase in the number of employee benefit plans, that the security of millions of employees is affected by these plans, and that industrial relations, interstate commerce and the federal taxing power are concerned as a result. To protect the interests of all affected and to compensate for any inadequacies and inequities, it has enacted the Employee Retirement Income Security Act.

Participation

The Act concerns "employee welfare benefit plans" or "employee pension benefit plans" which are in existence or to be established by an employer or by an employee organization.

An employee who qualifies may participate in such a plan, although a waiting period of one year may be required for a new employee, and he is required to attain the age of 25 before he may participate.

An employee who has 3 years of employment must be included in the plan. However, an employee who commences work within 5 years of his normal retirement age may be excluded.

Funding

The plan must establish a fund so that the contributions may be accumulated to satisfy the payment of benefits and the costs of servicing, operating and maintaining the plan.

Individual Retirement Accounts

A person who is not a participant in a qualified retirement or government plan may establish his own individual retirement account with tax deductible contributions.

A portion of the money deposited into a retirement income fund is tax exempt and may be taken as a tax deduction for the year when such deposit is made.

Earnings on the money in the fund which is being accumulated are not taxable until the time for retirement is reached, when the taxable income can be expected to be in a lower bracket.

The following retirement plans will qualify for tax incentive benefits:

1. Creation of a trust
2. Purchase of an annuity from a life insurance company
3. Deposit in a special custodial account
4. Purchase of special U.S. Government "retirement bonds"

Vesting

Contributions made by the employee to the plan are nonforfeitable and must be returned to him if for any reason he does not qualify for benefits.

Vesting of contributions made by the employer in the plan must occur in one of the following ways:

1. An employee having 10 years of service is fully vested. He is then entitled to all benefits for which he would ordinarily be qualified under the plan.

2. After 5 years of service, 25 per cent or one quarter of the employer's contributions are vested for the benefit of the employee. There is a 5 per cent increase each year until the 10th year of employment, and a 10 per cent increase for the next 5 years, so that at the end of 15 years the employee has full vested retirement interest.

3. An active participating employee must have at least 50 per cent vesting if he has 10 years of service or if he has at least 5 years of service and the total of his age and his years of service

equals or exceeds 45. An additional 10 per cent is to be added for each additional year thereafter.

Summation

Points to Remember about Financial Aid and Security Laws

There are many who feel that any help which the government gives to its people or its industries borders on socialism. Yet there are very few of us who have not received some benefit from government. Our public and compulsory education is government-given; few of us could afford to educate our children if we had to pay the actual cost. The food we eat, particularly the farm products, would be exorbitantly expensive were it not for the farm subsidies which help the farmer. These are but a few examples; there are many, many more. Government was created to help the people. Based on this principle, laws have been passed and programs created which help the people in their needs, give them an opportunity to be self-sufficient and not public charges. It is true, there are some who take advantage. However, the main purpose is achieved when those who need that helping hand regain their self-respect and places in the community.

What are those public benefits which government makes available?

For those who have no means of support for themselves and their families, the states and the local communities render public assistance. This may take the form of money, free lodging, free food and clothing or other necessary services. Application for such assistance should be made to the local welfare agency.

The aged, the blind, the totally and permanently disabled, as well as dependent children, are given assistance by a program of cooperative effort by the states and the federal government. Here again persons in need should apply to the nearest welfare agency and adequate provision will be made for their support, regardless of the source of the funds which make this help possible.

Having made provision for those who cannot support themselves, government then proceeded to protect the worker who, due to illness, industrial accident or unemployment, loses his sources of income. Workmen's Compensation laws protect the worker if he becomes ill or injured through his job. Unemployment insurance helps tide him over until he gets another job and even helps him find another job. Social Security attempts to provide for his retirement and to provide for his family in the event of his death or disability. A new adjunct to the Social Security benefits is health insurance which provides him with hospital benefits and, if he elects to pay an additional premium, will help him to pay the greater portion of his doctor's bills.

The veteran of the armed services of the United States is particularly favored by the federal, state and local governments in their efforts to prove their appreciation for his services. Application to the nearest Veterans Administration office will get him advice, guidance and assistance.

CHAPTER 16

Consumer Protection

The old attitude of "caveat emptor" (let the buyer beware) is being replaced, to a large degree, by a growing concern on the part of federal, state and local governments for the protection of the consumer. He is defined as a natural person who buys, leases or obtains goods, services or credit for personal, household or family purposes.

The protection offered includes steps taken to assure his personal safety in the use of products purchased, to prevent any unconscionable and deceptive practices by suppliers of such products, and to protect him from unfair practices in his consumer credit transactions.

The practical result of this concern is the enactment by the federal government of the Consumer Products Safety Act and the Consumer Credit Protection Act and the adoption by the states of the Uniform Consumer Sales Practices Act, the Uniform Consumer Credit Code and the Uniform Commercial Code. City and local governments have followed suit by enacting their own respective consumer protection laws in accordance with their own requirements.

THE FEDERAL CONSUMER PRODUCT SAFETY ACT

The Federal Consumer Product Safety Act was passed by Congress to protect the consumer from unreasonable risk of injury resulting not only from the ordinary use of products but from causes not anticipated by the user. This involves products produced or distributed for sale for personal use of consumers, as to their performance, composition, contents, design, construction, finish or packaging.

The Consumer Product Safety Commission has the power to regulate and enforce adequate standards of products which come within the purview of the Act. For example, mattresses and children's sleepwear, fireworks and spray adhesives are subject to its control and supervision.

The Commission has the authority to establish safety standards over the manufacture and distribution of products when it is reasonably necessary to prevent or reduce an unreasonable risk of injury.

The Magnuson-Moss Federal Trade Commission Improvement Act provides further protection for the consumer. It requires a manufacturer to indicate clearly the provisions of a written warranty he makes with his product. He must state whether it is a full warranty or a limited warranty. A full warranty gives the consumer the right to relief if he makes complaint within a reasonable time. It also gives the consumer the right to a refund or replacement without charge for installation if several attempts to remedy the defect have been made without satisfactory results.

UNIFORM CONSUMER SALES PRACTICES ACT

The Uniform Consumer Sales Practices Act is promulgated and recommended to the states by the National Conference of Commissioners on Uniform State Laws. When adopted by a state it becomes the law of that state. The purpose of this Act is to protect consumers from deceptive and unconscionable sales practices and to establish a standard of consumer sales practices consistent with the policies of the Federal Trade Commission.

Local governments conforming to federal and state legislation for the protection of the consumer have also enacted similar laws.

Consumer Protection Law of New York City

Thus, New York City has included a Consumer Protection Law as a part of its City Charter and Administrative Code to prohibit unfair, deceptive and unconscionable trade practices that take advantage of consumers in their transactions. Violations of regulations established by the Commissioner of Consumer Affairs are punishable by a civil penalty, and a knowing violation may be punishable by the payment of a civil penalty or a fine or both.

THE COURTS AND THE CONSUMER

The substantive law of contracts binds both the buyer and the seller to the terms of the contract. However, the courts look more closely into a transaction in which a consumer is involved.

Parties to a contract have the right to agree to any terms acceptable to them. Oppressive and unconscionable contracts will not be enforced against a party entering into a contract at a disadvantage. There is a duty on the party of one side to a contract to disclose information available to him which gives him an unfair advantage in the transaction.

Fraud continues to be the basis for the avoidance of liability or for a rescission if it induces the creation of the contract by reason of false statements made for that purpose.

Fine print in a contract may be construed under certain conditions as an intent to conceal. State statutes may require that in certain contracts certain important specific clauses be in large type.

Additional protections for the consumer under the law concern the warranty in a contract of sale. More particularly the consumer is protected in a sale of food for human consumption by the warranty, which permits him to recover for any loss sustained by reason of defective products. By relaxing the law as to privity of contract, the courts have permitted recovery for injury to a person despite the fact that he did not purchase the food but was an invited guest.

CONSUMER CREDIT PROTECTION ACT

The Consumer Credit Protection Act as enacted by Congress includes the Consumer Credit Cost Disclosure Act, also known as the Truth in Lending Act, Restrictions on Garnishment of Wages, and Consumer Credit Reporting, also known as the Fair Credit Reporting Act.

TRUTH IN LENDING ACT

The Truth in Lending Act is based on the finding by Congress that a consumer should have a disclosure of credit terms if he is to obtain credit on the most favorable terms.

Credit is the right granted to a debtor or consumer by a creditor to defer payment of a debt or to incur the debt and defer its payment. The creditor covered by the Act is a person or company who extends credit or arranges to extend credit in the course of his regular business.

Since the disclosure aspects of the Act involve financial institutions and the charge for the use of money, the Federal Reserve Board is charged with issuing regulations to carry out its purposes. Accordingly Regulation Z controls consumer credit disclosure and assures the consumer of meaningful information as to the cost of credit. This cost must be expressed in the dollar amount of the finance charge and also as an annual percentage rate computed on the unpaid balance of the amount financed.

The creditor must give the consumer-credit-customer a disclosure statement before he enters into the credit sale transaction. This statement should contain the total charge for the amount of money financed or for which credit is to be extended.

This finance charge is determined from the following facts, which must also be included in the disclosure statement:

The cash price of the goods or services

The total downpayment, including cash or trade-in allowance

The unpaid balance of the cash price

Other charges, itemized, such as taxes, fees and charges to perfect security interest, fees to examine title or to prepare a deed for real property

The unpaid balance of all above items
The finance charge in dollars and annual percentage rate

RIGHT OF RESCISSION

An important facet of the Truth in Lending Act is the right of the consumer-credit-customer to rescind the transaction within a stated period, depending upon the type of transaction involved. If there is such a right of rescission, then notice must be given to the customer of the time limit for such rescission. If no notice is given, then the customer may cancel at any time.

Examples of transactions which may be canceled are those which result in a lien or mortgage on real property or sales of personal property solicited at the home of the purchaser.

CREDIT CARDS

Under the provisions of the Act, credit cards may not be issued unless there was an application made. This does not apply to renewals.

A credit card issued but not requested or accepted by the person in whose name it was issued does not incur liability for its unauthorized use.

The unauthorized use of a duly issued credit card will expose the owner to a maximum liability of $50. However, if notice of loss is given to the issuer before any unauthorized use occurs, the owner is not liable. The issuer of a credit card must make the owner aware of the procedure to be followed in the event of loss.

RESTRICTION ON GARNISHMENT

A portion of the Consumer Credit Protection Act known as Title III is devoted to garnishments. Garnishment has the effect of withholding the wages or salary of a debtor by the employer to be used for the satisfaction of a debt. Such a withholding or garnishment may be accomplished by the consent of the debtor or by a legal proceeding such as a court order after judgment.

The Act attempts to restrict garnishment of salary on consent in order to obtain an extension of credit in a consumer credit sale.

Generally, the Act limits or restricts the withholding or garnishment of wages to 25 per cent of the disposable earnings of the employee for any work week. The Act does not supersede any state law which prohibits garnishment entirely or limits it to a lesser amount.

An employer may not discharge his employee for the reason that his earnings have been subjected to garnishment for any *one* indebtedness.

The provisions of this Act are enforceable by the Secretary of Labor acting through the Wage and Hour Division of the Department of State.

FAIR CREDIT REPORTING ACT

Title VI of the Consumer Credit Protection Act is concerned with consumer credit reporting for the purpose of having consumer reporting agencies adopt procedures for gathering and reporting information which are fair and equitable. Information obtained for consumer credit, personnel and insurance purposes must be accurately obtained and reported. The confidentiality of the report must be protected and its utilization must be for legitimate needs.

A consumer reporting agency may furnish a report:
  a. In response to an order of a court having jurisdiction to issue such an order
  b. Pursuant to written instructions of the consumer
  c. To a person or firm it has reason to believe will be used in a credit transaction, for employment purposes, insurance purposes, the issuance of a license or other legitimate business needs

On request in writing from the consumer, the consumer reporting agency must clearly and accurately disclose to him:
  a. The nature and sources of all information in its files at the time of the request

b. The sources of the information, under certain circumstances
c. The recipients of any report furnished for employment purposes within a two year period or for any other purpose within a six month period

A consumer report should not contain either the listing of a bankruptcy which is more than 14 years from the date of the report or judgments and any other financial information which antedate the report by more than 7 years.

UNIFORM CONSUMER CREDIT CODE

The Uniform Consumer Credit Code has been presented to the states for adoption to supplement the existing Uniform Commercial Code and to expand the scope of uniform consumer protection now afforded by federal statutes in the Consumer Credit Protection Act.

In its effort to standardize the dealings of a consumer-credit-customer with the professional creditor, the credit-vendor and/ or the financing institution, the Code:

a. Requires full disclosure of the cost of credit to the consumer at the time of the transaction
b. Prohibits certain practices and agreements which have been the basis of abuses by some creditors
c. Brings the creditor within the control of the Administrator of the Code and the courts in rendering unenforcible any provision of the transaction which is found to be unconscionable

Consumer Protection Assistance

Information concerning Truth in Lending is generally available from the offices of the Board of Governors of the Federal Reserve System at Washington, D.C. 20551, or the Federal Reserve Banks in the 12 districts or their branches.

Federal Reserve District 1—Boston, Mass. 02106
Federal Reserve District 2—New York, N.Y. 10045

Branch: Buffalo, N. Y., 14240
Federal Reserve District 3—Philadelphia, Pa. 19101
Federal Reserve District 4—Cleveland, Ohio 44101
Branches: Cincinnati, Ohio 45201
           Pittsburgh, Pa. 15230
Federal Reserve District 5—Richmond, Va. 23261
Branches: Baltimore, Md. 21203
           Charlotte, N.C. 28201
Federal Reserve District 6—Atlanta, Ga. 30303
Branches: Birmingham, Ala. 35202
           Jacksonville, Fla. 32203
           Nashville, Tenn. 37203
           New Orleans, La. 70160
Federal Reserve District 7—Chicago, Ill. 60690
Branch: Detroit, Mich. 48231
Federal Reserve District 8—St. Louis, Mo. 63166
Branches: Little Rock, Ark. 72203
           Louisville, Ky. 40201
           Memphis, Tenn. 38101
Federal Reserve District 9—Minneapolis, Minn. 55480
Branch: Helena, Mont. 59601
Federal Reserve District 10—Kansas City, Mo. 64198
Branches: Denver, Colo. 80217
           Oklahoma City, Okla. 73125
           Omaha, Nebr. 68102
Federal Reserve District 11—Dallas, Tex. 75222
Branches: El Paso, Tex. 79999
           Houston, Tex. 77001
           San Antonio, Tex. 78295
Federal Reserve District 12—San Francisco, Calif. 94120
Branches: Los Angeles, Calif. 90051
           Portland, Ore. 97208
           Salt Lake City, Utah 84110
           Seattle, Wash. 98124
Information and advice may also be obtained from:
  The Federal Deposit Insurance Corporation, 550 Seventeenth St. N. W., Washington, D.C. 20429

The Federal Trade Commission, Pennsylvania Ave. at Sixth
St. N.W., Washington, D.C. 20580
The Comptroller of the Currency, Fifteenth St. and Penn-
sylvania Ave. N.W., Washington, D.C. 20220
The Bureau of Federal Credit Unions in the Department of
Health, Education and Welfare, 6401 Security Blvd.,
Baltimore, Md. 21235
The Federal Home Loan Bank Board, 101 Indiana Ave.
N.W., Washington, D.C. 20552
The Civil Aeronautics Board, 1825 Connecticut Ave. N.W.,
Washington, D.C. 20250
The Agriculture Department, Fourteenth St. and Inde-
pendence Ave. S.W., Washington, D.C. 20250
The Interstate Commerce Commission, Twelfth St. and
Constitution Ave. N.W., Washington, D.C. 20423

Summation

Points to Remember about Consumer Protection

In all transactions, the buyer should know what he is buying,
what the reasonable price is for the item of purchase, what legal
commitments are involved, how and under what terms payment
is to be made, and what protections he has with regard to the
contents and performance of the item of purchase. He cannot
and should not rely upon the good conscience and honesty of
the seller. He must be aware and he should beware.

However, governmental agencies have been created to protect the unwary buyer from the unscrupulous seller.

By the use of observation, examination, intelligence and
reasoning, and aided by legislation enacted for his protection,
the consumer is in a better position to get full value for his
purchase, whether it is merchandise or credit.

CHAPTER 17

Taxes

Everyone pays taxes of one kind or another. They are imposed by a government—federal, state or local—to finance the cost of operation.

The chief source of federal revenue is the income tax. The balance is received from excise taxes, import taxes, estate and gift taxes.

State revenue may come from income taxes or property taxes or both, depending on the state law, and from sales, excise, license or franchise, estate or inheritance taxes.

City, county, town and village governments rely on property, sales and licensing taxes. Some have added income taxes as a means of revenue.

DEFINITIONS

An income tax is a levy and collection of a tax from a person based upon his income or earnings. Usually consideration is given to the size of the family by means of personal exemptions and to the amount of earnings by establishing a taxable minimum and a graduated tax rate on progressively increasing income brackets.

A property tax on real or personal property is determined by an assessment on the appraised value at a tax rate established by law or by budget requirements.

A sales tax is usually added by the seller to the cost of a consumer purchase and reported and paid by him to the taxing authority.

An excise tax is imposed on certain designated commodities or transactions for a specific reason determined by the taxing authority. Some examples of excise taxes are those levied on alcohol, tobacco and gasoline.

An estate tax is levied on the transfer of assets in the estate of a deceased person. It is not a property tax, nor does it tax the right of the person who receives the property. It is assessed against the net taxable estate before it is distributed and paid by the executor or administrator of the estate.

An inheritance tax is levied on the net taxable amount received by the legatee or beneficiary and is paid by him.

A gift tax is assessed and must be paid by the person who transfers property to another without consideration and as a gift during his lifetime. The purpose of this tax is to prevent the transfer of property during the lifetime of the donor to avoid the payment of an estate tax upon his death.

INCOME TAX

The federal income tax is the one tax which concerns all—the businessman, the professional, the manufacturer, the seller, the consumer, the employer, the employee and the wage-earner.

Essentially, it is based on individual self-assessment and voluntary compliance.

Every citizen or resident of the United States who during the previous year earned in excess of a designated amount must file an income tax return for that year. This amount may vary annually and does vary according to the marital status or age of the individual, such as single or married or over 65 years of age.

Payment of the tax due is made in accordance with the computations of the tax return with due credit being given to prepayment by withholding or estimated tax.

Form 1040A

Persons whose gross income, though unlimited in amount, consists only of wages, salary, tips, dividends and interest, may use Form 1040A. This is a simple single-sheet two-page form which does not require any attached forms or documents other than the W–2 form, which indicates earnings, tax withheld, and Social Security paid. It is not to be used if special deductions are claimed.

Form 1040

All others are required to use the basic Form 1040, with the W–2 and those schedule forms required to substantiate their return.

This two-page single-sheet form is a summary of all information presented in the accompanying schedules and is used for the final computation of the taxes due. In simplified form this computation consists of a statement of the gross income from all sources, less deductions as indicated in the schedules used as required, which results in the adjusted gross income. To obtain the taxable income of the individual, itemized deductions, or the standard deduction, and personal exemptions are subtracted.

Taxpayers with a gross adjusted income less than $10,000 who do not itemize their deductions and take the standard deduction will find their amount of tax due by referring to the column in the Tax Tables indicating the number of exemptions claimed and their taxable status. This tax amount has taken into consideration the standard deductions and the allowable exemptions as declared.

Taxpayers with an adjusted gross income greater than $10,000 who either use the standard deductions or itemize them, will, after the required computations, apply Tax Rate Schedule XY and Z to arrive at their tax amount on the basis of their taxable income.

States and local communities who levy an income tax generally use the figures submitted on the federal income tax return as the basis for their assessment of tax. There is cooperation between the respective taxing agencies. It is therefore important that the figures on all returns are consistent.

ESTIMATED TAX

Every citizen or resident of the United States must file a declaration of estimated tax if he can reasonably expect to earn more than $500 from sources other than wages or if his gross income may exceed $20,000 for the coming calendar year, and provided that the tax due exceeds the withheld amount by more than $100. This declaration is filed before April 15, usually at the time when the income tax return and payment for the previous year is made. The estimated tax, if due, is then paid in full or in quarterly payments, before April 15, June 15, September 15, and January 15 of the current year.

EXEMPTIONS

Each taxpayer is entitled to an exemption as determined by law for the taxable year on the basis of one exemption for each dependent. The amount of tax withheld by the employer during the tax year is usually based upon the number of exemptions claimed. An additional exemption is available to a taxpayer who is over 65 years of age or who is blind. Therefore a taxpayer who is over 65 and blind is entitled to three exemptions.

HEAD OF HOUSEHOLD

An unmarried individual who maintains a household for himself and at least one dependent during the taxable year qualifies to file under this category. The benefit is that the tax rate applied is less than that for single persons but greater than that for a joint return. The dependent must reside in the household during the taxable year. The only exception is a household which the taxpayer maintains for his parents while he resides elsewhere.

JOINT RETURN

A married couple has the option of filing a joint or separate returns. The joint return will result in a lower tax and may be filed even if only one spouse has taxable income.

The type of return filed becomes significant when computing medical deductions and the dividend exclusion. If one spouse has excessive medical expenses, a separate return will enable him to deduct more than under a joint return. Dividends received by a married couple from jointly-owned investments will entitle them to the full $200 exclusion, $100 for each.

A joint return may be filed by a surviving spouse for himself and the decedent for the year in which the death occurred.

If the surviving spouse remains unmarried and maintains a household for a dependent child for whom an exemption is taken, he may file a return for 2 years following the year of death of his spouse and joint return rates will apply, despite the fact that he does not file a joint return.

LIFE INSURANCE

Proceeds from life insurance policies received by a beneficiary on the life of the deceased are not taxable as income. However, they may be taxable as a part of the estate of the decedent as an estate tax. If the insurance application is made by the beneficiary on the life of the decedent and premiums are paid by him, the proceeds are not taxable to the estate.

Payment of life insurance benefits made in installments, which include interest on the proceeds retained, will require that the interest be reported and the tax paid. If the beneficiary of such a policy is the surviving spouse, then such interest may be excluded as taxable income up to $1,000 annually.

PERSONS OVER 65

Tax rates apply equally to all taxpayers regardless of age. However, persons over 65 have certain benefits available to them. For example, a person over 65 is permitted to earn more money before he is required to file a return. He is also entitled to an additional personal exemption, beginning with the year he attains 65.

Under a recent change in the law, a person over the age of 55 who sells his residence which he has used as such for at least three of the five years before the sale, may exclude up to $50,000 of the profit realized from his taxable income. If the home was owned jointly with his spouse, then the exclusion may be up to $100,000 if they file a joint return. This is a once-in-a-lifetime election and cannot be used again.

RETIREMENT INCOME CREDIT

Retirement income credit is available to retired persons 65 years of age or older who receive a retirement income from pensions, annuities, interest, dividends or rents, which are ordinarily taxable. The purpose of this income credit is to give such persons the benefit of a tax exemption equivalent to that available to persons receiving tax-exempt Social Security retirement payments. To report and obtain the benefit of this income credit, the taxpayer must complete Schedule R and attach it to his Form 1040.

SELF-EMPLOYMENT TAX

An individual who is in business for himself or in a profession is subject to the required payment of a self-employment tax for the purpose of providing for Social Security benefits. A self-employment Social Security tax is imposed on net earnings of $400 to a maximum earnings amount set for regular Social Security wage deductions. The tax is computed and reported on Schedule SE and attached to Form 1040.

SELF-EMPLOYED RETIREMENT BENEFITS

A self-employed person may set up a qualified retirement plan for himself similar to pension or other types of employee benefit plans and deduct the contributions. Employees of this self-employed individual, who have 3 or more years of service, must be included in the plan, which must be funded by a trust or custodial account with a bank or by investment in annuities or special U.S. bonds. However, employees who begin service within 5 years of the regular retirement age may be excluded from a defined benefit plan.

WITHHOLDING TAX

In order to avoid an undue delay in the collection of taxes and to facilitate the "pay-as-you-go" principle of tax collection, an employer is directed to withhold a percentage of the earnings of an employee at the time of payment. The employee-taxpayer files a W–4 form withholding exemption certificate with his employer to indicate the number of exemptions he claims. The amount of money withheld is dependent upon the number of exemptions reported.

An employee who anticipates no income tax liability for the coming tax year may file a W–4E form withholding exemption certificate and thus avoid withholding and the subsequent bother of filing a return to obtain a refund.

The employer must furnish the employee before January 31 of the subsequent year with a W–2 form which sets forth the gross earnings, the amount of tax withheld, and the amount of Social Security withheld to be forwarded by the employer. This form must be attached to the form by the employee-taxpayer when he makes his tax return.

A W–2 copy indicating the amounts withheld is also given to the employee for use in filing his state and local income tax returns.

INCOME TAX COLLECTION AND ENFORCEMENT

As indicated, income tax is based on self-assessment and voluntary compliance. However, an enforcement procedure is necessary and the Internal Revenue Service is charged with the responsibility of determining, assessing and collecting internal revenue taxes and enforcing the internal revenue laws.

If on examination of a taxpayer's return it appears that a deficiency exists and that he owes an amount in excess of the tax paid, he will be so advised. An audit may be requested of the taxpayer's books and the amount of the deficiency confirmed. The taxpayer is given the opportunity of appealing to the United States Tax Court and subsequently to the United States Court of Appeals.

Failure to pay a tax after notice and demand may subject the property of the taxpayer to seizure to enforce collection.

Federal Tax Calendar

January 15	Final payment due on estimated tax for previous calendar year.
January 31	Individuals may file final returns for previous calendar year instead of amending estimated tax for that year. Employer to furnish W–2 form to employee. Employer to file Form 940 for prior year. Last quarterly return by employer of tax withheld under Form 941, also Form W–2 Copy A and Form W–3.
April 15	Income tax and self-employment tax returns for individuals for previous calendar year due. Individuals' estimation date; file declaration and pay first quarter of estimated tax for current tax year. Last day to file gift tax return and payment of tax on any gift made in previous calendar year to any one person in excess of $3,000.
June 15	File amended declaration of estimated tax and pay second quarter of estimated tax for current tax year.
September 15	File amended declaration of estimated tax and pay third quarter of estimated tax for current tax year.

ESTATE, GIFT AND INHERITANCE TAXES

One substantial source of revenue for federal and state governments is the excise tax imposed upon the transfer of property by will, by intestacy or by gift without a valuable and full consideration therefor.

FEDERAL ESTATE TAX

This tax is imposed by the federal government through the Internal Revenue Service on the estate of every deceased citizen or resident of the United States or of every nonresident, noncitizen who at his death owned property in the United States. The subject of the tax is the property owned by the decedent which is to be transferred and distributed to the various heirs and beneficiaries either by direction of his will or by the laws of descent and distribution. Payment of the tax is made by the estate.

The taxable estate is determined by deducting an exemption and certain other allowable deductions from the value of the gross estate.

The Gross Estate

Any property in which the decedent had a valuable interest at the time of his death must be included in his gross estate. Thus real property, including mineral rights and royalties are included. Stocks, bonds, negotiable instruments, works of art, an interest in a business—all assets form a part of his gross estate.

Any interest which the deceased owned jointly with another person in real or personal property is included as a part of his estate to the extent of its value. This applies to a joint tenancy, a tenancy by the entirety with his wife, or a joint account in a bank, payable to either or survivor.

Despite the fact that ownership of this property by law passes to his co-owner, the extent of his interest is computed as a part of his estate and is taxable. If it is shown that he owned all of the property and that the co-ownership was merely as a convenience, then the entire value of the deceased's property will be included in his taxable estate.

The proceeds of life insurance on his life, payable to a designated beneficiary, are included in his gross estate if he retained the incidents of ownership.

Any trust created in the will or prior to his death, not based on valuable and full consideration, will be considered as a part of his gross estate.

Dividends and interest which became due and payable before his death are a part of his gross estate. If payable after his death, this money is considered as income to the estate and is subject to income tax to be paid by the estate.

Community Property

In those states where community property laws are in effect, in the event of death of one spouse, one half of the value of the property is subject to testamentary or intestate disposition and the other half belongs to the surviving spouse.

Marital Deduction

A decedent may leave to his surviving spouse one half of his adjusted gross estate; this will be excluded from his gross estate and will not be subject to the estate tax.

The Taxable Estate

The taxable estate of a deceased citizen or resident of the United States is determined by subtracting the debts, obligations and liabilities as well as the deductible expenses in the proceeding and then also deducting the estate tax exemption which is established at $147,000 for 1979, $161,000 for 1980 and $175,000 for 1981 and thereafter.

Deductions

Funeral expenses are deductible from the gross estate. These include reasonable expenditures for the funeral, burial plot, monument, transportation of the body to the place of burial and the cost of perpetual care. The amount of the deduction will be reduced by any Social Security or Veterans Administration death benefits received.

Administration expenses, if actually incurred, may be deducted; these include expenses incurred in connection with the transfer of estate property to the beneficiaries, commissions to executors and administrators, attorneys' fees, court costs and fees, and the cost of storing, maintaining and preserving the estate property.

Procedural Requirements

On the death of a citizen or resident with a gross estate in excess of $60,000, a preliminary notice must be filed with the Commissioner of Internal Revenue advising him of the possibility of an estate tax liability. This should be done within 2 months after the death or 2 months after the executor or administrator qualifies to administer the estate.

The second form to be filed is the Estate Tax Return which must be filed within 15 months of the date of death and must accompany payment of the tax. In the event that final computations are not available, a request should be made for an extension of time. To avoid liability for the payment of interest penalty, a tax payment should be made based upon an estimate of the tax liability, for which credit will subsequently be given by the Internal Revenue Service.

Those states which impose an estate tax have their own procedures and requirements which must be complied with if the estate property is within their jurisdiction.

INHERITANCE TAXES

An inheritance tax is also an excise tax which is imposed upon the transfer of property from the estate of a decedent to a beneficiary. However, payment of the tax is the responsibility of the beneficiary and is deductible from his share.

FEDERAL GIFT TAX

The gift tax, like the estate tax, is levied on the transfer of property. However, this tax is imposed upon the person who

makes a gift of money or property to another without adequate
and full consideration having been given for it.

The purpose of this tax is to prevent the transfer of property
during the lifetime of the donor in anticipation of death to avoid
the payment of an estate tax. However, in order not to discourage gifts and intervivos transfers, the tax rate on gifts is
3/4 that of the estate tax rate.

When Tax is Applicable

The gift tax is imposed upon the transfer of property valued
in excess of $3,000 to any one person in any one taxable year
from one donor. There is a lifetime exemption of $30,000 to any
one person from one donor. Thus payments in excess of $3,000
in any calendar year or in excess of $30,000 during the lifetime
of the donee become taxable.

Gift Splitting

Gifts from a married couple may be considered as one half
from each, thus doubling the annual and lifetime exemptions.

Filing of Return

Each individual citizen or resident of the United States who
during a calendar year made gifts to any one donee of more
than $3,000 in value is required to file a gift tax return on Form
709.

Penalties

Any person required by the gift tax law to pay a tax or file
a return who wilfully fails to do so is guilty of a misdemeanor and
on conviction may be fined not more than $10,000 or imprisoned
for not more than one year or both, with costs of prosecution.

Any person who wilfully attempts to evade or defeat any
gift tax is guilty of a felony and on conviction may be fined not
more than $10,000 or imprisoned for not more than 5 years or
both, with the costs of prosecution.

Summation

Points to Remember about Taxes

The constantly increasing complexity of government results in increasing costs of operation, and this in turn increases the tax bite on income.

A reasonable knowledge of the type of taxes to which income earners and property owners are exposed should be regularly maintained and replenished. Coping with taxes should not be a once-a-year panic-stricken flurry of frustrated activity.

Although it is suggested that all technical and legal matters pertaining to taxes be referred to professionals for advice, guidance and execution, it is after all the taxpayer who is the primary source of the financial and fiscal information. He is the one who will pay the taxes or suffer the consequences. He should know the extent of his responsibility so that he can instruct the professionals intelligently.

CHAPTER 18

The Law and Business

As explained in Chapter 1, the law governing this country consists of enactments by the many government lawmakers in the United States Congress and in the legislative bodies of the various states, counties, cities and towns. These laws are interpreted by the courts and by quasi-judicial agencies.

The composition of these legislative and judicial bodies, of course, changes with time through elections and new appointments. The law is continually being amended to fit new situations and to keep up with the needs of the time.

New legislation is often introduced to conform to changing business and economic conditions. These new laws affect both the business community and the individual, both as a member of that community and as a consumer.

Some current legislation relating to business enterprise is summarized here.

STARTING A BUSINESS

The general legal principles applicable to business and business organization have been discussed in Chapter 8, "Forms of Business Ownership." Specifically, the essentials in the operation of a business enterprise concern credit and financing, locating the business, employment of personnel and wages.

The considerable investment of time, effort and money involved in launching a business makes thorough preparation and investigation imperative. There can be no doubt that relevant legal and accounting advice and guidance is important and should be obtained before any commitment is made.

However, while a new business is still in the exploratory and planning stage, certain basic legal and practical problems should be understood.

THE SMALL BUSINESS ADMINISTRATION

To assist and facilitate the formation of a small business, to protect its interests, to give financial guidance and assistance and to develop and improve management skills, federal legislation created the Small Business Administration (SBA).

A small business is defined as a small concern, independently owned and operated, not dominant in its field of operation, having a small number of employees and a comparatively low dollar value.

The SBA renders assistance to existing and prospective small business enterprises, both directly, through its regional and district offices distributed throughout the country, and through state agencies. There are ten regional offices located as follows:

I. Boston, Mass. 02110
II. New York, N.Y. 10007
III. Bala Cynwyd, Pa. 19004
IV. Atlanta, Ga. 30309
V. Chicago, Ill. 60604
VI. Dallas, Tex. 75202
VII. Kansas City, Mo. 64106
VIII. Denver, Colo. 80202
IX. San Francisco, Calif. 94102
X. Seattle, Wash. 98104

The SBA provides direct participation loans to help finance plant construction and expansion and to create working capital, if required.

Another function of the SBA is to render disaster relief in the form of loans to assist in the rehabilitation of small businesses which have sustained substantial economic injury as a result of a major disaster.

To further the progress of small business, the SBA has established procedures which are intended to increase the number of government contracts.

In addition, the SBA co-sponsors workshops and conferences

and distributes literature to help the small businessperson solve his or her management problems.

TERMINATING A BUSINESS

Essentially, there are two ways in which any business may be terminated: voluntarily or involuntarily. It may be voluntarily terminated by the consent and agreement of all of the parties interested in the business after all of the business debts and obligations have been satisfied.

Termination may come involuntarily as a result of action of the creditors in their efforts to be paid. A business may also be terminated by a court proceeding instituted by one of the interested parties when he can prove that the business is deadlocked and cannot proceed by reason of dispute, disagreement or illegality. It may, in addition, be terminated by government action if the business is in violation of law.

Voluntary Termination

When an individual owning and operating a company, either in his own name or under a trade name, decides to close up shop, he merely pays off all of his creditors, sells his inventory, fixtures and "goodwill," and collects all of the money due him from his debtors.

The sale of a business is discussed under the heading "Bulk Sales and Transfers" in Chapter 3, "The Sale of Property."

When all of the members in a partnership agree to terminate their business, the procedure is similar to that of a sole proprietorship.

In the event that only one of the partners withdraws from the firm, he becomes liable for any commitments he has made to the partners or to creditors who have not been paid. The partnership is then considered to be legally dissolved subject to the financial adjustments to be made depending upon the financial status of the business. The death of a partner is another reason for partnership to be technically dissolved. The credit also requires a financial adjustment in order that the estate or the next of kin of the deceased partner be paid out his or her share of the solvent business. This problem can be avoided if the partnership takes insurance coverage on the lives of the partners with the proviso that the proceeds from the policy shall be in satisfaction for any claims against the firm.

A corporation may be dissolved by the unanimous consent of all stockholders. All debts of the firm must be paid before the dissolution, or there will be personal liability against all members of the firm at the time of the dissolution. Technically, a certification of dissolution must be filed with the Secretary of State.

Involuntary Termination

A sole proprietorship, a partnership or a corporation must proceed in accordance with the Law of Bankruptcy if they are insolvent and are unable to pay their creditors.

This does not preclude the possibility of making a settlement with the creditors, who will then accept the term of the settlement and permit the debtor to continue in business.

If such a settlement is not acceptable to the creditors, then either the debtor or the creditors must proceed through the Bankruptcy Court.

Bankruptcy

When confronted with the problem of insolvency, that is, the inability of the business to pay its debts or the excess of debts over assets, the operators of the business have the option of filing a voluntary petition in bankruptcy or waiting for the creditors to file a petition of involuntary bankruptcy.

A person with residence, business or property in the United States may file a voluntary petition requesting the Bankruptcy Court to have him declared a bankrupt and thus to be relieved of his financial obligations. With the petition, he must also file schedules setting forth all of his assets and listing all of his creditors and the amounts he owes.

If the debtor does not file a voluntary petition, his creditors may file a petition requesting the court to have him declared a bankrupt. This can be done only if the debtor owes at least

$5,000 and has not been paying his obligations or is unable to do so. Such a petition may be filed by 3 of his creditors if he has more than 12. Otherwise, one or more may file such a petition.

After such a petition has been filed, the debtor is required to file schedules listing his assets, his creditors and the amounts he owes them.

He must then turn over all of his property to a person appointed as a temporary trustee until a permanent trustee can be appointed who will then administer the proceeding, liquidate the assets, collect any moneys due the debtor and distribute the money realized proportionately to each of the creditors who have filed claims against the bankrupt.

Prior to the transfer of his assets, the debtor may make an offer of settlement of all of the claims against him. If this is accepted by the creditors, the debtor may be permitted to remain in possession of his property and the petition in bankruptcy will then be dismissed.

Unless there is an objection by the creditors, the debtor will be declared a bankrupt, and within a reasonable time he will be discharged of all debts which he incurred prior to the filing of the petition.

He will not be discharged if he had previously been discharged in bankruptcy within 6 years from the date of the filing of the petition, or if the objecting creditors present proof within a 30-day period that he concealed property or committed other acts in fraud of his creditors.

There are certain debts which cannot be discharged in bankruptcy. Unpaid taxes are not dischargeable, neither are obligations due for the support of a former spouse or a child in connection with a divorce or maintenance agreement.

Educational loans owed to a government agency or to a nonprofit institution of higher learning are not dischargeable for a period of 5 years after the debt first becomes due.

A debtor in bankruptcy is entitled to certain exemptions from the claims of his creditors. His interest in real property used as a residence up to the value of $7,500 is exempt. His interest in a motor vehicle up to the value of $1,200 and his interest in any particular household item up to $200 are also exempt. He must file a list of the exemptions which he claims.

Individual Payment Plans

In order to provide a meaningful alternative to bankruptcy liquidation, the bankruptcy laws permit an individual with a regular income who has obligations which he cannot pay to develop and present to his creditors a plan for full or partial repayment of his debts over an extended period of time.

The plan may propose an extended repayment from his income for a period of 5 years. Under this procedure all actions against him will be stayed and creditors will be prohibited from taking legal action against him or his property to satisfy consumer debts.

Corporate Reorganization

When confronted with the pressure of financial obligations which cannot be met, corporate management may seek the assistance of the Bankruptcy Court to propose a plan of reorganization and repayment of its debts by means of an extension of time and the consent of its creditors. This process assures the creditors of some plan for payment and assures the debtor corporation of an opportunity to avoid liquidation.

PRODUCTS LIABILITY

A businessman manufacturing or selling a product must be alert and aware of the potential liability for damage or injury resulting from a defective product.

This potential financial responsibility has been developed by court decisions in situations which involve the manufacture and distribution for sale of products which may be inherently defective and therefore dangerous. The basis for this legal principle is the fact that the product, though not ordinarily dangerous, when in use becomes a source of unexpected danger to the purchaser, the user or the bystander by reason of its inherent defective condition.

Responsibility of the manufacturer or the seller of a product is imposed under the legal principles of negligence, as has been previously discussed in Chapter 10, "Torts." The product may also be attached, as previously discussed in Chapter 3, "The Sale of Property."

It is important at this time to distinguish the extent of the manufacturer's or seller's responsibility and the proof required to recover damages under the Law of Torts and Negligence, and the Law of Sales and Warranties and Products Liability.

In order to recover for personal injury or property damage based upon negligence, it is necessary to prove (1) that the product was negligently constructed; (2) that the injury or damage was the direct result of this negligent construction; and (3) that there was no intervening factor which was responsible.

To recover for damages sustained as a result of a breach of warranty pursuant to a sale of the product, it is necessary to prove (1) the sale; (2) an express or an implied warranty indicating that the product was safe, proper and adequate for the use to which it was intended; and (3) that the occurrence of the accident which resulted in the damage was not due to any other intervening cause but was due entirely to the existing defect in the product. The defect should have been discovered by the application of proper testing procedures; had those procedures been used, the defect would have been corrected and the damage avoided.

However, to recover in a lawsuit for injury or damage on the principle of products liability, it is not necessary to prove negligence. This liability may be imposed despite the fact that all possible care was exercised.

The elements which must be proved to establish the responsibility of a manufacturer for his products are:

1. The product, its construction or its packaging is defective.
2. By reason of this defect it is not fit for the use or purpose which can be reasonably expected or foreseen.
3. The existence of this defect is latent and not obvious to the prospective user.
4. The defect was created while it was in the control of the manufacturer.

5. This condition was the direct and proximate cause of the personal injury or property damage for which the lawsuit is brought.

This risk of responsibility has also been extended by the courts to any person or business which sells, distributes for sale or retails the product.

A lawsuit brought on the ground of products liability may be defended by proving (1) that the product was not used for the purpose for which it was intended or which was reasonably foreseeable; (2) if it was used for the proper purpose, it was not used properly in accordance with the instructions; or (3) that the user knew of the defective or dangerous condition and proceeded to use it nevertheless.

THE EQUAL CREDIT OPPORTUNITY ACT

Credit is the basic and primary requisite in the formation and operation of any business. The Equal Credit Opportunity Act was passed to assist and to foster the expansion of business activity without discrimination.

Business people, both as applicants for credit and as extenders of credit to customers, should be aware of the requirements of the Act.

It is unlawful for any creditor to discriminate against any applicant on the basis of race, color, religion, national origin, sex, marital status or age, provided that the applicant has the other requisites necessary to enter into a contractual commitment.

Credit shall not be refused to an applicant because his income is derived from any public assistance program or because the applicant has in good faith exercised his rights available under the provisions of the Act.

The applicant is to receive notice of the action taken on his application for credit within 30 days from the date of its receipt. If credit is refused, the applicant may request a reason for the refusal within 60 days from the date of the notice, if such reason was not provided. The reason for the refusal must then be given within 30 days from the date of the demand.

Failure to comply with these provisions may subject the creditor to a civil action for the actual damages sustained by the applicant. Under certain circumstances, punitive damages may be assessed by the federal district court having jurisdiction of the case. However, these punitive damages shall not be greater than $10,000 for an individual or $500,000 in a class action. The court may also add costs and reasonable attorneys' fees.

An action based upon discrimination and a violation of the provisions of the Act must be brought and instituted within two years from the date when the extension of credit was refused.

THE OCCUPATIONAL SAFETY AND HEALTH ACT (OSHA)

In the physical layout of the operating plant of a new business, it is important to keep in mind the provisions of the OSHA to protect the workers' health, safety and sanitary conditions.

OSHA was enacted because the loss to national productivity, as well as to the employer and the workers, resulting from harmful and unsafe working conditions was alarmingly substantial and continually increasing. It is the purpose of the Act to encourage employers and employees to reduce dangers to health and safety by creating and maintaining improved working conditions.

The employer must furnish his employees with a place to work which is free from recognized hazards that might cause serious physical injury. Employment standards are established by the Secretary of Labor within each type of employment to assure compliance by both employers and employees for their own benefit and safety.

The employer must keep records subject to inspection by an OSHA compliance officer to show each specific injury suffered by a worker on the job. He must keep an annual summary of all injuries sustained in the plant. He must report within 48 hours to the nearest OSHA office the occurrence of an industrial accident which is fatal to one or more employees or which results in the hospitalization of 5 or more employees.

The employer must give notice to his employees of their

rights under the law. He must establish safety programs and constantly inspect and supervise conditions to see that there is compliance with the Act.

Despite the fact that the law requires the employer to permit inspections by OSHA compliance officers, there is some question as to the right and the extent of this inspection, since it is made without a warrant and may thus be in violation of the Constitution. If such an inspection is objected to and opposed, there will be a court determination in each case as to its validity and admissibility.

There are civil and criminal penalties for failure to comply with the requirements of the Act. An employer may be fined up to $10,000 for each willful or repeated violation. If a willful violation results in the death of an employee, the employer, on conviction, may be liable to a fine up to $10,000 and imprisonment up to 6 months, in addition, of course, to civil actions for damages by the injured or his kin.

In determining penalties, the court will take into account the size of the business, the seriousness of the violation, the prior history of violations and the good faith of the employer.

THE EQUAL EMPLOYMENT OPPORTUNITY ACT

This civil rights legislation makes it unlawful to deprive any person of an equal opportunity for employment by reason of race, color, religion, national origin or sex. It is also unlawful to discriminate on such a basis with respect to compensation, terms, conditions and privileges of employment.

The definition of the term "by reason of or on the basis of sex" has been defined to include, "on the basis of pregnancy, childbirth and related medical conditions." Women affected by these conditions shall be treated for all employment-related purposes, including fringe benefits and benefit programs, the same as other persons, depending on their ability or inability to work.

The provision as to discrimination applies not only to prospective employers but also to labor organizations and to employment agencies.

A labor union is prohibited from excluding or expelling a person from membership for the reasons listed. Nor may it classify or segregate its members into categories which may deprive them of equal employment opportunity.

An employment agency must not refuse to refer a person for employment on the basis of these classifications. Advertisements of employment opportunities in the news media must not segregate or classify on the basis of sex. The advertisers must list their available jobs under the general heading of "Help Wanted." In the event that the nature of the job requires a person of one sex or the other, the advertisement must indicate that the sex preference is a bona fide occupational qualification (BFOQ) for the specific job offered.

Other exceptions to the anti-discrimination provisions of the Act include:

1. The requirement of a person of a particular sex or religion by an educational or religious institution
2. The exclusion of a person who is a member of the Communist Party
3. Discrimination justified by national security
4. Laws giving preference to veterans
5. Laws giving preference to Indians

Training programs instituted by an employer, a labor organization or a joint labor-management committee must not discriminate and must make access to such opportunities available to all persons otherwise qualified.

Any person who claims to be a victim of discrimination may file written charges with the office of the Equal Employment Opportunity Commission. Notice of the charge will be sent to the person against whom the claim is made within 10 days. An investigation will be made by representatives of the commission. This may include fact-finding conferences in an effort to establish a framework for a negotiated settlement.

After the investigation is completed, if there is a reasonable cause to believe that the charge is true, the district office will attempt to remedy the alleged unlawful practice through conciliation, conference and persuasion.

If an acceptable agreement is not reached, the commission may bring suit in the federal district court. If such a suit is not instituted, a Notice of Right to Sue will be issued by the commission allowing the person making the charge to institute suit in his own name in a federal district court within 90 days.

THE FAIR LABOR STANDARDS ACT

By the authority of the U.S. Constitution, Congress is authorized to legislate in matters pertaining to interstate commerce. Congress has determined that labor conditions which are detrimental to the health and welfare of workers affect interstate commerce. It has also determined that the lack of minimum-wage standards affects the free flow of goods, constitutes an unfair method of competition, leads to labor disputes and thus interferes with the orderly marketing of goods.

Congress has therefore established minimum-wage standards which are currently as follows:

An employer shall pay to each of his employees who in any work week is engaged in interstate commerce not less than $3.10 an hour, starting January 1, 1980.

The Wage and Hour Division of the Department of Labor is designated to supervise compliance with these established standards.

MANAGEMENT-LABOR RELATIONS

Labor law is the general term which covers all laws, regulations, rules and court decisions concerned with labor relations.

Labor relations is the general term which includes employer-employee and employer-union negotiations, unions and their organization and control, collective bargaining, strikes, picketing and unfair labor practices either by the employer or by a union.

The Norris-LaGuardia Act

Passed in 1932, this was the first federal law to deal with labor relations and, more specifically, with injunctions by the court against union activities. Its main purpose was to prevent the federal courts from issuing injunctions against unions in their efforts to organize by means of strikes and picketing.

The National Labor Relations Act (Wagner Act)

This law was intended to protect unions in their efforts to increase their membership and to organize those shops which did not have union representation. It established the machinery by which elections by employees in each shop determined the union to represent them. It promoted and encouraged collective bargaining between union and employer. It declared as an unfair labor practice any act by an employer which interfered with union organization:

Unfair Labor Practices by the Employer

1. To interfere with employees in the exercise of their rights granted by this law
2. To dominate a labor organization
3. To encourage or discourage membership in a labor union by discrimination in hiring, tenure or conditions of employment
4. To discriminate against employees who file charges or testify in National Labor Relations Act (NLRA) proceedings
5. To refuse to bargain collectively
6. To enter into a "hot cargo" agreement by which an employer, in collusion with a union, agrees to discontinue doing business with another employer or deal in the products of that employer (This subdivision was added by the Labor-Management Reporting and Disclosure Act, to be discussed later.)

The Labor-Management Relations Act (Taft-Hartley Act)

This Act, which was an amendment to the National Labor Relations Act, declared certain actions by unions to be considered as unfair labor practices. Under the Taft-Hartley Act unfair labor practices by unions are defined as follows:

Unfair Labor Practices by a Union

1. To restrain or coerce employees or employers
2. To coerce employers to discriminate against employees
3. To refuse to bargain
4. To engage in strikes or boycotts for certain purposes
5. To impose excessive or discriminatory initiation fees
6. To exact money for work not performed, known as featherbedding
7. To picket or threaten to picket certain candidates
8. To enter into "hot cargo" agreements
9. To strike or picket, in the health-care industry, without giving 10 days' notice

Employees' Rights

The NLRA declares the right of employees not only to engage in concerted activities but also to refuse to engage in such activities. Neither the union nor the employer may interfere with these rights of an employee.

Procedure in Unfair Practice Cases

When there is a complaint of an unfair labor practice, a charge is filed with the regional office of the National Labor Relations Board (NLRB). It may be filed by an employee, a union or an employer. It must be served on the party being charged within 6 months from the date when the alleged unfair labor practice was committed.

The charging party must submit evidence to substantiate its allegation, and the other side is requested to make a statement in response. The matter is referred to a field agent for investigation. When the charged party is interviewed, he has a right to have his attorney present. If the charge is unsupported, it will be dismissed, giving the charging party the right to appeal to the NLRB general counsel.

If the charge is sustained, then an effort is made to settle the matter by the charged party's agreement to discontinue the practice. If no settlement is possible, then formal proceedings are instituted by the issuance of a complaint and a notice of hearing. A hearing is held before an administrative law judge giving all parties the rights essential for the presentation of their claims and their proof. The administrative law judge renders his report. This is reviewed by the NLRB if there is objection to the judge's order within 20 days. The NLRB then renders a decision and order. To be enforceable this order must be confirmed by the court.

The Labor-Management Reporting and Disclosure Act (Landrum-Griffin Act)

Following congressional investigations in the labor and management fields, this law was passed primarily to protect the rights and interests of employees and the public as they relate to the activities of labor organizations, labor relations consultants and their officers and representatives.

Labor organizations are required to adopt constitutions and bylaws and to file copies of these documents with the Secretary of Labor. Reports and other information filed by a union must be made available to its members, and under certain circumstances, the books and records of the union may be required by the Department of Labor to verify these reports.

DEBT COLLECTION PRACTICES

After committee findings that debt collectors indulged in abusive, deceptive and unfair practices, Congress passed legislation to restrict and control them by the following provisions:

A debt collector shall not reveal his purpose or his identity when he communicates with a person other than the debtor. He is not to communicate with the same person more than once and is not to do so by postcard.

If the collector knows that the consumer-debtor is represented by an attorney, he is to communicate with the attorney.

A debt collector shall communicate with a debtor at a reasonable and convenient time and not at the debtor's place of employment. If the debtor indicates his refusal to pay, there is to be no further communication from the collector, no harassment, no abuse.

The next step is to proceed to collect the claim by legal action. Failure to comply with these rules will subject the collector to civil liability for the actual damages sustained by the debtor.

THE COPYRIGHT ACT OF 1976

This law, which came into effect January 1, 1978, established a single system of statutory protection for all copyrighted works, both published and unpublished.

The law provides protection to an author (creator) of a work or works during his lifetime and to his heirs for a period of 50 years after his death.

Copyright protection is not dependent upon registration of the work by the author.

Copyright protection is achieved by means of the notice of copyright which must be present on all published copies.

The copyright notice may take one of the following forms:

Copyright, (the year of first publication), (the name of the owner of the work)

Instead of the word "copyright" either the abbreviation "copr." or the symbol "©" may be used:

Copyright, 1980, Martin J. Ross
Copr., 1980, Martin J. Ross
© 1980, Martin J. Ross.

The copyright notice of records or sound recordings should take the following form:

℗ 1980, Martin J. Ross

Though the registration of a work is voluntary and not mandatory, the failure to register it may deprive the owner of certain rights and remedies. It is a prerequisite to bringing a lawsuit for infringement. The remedy of statutory damages and attorneys' fees will not be available for any infringement which occurs before registration.

The effective date of a copyright registration is the date when an acceptable application has been filed in the U.S. Copyright Office together with the required fee and the necessary number of copies of the work.

There are five specific categories for registration and a separate and specific application must be filed for each category.

1. Non-dramatic literary works which are published or unpublished, written in words, numbers or other symbols. These are registered by Application Form TX.
2. Works of the performing arts, published or unpublished, and prepared to be performed directly before an audience or indirectly by a device or process. Application Form PA.
3. Works of the visual arts, published or unpublished, pictorial, graphic and sculptural. Application Form VA.
4. Sound recordings, published or unpublished, where the claim is for the sound recording itself or where the same claimant wants to register also the musical, dramatic or literary work embodied in the recording. Application Form SR.
5. Applications for renewal of copyrights issued under the old copyright law are filed by means of Form RE.

The owner of the copyright has the legal obligation to file the required copies of the work, usually two, within a specified time, usually within three months of the publication. Failure to file can result in fines and penalties by the Copyright Office.

PATENTS AND TRADEMARKS

The United States Constitution authorizes the establishment of the patent and copyright legislation in order "to promote the progress of science and the useful arts."

Patents are issued to grant the inventor exclusive rights to produce, use and sell his invention for a specific period of time. They thus provide an incentive for the inventor to continue in the research, development and commercialization of new technology.

Applications for patents to protect designs, constructions and processes from competitive infringement and exploitation are filed with the U.S. Patent Office.

Patents for designs are obtained for a maximum of 14 years. Protection for other types of inventions is for a period of 17 years.

A Trademark is a distinctive feature, such as a name, device or symbol which is used by a manufacturer or merchant to identify his business, product or service and to distinguish it from that of his competitors. Trademarks are registered for a period of 20 years with the right of renewal.

THE FREEDOM OF INFORMATION ACT

Under this law a person has the right to request any government agency to make available for his inspection all information concerning him which the agency has in its files.

The government must publish in the federal register a list of agencies where these records are kept, and each agency must make these records available for public inspection and copying. There is a schedule of fees and charges for document search and duplication.

Each agency may classify certain categories of material which are exempt from the requirements of the Act and which are not to be disclosed.

However, this determination is not final. Any person to whom access to his records was denied may challenge this in a federal court. If the court decides that the withholding was unjustified, the agency may be required to pay the actual damages suffered.

Any officer of any agency who illegally withholds this information will be subject to disciplinary action.

THE PRIVACY ACT OF 1974

This law was enacted to uphold the fundamental right of privacy of the individual derived from the Constitution of the United States. It establishes safeguards to prevent the misuse of personal information accumulated by the federal government.

The Act gives the individual access to records containing

such personal information and the right to control the transfer of these records to other agencies.

It also gives the individual the right to object to information which is not material or pertinent to the function of the agency. He may request that the records be amended in accordance with his claim, and he has the right of appeal from an adverse determination by the agency.

Any employee of a government agency who violates the privacy of the information contained in the records by disclosing or revealing it may, if found guilty, be charged with a misdemeanor and fined up to $5,000.

GOVERNMENT "IN SUNSHINE"

A congressional enactment declares it to be the policy of the United States that the public is entitled to full information of the decision-making process of government. Thus all meetings of government agencies are required to be public unless they come within a category which exempts them from public disclosure.

This requirement is subject, however, to the individual's right of privacy and the government's responsibility to protect the nation's security interests.

The time, place and subject matter of all meetings must be announced in advance, together with the name and the telephone number of a person who is competent to answer questions about the meeting. Minutes or a transcript of each meeting must be made available to the public.

Appendix

A DO-IT-YOURSELF LIST

Your will is not enough. You must keep accurate records of your transactions and your property and a list of those persons who are responsible for them.

Every individual—employee or businessman—of modest or considerable financial resources is aware that his estate will be left at loose ends if an emergency leaves him unable to act for himself. Money, property or benefits may be lost because there was no record available to make a proper claim for their recovery.

To avoid such unnecessary financial loss, it is urgently suggested that a check list be kept in a safe but accessible location. The following basic information is necessary, in addition to any information which applies to each individual's situation:

Name and Address of:
> Lawyer
> Accountant
> Insurance broker
> Stockbroker
> Bank accounts
> Bank vaults
> Employer

Location of:
> Will
> Insurance policies
> Bank books
> Stocks and bonds
> Vault keys
> Military discharge papers

Birth certificates
Real estate deeds and records
Proof of citizenship
Books of account
Tax records
Cemetary plot

Additional information:
Funeral arrangements
Interment instructions
Loans outstanding
Moneys due
Membership in organizations
Persons or organizations to be notified at once
Social Security number
Pension fund and number

OTHER DO-IT-YOURSELF SUGGESTIONS

CONTRACTS Read every word of any contract or document you are asked to sign. Make certain that the words, as written, mean exactly what you agreed upon.

It is the writing with your signature on it which will be binding, not the oral promise made before the signing.

SALES AND BAILMENTS When the purchase you are making or the repair job you have ordered is accompanied by a written document which you are asked to sign and which contains small print on the back or refers to other documents, make certain that you agree with the contents of that small print or the other documents.

INSURANCE When obtaining insurance through an insurance broker or a company agent, make sure that you are getting the coverage you require as to description and quantity of the merchandise, the value and the risks against which you are insuring.

Read your policy when you get it, so that there will be no doubt in your mind.

TORTS If you are involved in an accident, make a careful note of all information about the accident: the cars, the people, the conditions of weather and roadway, names of witnesses. *As soon as possible notify your insurance broker or your insurance company agent.*

REAL ESTATE When buying a house, don't sign a binder with the broker if you can merely get a receipt for your deposit with a description of the house, the cost of the house and the statement that your lawyer and the seller's lawyer will arrange for signing of a contract.

Before you sign a lease, read it carefully to make sure that you agree with all of the printed provisions and the "Rules and Regulations" on the back. If you don't agree with some of the rules, corrections should be made *before* you sign. They are not likely to be made after.

Glossary

AB INITIO is a Latin term meaning "from the beginning."

ABANDONMENT is a ground for a legal separation when one spouse leaves the other without any intention to return.

ABATEMENT is the term used to indicate a suspension of a legal proceeding.

ANNUITY is the annual payment of money in accordance with an agreement between the donor and the recipient.

ANNULMENT is a declaration by a court that a marriage presumed to be binding is a nullity and ineffective.

ANSWER is the document which the defendant in a civil lawsuit serves on the plaintiff or his attorney in answer to the summons and complaint.

APPEAL is the proceeding by which a party to a lawsuit defeated in a lower court applies to a higher court to determine the correctness of that decision.

ARBITRATION is a proceeding established by previous agreement in which both sides to a controversy submit their dispute to persons designated or to be chosen.

ARRAIGNMENT is that part of a criminal case in which a person charged with a crime is brought before the court and advised of the charge against him.

ARREST is the legal apprehension and restraint of a person charged with a crime so that he may be brought to court to stand trial.

ASSIGNMENT is the transfer of a right or interest in property by one person to another.

ASSIGNMENT FOR THE BENEFIT OF CREDITORS is the transfer by an insolvent debtor of all of his property to another for the purpose of arriving at an adjustment with his creditors.

ATTACHMENT is the proceeding by which a person or his property are restrained in accordance with a direction of a civil court to secure payment of a judgment or the presence of the person when the case is being tried.

ATTESTATION CLAUSE is the formal legal language used at the end of a will, below the testator's signature, which declares that the requirements for the proper execution of the will have been complied with.

ATTORNEY IN FACT is a person who has been appointed by another to transact business for him and in his name. He does not have to be a lawyer.

AUCTION is a public sale of property to the highest bidder by a person called the AUCTIONEER, who must be licensed to carry on such a business.

AWARD is the determination of a judicial body which grants a sum of money to the winner.

BAIL is security given to a court in exchange for the release of a person in custody to assure his presence in court later.

BAIL BOND is an undertaking by which someone obligates himself to pay the amount of the bail if the person out on bail fails to appear when required.

BAILMENT is the relationship created when the owner of property, the BAILOR, delivers it to another, the BAILEE, for some specific purpose.

BANKRUPTCY is a proceeding under the federal laws, dealing with the property and debts of an insolvent debtor and his creditors.

BARRATRY is the act of encouraging lawsuits and inciting quarrels which ultimately end in litigation.

BASTARDY or FILIATION PROCEEDINGS are brought by the mother or a public welfare agency to establish the paternity of an illegitimate child.

BEARER PAPER is any negotiable instrument which can be negotiated by delivery and does not require indorsement.

BENCH WARRANT is a process issued by a court ordering the apprehension and arrest of a person guilty of contempt of court or indicted for a crime.

BEQUEST or LEGACY is a provision in a will giving property or money to a designated person.

BIGAMY is the crime committed when a person has two husbands or two wives living, without being divorced from one of them.

BILL OF ATTAINDER, forbidden by the Constitution, is any law which creates a forfeiture of a person's property.

BILL OF EXCHANGE or DRAFT is a negotiable instrument which requires the drawee to pay a designated sum of money to the payee or subsequent holder.

BILL OF LADING is an agreement between a shipper of freight and a common carrier.

BILL OF PARTICULARS is a document in a lawsuit which amplifies the information set forth in the complaint.

BINDER, used in insurance and real estate, is a preliminary agreement.

BLANK INDORSEMENT results when an indorser of a negotiable instrument merely signs his name without specifying the person to whom he is negotiating it.

BLUE SKY LAWS are enacted by state legislatures to protect their citizens from investing in stock of spurious corporations.

BONA FIDE PURCHASER FOR VALUE, used in contracts and negotiable instruments, describes any person who acquires property or negotiable instruments in good faith and for a valuable consideration.

BOND is an undertaking, an obligation assumed by the person who executes it.

BREACH OF THE PEACE is any act committed by a person in a public place which disturbs the public peace and tranquility.

BULK SALE is the acquisition of all or a greater part of the stock and fixtures of a business in a manner other than in the ordinary course of its business.

BURDEN OF PROOF is the duty of a party in a lawsuit to present sufficient proof to sustain the charges that he made.

BURGLARY is the crime committed by a person who breaks into and enters the home of another without permission and with intent to commit a crime.

CALENDAR is the list of cases which is established in each court to determine their orderly disposition and trial.

CAPACITY is the ability under the law to take recognized legal action.

CAPITAL CRIME OR OFFENSE is one which is punishable by death.

CAPTION is the title of a lawsuit as used to describe it, containing the names of the plaintiff and defendant and the court in which it is being tried.

CASH ON DELIVERY (C.O.D.) transactions require the buyer to pay for the merchandise in cash when it is delivered to him.

CAUSE OF ACTION is the legal basis on which the plaintiff relies for his recovery against the defendant.

CAVEAT EMPTOR means "Let the buyer beware."

CERTIFICATE OF DEPOSIT is a written receipt by a bank which indicates that there is a certain sum of money on deposit in the name of a designated person.

CERTIFICATE OF DOING BUSINESS is generally required when an individual or a partnership operates a business under an assumed or firm name.

CERTIFICATE OF INCORPORATION, also called a CHARTER, is the document which creates the corporation.

CESTUI QUE TRUST denotes the person who benefits from the trust.

CHALLENGE is the right of a party to a lawsuit to object to a juror during the selection of the jury before the trial.

CHARGE in criminal law is the accusation made against a person that he committed a crime. In a civil action, it is the instructions on the law which the court gives the jury at the end of the trial.

CHARTER is another name for the CERTIFICATE OF INCORPORATION.

CHATTEL is any item of personal property as distinguished from land, which is real property.

CHATTEL MORTGAGE is a document executed and delivered by the owner of personal property, transferring ownership to secure re-payment of a loan.

CHECK is a negotiable instrument, a written order to a bank by its depositor requesting payment of a definite sum of money to the order of the named payee.

CITATION is a process of a probate or surrogate's court bringing the the parties within its jurisdiction.

CLOSING OF TITLE in real property is the time when the buyer of a piece of real estate pays the money due under the contract in ex-change for a deed to the property.

CODICIL is a document, executed with all the formality of a will, used to make minor changes in an existing will.

COHABITATION is the act of a man and woman living together as hus-band and wife, with all of its consequent rights and obligations.

COINSURANCE is a provision in fire insurance policies which requires the premises to be insured for an agreed proportion of their value.

COLLUSION is an agreement between two or more persons to proceed fraudulently to the detriment and prejudice of an innocent and ignorant third party.

COMITY AMONG NATIONS is the friendly relation existing between them so that the laws and institutions of each are recognized by the other.

COMMITMENT is the order of a court which directs a person to be kept in custody either in a penal or a mental institution.

COMMON CARRIER is any transportation facility which publicly under-takes to transport persons or property for a stated price and with-out restriction.

COMMON LAW is the body of law which was accumulated and col-lected from the decisions of the English courts and adopted as the basis of law in this country.

COMMON-LAW MARRIAGE is a relationship between a man and woman living together as husband and wife and recognized by law as a valid marriage.

COMMUTATION is a reduction of punishment or sentence after convic-tion for a crime.

COMPARATIVE NEGLIGENCE is a principle of law which takes into account the negligence of both sides in an accident.

COMPENSATORY DAMAGES is a sum of money awarded to a plaintiff by a court or a jury as a fair and just recompense for injury sustained to person, property or reputation.

COMPLAINANT in a criminal action is the person who, as a victim of a crime, brings the facts to the attention of the police authorities.

COMPLAINT is the document prepared and submitted by the plaintiff in a lawsuit which sets forth his claims for recovery against the defendant. A complaint may contain several "causes of action."

COMPOSITION OF CREDITORS is an agreement by the creditors of a person who is financially insolvent to accept a sum' less than the full amount of his indebtedness.

COMPREHENSIVE AUTOMOBILE INSURANCE COVERAGE is a policy of insurance which covers the owner of an automobile for damage to his car resulting from certain stated risks.

CONDEMNATION is the legal machinery by which an authorized governmental agency takes private property for public use.

CONDITION is a provision in a contract which must be performed to make it effective.

CONDITIONAL SALE is an agreement which gives the buyer possession of personal property but not ownership until full payment is made.

CONDITIONAL WILL is a will which disposes of a person's property only in the event of death under certain specified conditions.

CONDONATION by a husband or wife forgives an act of infidelity by the other.

CONFESSION of a debt by a debtor in a civil action under certain conditions gives the creditor the right to enter judgment for the debt. In a criminal action, it is the acknowledgment and admission of guilt to a crime with which a person is charged.

CONFINEMENT is restraint or restriction of a person's freedom of movement.

CONFISCATION is the act of taking private property as a penalty and a forfeit for public use.

CONFRONTATION is the right of a person to face the witnesses who charge him with a crime.

CONSANGUINITY is the relationship of persons by blood and by descent from a common ancestor.

CONSENT is a voluntary accord between two people in their contractual relationship.

CONSIGNMENT is the delivery of merchandise by the owner to the

CONSIGNEE to be sold and the proceeds, less commission, to be returned to the CONSIGNOR.

CONSOLIDATION is the combination of two or more corporations into one, or the combination of two or more lawsuits between the same parties to be tried together.

CONSORTIUM is the right which a person has to the affections, services and society of his spouse.

CONSPIRACY is an agreement between two or more people to commit an illegal act.

CONSTRUCTION of a contract or a will is the interpretation which the court gives to its terms to arrive at the intention.

CONTEMPT is the disobedience of the rules, orders and processes of the court or a legislative body.

CONTINUANCE is the adjournment or carry-over of a legal proceeding to another scheduled date.

CONTRABAND is any article which has been declared illegal for export or import.

CONTRACT is an agreement between two or more people enforcible in a court of law.

CONTRIBUTION is the right to enforce payment of a share in a common loss or obligation.

CONVEYANCE is a document by which ownership in real estate is transferred.

CORPORATION is a form of business organization created by state authority as a legal entity.

CORPUS DELICTI is the legal term for the actual tangible evidence to prove that the crime was committed.

COST, INSURANCE AND FREIGHT (C.I.F.) are terms in a contract for the sale of merchandise which requires the seller to pay the insurance, cost and freight of the goods to the point of destination.

COUNTERCLAIM is the claim for relief made by the defendant in a lawsuit as part of his defense to the plaintiff's action.

COVENANT is a specific provision in a deed or lease relating to the use of the property.

CREDIBILITY is the believability of a witness at a trial as to his testimony.

CRIMINAL CONVERSATION is illegal sexual intimacy between a man and a woman.

CROSS-EXAMINATION is the questioning by a party or his attorney to test the witnesses of his opponent.

CURTESY is the right given to a widower in the real estate of his deceased wife which she owned at her death.

CUSTODY is the legal right given to a parent or another person to live
with, control, educate and guide children.

DAMAGES are the award of money assessed to compensate for financial loss to the injured party in a lawsuit. GENERAL or COMPENSA-
TORY damages are awarded to pay in money for the pain, suffering
and injury which was sustained. SPECIAL DAMAGES are awarded for
any financial loss which flows directly from the other injury sustained. This would include medical and hospital expenses and actual loss of earnings. PUNITIVE OR EXEMPLARY DAMAGES are
awarded in a tort action where a willful or malicious act was involved. The purpose of such damages in addition to others imposed is to punish the responsible party. This may occur in
defamation where the act was particularly vicious and malicious.
NOMINAL DAMAGES are imposed when the injury is negligible yet
the responsibility of the party at fault must be established.

DECEDENT in wills and estates is used to denote the deceased person
whose estate is involved.

DECISION is the determination of the court which disposes of the case
under consideration.

DECREE is a formal determination of a court, usually made in writing.

DEED is a document which transfers ownership to real estate.

DEFAMATION is a statement made orally or in writing which injures
a person's reputation in the community.

DEFAULT is a legal term meaning the failure to appear and defend
a lawsuit.

DEFENDANT is the person in a lawsuit who is charged with responsibility for creating a situation against which the plaintiff wants
relief.

DEFENSE is the justification interposed by the defendant of a lawsuit
which is intended to relieve him of blame and of financial obligation.

DELIBERATION is the consideration given by the jury to a case so that
it may arrive at its verdict.

DEMURRER is the answer of a defendant to a charge made against
him which denies legal responsibility though it may concede the
plaintiff's contention.

DEPOSITION is a written statement made under oath. The person
making it is called the DEPONENT.

DESTITUTE is the term applied to persons who do not have the necessaries of life and have no means of obtaining them.

DEVISE is a grant or transfer of real estate by will. The person getting
such land is known as the DEVISEE.

DISABILITY is disqualification in law for lack of necessary legal requirements.

DISAFFIRM in law means to renege or to refuse to go through with an agreed transaction.

DISHONOR in law means a refusal to accept an obligation such as negotiable instruments when presented for acceptance or payment.

DISMISS is to throw a case out of court.

DISPOSSESS is the term used when a tenant of real estate is ousted from possession by an order of a court at the request of the landlord.

DISTRIBUTEE is a person who shares in the estate of anyone who died without leaving a will.

DIVORCE is a legal dissolution of a marriage, so that each partner is freed from the bonds of matrimony with the right to remarry.

DOMICILE is the place of permanent residence of an individual.

DOUBLE or FORMER JEOPARDY prevents a person from being tried twice for the same offense.

DOUBLE INDEMNITY is a separate agreement in an insurance policy which obligates the company to pay twice the face amount of the policy if the insured dies as a result of "violent and accidental means."

DOWER is the provision in the law which entitles a widow to a share of the real estate owned by her husband at his death.

DRAFT is a negotiable instrument, a written demand made by one person to another to pay a designated sum of money to a named third person known as the "payee."

DUE PROCESS guarantees that no person shall be deprived of his life, liberty or property without "due process of law."

DURESS is force, pressure or threats which induce a person to act in a manner contrary to his own wish.

EASEMENT is the right of a landowner to use the land of his neighbor.

EJECTMENT is the legal remedy available to the owner of real estate to remove persons in possession who have no right to be there.

EMINENT DOMAIN is the power of the government to acquire land or property of a private individual for a necessary public purpose.

ENDOWMENT in life insurance provides for the payment of the face amount of the policy if the insured survives the agreed term of the policy or dies while it is in effect.

ENOCH ARDEN is the name given to a proceeding which permits the dissolution of a marriage when one of the parties disappears and is absent for a designated period of time, creating the legal presumption that he is dead.

EQUITY grants relief to a party in cases when the mere payment of money is not adequate to help him.

ESCHEAT is the return of land and property to the state if there is no person legally entitled to inherit.

ESTATE consists of the property belonging to a recently deceased person which must be administered and distributed in accordance with a will or the laws of intestacy.

ESTOPPEL results when a person by his prior attitude caused someone to act in reliance upon it. A subsequent change of attitude will not be permitted or recognized by the court.

EVICTION is the act which deprives a person of the use and enjoyment of property.

EX PARTE indicates that an application has been made by one litigant without notice to the other.

EX POST FACTO LAW designates an act to be a crime although it was not a crime when it was committed.

EXAMINATION BEFORE TRIAL is a part of legal procedure which permits one litigant to make the other answer questions under oath before the actual trial of the case.

EXCEPTIONS are objections which a litigant may make to the court's ruling or its charge to the jury.

EXECUTED means that all of the terms of a contract have been fulfilled. An EXECUTORY contract still has some provisions to be complied with.

EXECUTOR (feminine: EXECUTRIX) is a person named in a will to take charge of the administration of the estate subject to the supervision of the court.

EXHIBITS are documents or other tangible evidence used at a trial to prove certain facts to the court and jury.

EXPRESS CONTRACT is one which has all of its provisions agreed upon by the parties. A contract is IMPLIED when it is created by the behavior of the parties.

EXTENDED COVERAGE is an agreement of insurance which covers damage resulting from windstorm, hail, riot, explosion and similar stated risks.

EXTORTION is the offense of taking money or property from a person by threat or duress or under pretense of authority.

EXTRADITION is the process by which fugitives from one state are returned by the authorities of another state in which they were apprehended.

FACTOR, also known as a commission merchant, is a person who takes property or merchandise of another to sell for him. It is also a person (or company) who takes over the accounts receivable of a business to collect the moneys due.

FAIR PREPONDERANCE OF THE CREDIBLE EVIDENCE is the measure of evidence required in a civil case for the plaintiff to prevail over the defendant. This is to be distinguished from the requirement in a criminal case that the defendant be found guilty BEYOND A REASONABLE DOUBT.

FALSE ARREST is the detention of a person by another who claims to have official authority which is in fact invalid.

FALSE IMPRISONMENT, also known as UNLAWFUL DETENTION, is the act of depriving a person of his liberty without any authority or justification.

FELONY is a crime which is punishable by a term in a state prison. Conviction of a felony deprives a person of his civil rights. A person convicted of such a crime is known as a FELON.

FIDUCIARY is a person who because of his position or relationship owes a duty of trust and confidence.

FIXTURES are items of personal property which may become a part of the real property when they are attached and cannot be removed.

FILIATION PROCEEDINGS, also known as BASTARDY PROCEEDINGS, are instituted to prove paternity of a child born out of wedlock.

FIT FOR HUMAN CONSUMPTION is a promise implied by the seller of food.

FORGERY is the act of making, counterfeiting or altering any writing with an intent to mislead and deceive.

FORECLOSURE is a proceeding in a court of law by which the right of a person against real or personal property is determined and enforced.

FRAUD is a false statement of a material fact made to induce someone to rely upon it to his financial loss.

FREE ALONGSIDE SHIP (F.A.S.) is a provision in a contract of sale which requires the seller to deliver the merchandise at a designated place for loading aboard ship.

FREE ON BOARD (F.O.B) is a provision in a contract of sale which requires the seller to deliver the merchandise at a designated place, usually to a carrier.

GARNISHEE (GARNISHMENT) is a notice or proceeding which requires a person who owes money to a judgment debtor to pay the judgment creditor instead.

GRAND JURY is a body of citizens properly selected according to law.

It examines the evidence against a person suspected of a crime and determines if he is to be held for trial.

GRANT is a transfer of real property or an interest in real property. The GRANTOR transfers the property to the GRANTEE.

GUARDIAN is a person appointed to be a protector of the interests of a minor. A GUARDIAN AD LITEM must be appointed for a minor if he is to prosecute or defend a lawsuit.

HABEAS CORPUS, a legal proceeding instituted by a writ, requires the person upon whom it is served to prove that he has a legal right to the custody of the person in whose name the writ was brought.

HEARSAY EVIDENCE is evidence brought out by the testimony of a witness at a trial which is not based upon his personal knowledge but rather on information he obtained from someone else, someone not available for cross-examination. This evidence is generally not acceptable.

HOLDER IN DUE COURSE is a person who has obtained a negotiable instrument in a regular business transaction for a valuable consideration and without knowledge that it has any defects.

HOLDOVER TENANT is one who continues in possession of leased premises after his lease has expired.

HOLOGRAPHIC WILL is one which is written in the handwriting of the maker or testator.

HOMICIDE is the killing of one human being by the act of another human being.

INCORPORATORS are persons who form a corporation and sign the certificate of incorporation.

INDEMNITY in insurance is the reimbursement for loss sustained.

INDICTMENT is a document prepared by the district attorney and approved by the grand jury which charges a person with the commission of a crime.

INDORSEMENT is the notation made on the back of a negotiable instrument by a person who owns it and is about to transfer it to someone else. The person making it is called an INDORSER.

INFANT, also known as a MINOR, is a person under legal age, generally 21.

INFORMATION is the written document which contains a charge that the person named in it committed a crime.

INJUNCTION is an order of a court which prohibits a named person from performing certain acts.

INSANE is the term applied to a person who is suffering from a mental disease which prevents him from knowing the consequence of his acts or that they are wrong.

INSOLVENT denotes the condition of a business when the liabilities are greater than the assets, so that the claims of the creditors cannot be paid.

INSURABLE INTEREST is the required ownership or interest a person must have to be able to take out insurance.

INTEREST is the charge made for the loan and use of money.

INTESTACY results when a person dies without leaving a valid will.

JOINT TENANTS are persons who each own an equal interest in the same property, either real or personal.

JOINT WILL is drawn and executed by more than one person with the intention that it be the will of each of them.

JUDGMENT is the formal entry of the court's decision between the plaintiff and the defendant. The winner to whom money is to be paid is the JUDGMENT CREDITOR. The one who owes the money is the JUDGMENT DEBTOR.

JURISDICTION is the legal authority which a court has to try a lawsuit.

JURY (sometimes called PETIT JURY) is a body of citizens of the county who are selected to hear and decide a case in a civil or criminal court.

LAST CLEAR CHANCE is a doctrine on which recovery for injury due to negligence is based. In those states where contributory negligence by the plaintiff defeats his right to recovery, this theory may be used as an exception if the defendant, the person causing the injury, had sufficient notice of the danger to which the plaintiff was exposed and had sufficient opportunity to avoid the accident but did not do so. If these facts can be proved, the plaintiff may still recover.

LAW MERCHANT is a collection of rules established by traders and men of commerce through the centuries, subsequently incorporated into the common law.

LEASE is an agreement by which the owner of real estate rents and permits it to be used by a tenant or LESSEE on payment of a consideration called rent. The landlord is also called the LESSOR.

LEGACY is a provision in a will which leaves certain personal property to a named individual. It is also known as a BEQUEST.

LETTERS OF ADMINISTRATION are documents issued by a probate or surrogate's court which gives a person named as the ADMINISTRATOR, or ADMINISTRATRIX if it is a woman, the authority to administer the estate of a person who died without leaving a will.

LETTERS TESTAMENTARY are documents issued by a probate or surrogate's court giving a person named as EXECUTOR, or EXECUTRIX if it is a woman, in a will the authority to administer the estate of the testator.

LIBEL is any statement made in writing which is defamatory and injures the reputation of an individual in the community. If the statement is such as to hold him up to contempt or ridicule or to charge him with the commission of a crime, it is LIBEL PER SE.

LICENSEE is a person who has been given permission to enter upon the land of another for a specific purpose.

LIEN is a claim which a person has against the property of another which is in his possession.

LIMITED PARTNERSHIP is composed of general partners and limited partners. The latter are only responsible for the amount which they actually agreed to invest in the business.

LIS PENDENS is a notice filed in the office of the county which advises that a lawsuit is pending against the owner of the designated property and involves that property.

MAKER is the person who makes, signs and delivers a promissory note to a payee.

MERGER is the absorption of one corporation by another, including all of its assets. Its individual existence is subsequently discontinued.

MISDEMEANOR is a crime which is less grave than a felony, tried before a court of special sessions and punishable in accordance with the law.

MISTAKE prevents consent and a "meeting of the minds" in the formation of a contract.

MORTGAGE is a contract which places real property as security for the repayment of a loan.

MOTION is a formal application made to a court asking for incidental relief during the progress of a lawsuit.

MOTIVE influences and induces the commission of a crime.

MULTIPLE WILLS are copies of the same will, each executed as if it were an original.

MURDER is the killing of one human being by another with a deliberate and premeditated design to cause his death.

MUTUAL and RECIPROCAL WILLS are separate instruments executed by individual testators and containing reciprocal provisions for the disposition of their individual property in accordance with an agreement between them.

NECESSARIES are those essentials which every person needs to exist, such as food, shelter, clothing and education.

NECESSARY PARTIES to a litigation must be joined as parties plaintiff or defendant in order that all issues between them may be litigated without the need for subsequent lawsuits.

NEGLIGENCE is the failure of a person to use that degree of care in a certain situation which he is by law obligated to use in order to protect the rights and property of others.

NEGOTIABLE INSTRUMENT is a written document which, when properly executed and delivered, can be used as a means of exchange and credit in place of money.

NEGOTIATION is the transfer of a document, particularly a negotiable instrument, from one owner to another by indorsement and delivery.

NON COMPOS MENTIS is a Latin phrase indicating that a person does not have the ability, due to his mental condition, to know the nature of his act.

NONJOINDER is the failure to make necessary persons parties to a lawsuit.

NON SUI JURIS means that a person, not of legal age, does not have legal capacity.

NONSUIT means that a lawsuit was dismissed because it was not properly proved.

NOTARY PUBLIC is a person authorized under state law to administer an oath. He also is authorized to present negotiable instruments for payment and to record a PROTEST in the event that they are not paid.

NOVATION results when a new contract, entered into by the same parties, supersedes a previous one made by the same parties concerning the same subject matter.

NUISANCE is the tort which results when a person uses his land in such a manner as to cause damage, danger and discomfort to his neighbors.

NUNCUPATIVE WILL is an oral will by which a person disposes of his property in the event of his death.

OBJECTION is the formal protest made by a litigant at a trial to record his disapproval of a question asked by his adversary.

OFFENSE is not a crime but a violation of some ordinance or some local municipal regulation.

OFFER is the initial step in the formation of a contract. It contains certain terms which, if accepted, may result in a contract.

OFFICE FOUND is a term often used to denote the adjudication of a person to be mentally incompetent.

OPEN TO THE JURY is a part of the procedure of a civil or criminal trial in which each side has an opportunity to present his position to the jury and outline what he intends to prove.

OPINION OF THE COURT is a statement by which the court sets forth the factual and legal reasons for its decision.

OPINION EVIDENCE is not based on provable fact but rather upon the opinion of the witness. Generally such evidence is not admissible at a trial.

OPTION is a collateral agreement in a transaction which gives one of the parties, or both, the right to choose a course of action. Examples are: an option to renew a contract, or an option to keep an offer open for a specific period before the offer is terminated.

ORDER OF A COURT is a formal direction requiring that a certain act be performed or restrained.

ORDINANCE is a regulation established by a local government to enforce and control certain necessary activities of the members of the community.

PARDON, by the governor of a state, releases a person convicted of a crime from punishment imposed by the sentence of a court.

PAROL EVIDENCE is that oral evidence introduced at a civil trial with the intention of altering and changing the terms of a written contract.

PARTITION is the relief available to persons jointly owning property so that their individual rights in that property may be determined.

PAYEE is the person named in a negotiable instrument to whom the money is directed to be paid.

PENDENTE LITE is a Latin phrase which means "during the period while the action is pending."

PLEADING is the formal written document which states the position of a litigant in a lawsuit. It may be a complaint, an answer or, if there should be a counterclaim interposed by the defendant, a reply.

PLEDGE is the use of personal property as security for the payment of a loan.

POLLING THE JURY is a part of trial procedure which permits that each juror be asked if the nonunanimous verdict of the jury is his verdict.

POSTDATED CHECK is one which is complete in all respects but dated in the future. It is not payable until that later date is reached.

POWER OF ATTORNEY is a document executed by one person giving another the right and authority to act for him in certain specific situations.

PRETRIAL PROCEDURE has been established in many courts to speed up the disposition of cases by encouraging and assisting settlements before trial.

PREMIUM is the consideration paid by the insured to the insurance company in return for which the company agrees to reimburse him for the loss agreed upon in the policy.

PRESCRIPTION is the technical term for the means by which a person may acquire a right to an easement.

PRIMA FACIE CASE is that amount of proof which the plaintiff must show at the trial before the defendant will be required to prove his defense to the action.

PRIVILEGED COMMUNICATION is a statement made by a party litigant to a person of trust, such as a lawyer, a doctor or priest. This statement may not be revealed at a trial by such confidant without the permission of the litigant.

PRIVITY OF CONTRACT is the relationship that is created between the parties to a contract to permit recovery for a breach of warranty of that contract.

PROBATE OF A WILL is the judicial procedure to determine that a certain document claimed to be a will of the decedent is valid and properly executed so that it can be enforced to dispose of the estate according to its provisions.

PROBATION is the sentence given to a defendant in a criminal prosecution when it is felt that he has a good chance for rehabilitation without being sent to prison.

PROBATIVE VALUE is the weight and belief which a judge or jury will give to evidence presented at a trial.

PROCESS is a course of proceedings in a lawsuit. It is also that legal document which brings the case or its participating parties into court.

PROMISSORY NOTE is a written document by which one person promises to pay money to the proper owner at a definite time.

PROMOTERS are those persons interested in selling the stock of a newly formed corporation.

PROOF is that evidence presented at a trial which is believed by the judge or jury.

PROTEST is the formality of recording that a negotiable instrument was presented for payment and that such payment was refused.

PROXY is the authority given by a stockholder of a corporation to another to vote at the annual meeting of the corporation.

PUTATIVE FATHER is the father of an illegitimate child.

QUALIFIED INDORSEMENT on a negotiable instrument is an indication that it is made without incurring liability on the instrument.

QUANTUM MERUIT or "amount deserved" is the relief in money which is awarded to a plaintiff in an action based on a contract implied by law.

QUASH is to annul or to set aside for insufficiency. An indictment is quashed if there is insufficient evidence to hold a suspect for trial.

QUASI-CONTRACT is a relationship created by law with the obligations of a contract.

QUORUM is the number of people which must be present at a meeting of any organization before the business of the meeting can be properly transacted.

RATIFICATION is approval or confirmation.

REAL ESTATE, REAL PROPERTY or REALTY is land, an interest in land or any article which is so attached to land as to become a part of it.

REBUTTAL is that proof presented at a trial by the plaintiff intended to overcome the evidence introduced by the defendant.

RECEIVER is a person appointed by the court to gather and hold property to be disposed of by order of the court.

RECIDIVIST is a person who reverts to criminal activity.

REFEREE is a person appointed by the court to take testimony and hear evidence presented by both sides.

REMAND is to recommit, as when a prisoner's habeas corpus application is dismissed and he is remanded to prison.

REPLEVIN is the process by which personal property is recovered when it is unlawfully detained.

REPLY is the document submitted by the plaintiff to a lawsuit in answering the counterclaims of the defendant.

REPRIEVE is the temporary suspension of death sentence.

RES IPSA LOQUITUR is a theory of recovery for personal injury which presumes that under certain conditions the injury would not have occurred if the defendant had been careful.

RES JUDICATA is the legal defense that the issue presented has previously been adjudicated between the same parties.

RESPONDEAT SUPERIOR is the principle in law which transfers liability to a principal for the negligent acts of his agent.

REST is the term used in a trial when each side has completed its submission of the evidence.

RESTRICTIVE INDORSEMENT is used in negotiating a negotiable instrument to a person for a specific task such as "for collection."

REVOCATION OF A WILL is an act by the person who has drawn a will that indicates his intention and desire that the will shall no longer be effective.

RISK in insurance is the specific event covered by the policy which may cause loss or damage to the property insured.

SALE BY DESCRIPTION refers to a transaction in which the merchandise is described in detail and the bulk must conform to that description.

SALE BY SAMPLE occurs when the buyer is shown a sample of the merchandise he is buying. When the merchandise is delivered, the bulk must conform in quality to the sample.

SALE OR RETURN is an agreement that goods are delivered with an option to purchase or return the merchandise.

SATISFACTION OF JUDGMENT is a document which states that a recorded judgment has been paid and satisfied.

SATISFACTION PIECE is the document which states that a recorded mortgage has been satisfied.

SEAL is the stamp, mark or other formal indication used on a contract to create a presumption of consideration. By legislation, the presence of a seal on a contract now has no additional legal effect.

SEIZIN is the ownership of land.

SEPARATION or DIVORCE FROM BED AND BOARD is a determination by a court authorizing a husband and wife to live apart although most of their marital obligations continue.

SEQUESTRATION is the proceeding by which property belonging to a judgment debtor, or to a husband ordered to pay alimony, is taken and sold to satisfy his obligation.

SERVICE OF PROCESS is the term used for properly delivering a summons, subpoena or citation upon a person in a legal proceeding.

SLANDER is a defamation of a person's reputation made orally. If the statement accuses him of a crime or holds him up to ridicule and it is not true, it is called "slander per se."

SPECIAL INDORSEMENT is an indorsement of a negotiable instrument which transfers it to a named person.

SPECIFIC PERFORMANCE is a remedy in equity available to a person who has no adequate remedy at law.

SQUATTER is a person who takes possession of land without any claim or color of title.

STATUTE is any law passed by a legislative body.

STATUTE OF FRAUDS is a series of legal provisions which require a contract to be in writing.

STATUTE OF LIMITATIONS is a series of legal provisions which limit the time when a plaintiff may bring a lawsuit.

STAY OF EXECUTION is a temporary period during which the execution of the judgment of the court is delayed.

STAY OF PROCEEDINGS is a temporary delay in the proceedings of an action, usually ordered by the court to compel one of the parties to comply with its requirements.

STIPULATION is an agreement between the parties or their attorneys.

SUBPOENA is a process issued out of a court requiring a witness to attend. If he has any books or records in his possession, he will be served with a *subpoena duces tecum* ordering him to bring them with him.

SUBROGATION is the substitution of the person who pays the injured party so that he may proceed to recover against the person who was responsible for the damage.

SUMMARY PROCEEDING is usually used in dispossessing a tenant to give the landlord back his property without undue delay.

SUMMATION is the closing statement to the jury made by each side in a lawsuit.

SUMMONS is the process by which a case is brought before the court by advising the defendant that there is a claim against him.

SURETY is the person who promises to make good the obligation of another.

SURROGATE is a judge who presides in the court where estates of deceased persons are administered.

TENANT is a person who rents or leases land or real estate from the landlord.

TENANTS BY THE ENTIRETY are a husband and wife who have an equal interest and ownership in property.

TENANTS IN COMMON are persons who share ownership in the same property.

TENDER OF PERFORMANCE in a contract is the offer by one of the parties to perform his obligations under it.

TESTAMENTATION is the privilege given to a person to devise and dispose of his property by will, to become effective upon his death.

TESTATOR (feminine: TESTATRIX) is a person who leaves and disposes of his property by will.

TESTIMONY is the presentation of evidence by a witness under oath.

TITLE is ownership in property.

TORT is a civil wrong committed when a person's private right is interfered with.

TRADE ACCEPTANCE is a negotiable instrument, a draft used in connection with the sale of merchandise.

TRESPASS is the act of coming upon the land of another without permission.

TRUE BILL is the indictment after it has been "found," or indorsed, by the foreman of a grand jury.

ULTRA VIRES is any act committed by a corporation through its agent which is not empowered or authorized by its charter.

UNDERTAKING is a bond or an assumption of an obligation.

UNDUE INFLUENCE is any threat or persuasion which overcomes or destroys a person's consent or will to act for himself.

USURY is that rate of interest charged for the loan of money which is in excess of the rate authorized within the state.

VENDEE is a buyer or purchaser.

VENDOR is the seller.

VENUE is the court which has jurisdiction to try a case.

VERDICT is the determination of a jury.

VERIFICATION is a statement made under oath which confirms the contents of an accompanying document.

VOID means "without any legal or effectual force to bind."

VOIDABLE refers to an agreement that is valid and binding but in which one of the parties has the right to avoid his responsibility.

VOIR DIRE is a preliminary examination, as of a juror before he is chosen to act as such.

WAREHOUSE RECEIPT is a statement which sets forth that certain described merchandise is being stored in the warehouse.

WAIVER is the act of relinquishing a right which a person has.

WARRANT is a process of a criminal court which authorizes search or seizure of persons or property.

WARRANTY is a collateral promise related to a contract.

WASTE is damage or injury done to real property.

WITNESS is any person who testifies in a judicial proceeding.

WRIT is a process of a court ordering a public officer or a private person to do a certain act.

Index

ab initio, 149
abandonment, 184, 193, 195
abortions, 297
abutting owner, 218
acceleration clause, 138
acceptance, 23, 24, 28, 140, 146
accident insurance, 124
accused, 293
action, cause of, 10
ad damnum, 10
adjudication, incompetent, 38, 39, 41, 109
adjusters, 109
adjustments, 249
administration, proceedings, 43, 238, 239
administrative agencies, 19
administrator, administratrix, 43, 238
adverse possession, 245
advertisements, 26
affirmation, 15
affirmative defenses, 10
aged, 298
agency, 151
agents, 103, 109, 115, 136, 152, 153
agistor, 91
aliens, 41, 42
alimony, 192–194, 196
alteration, 60, 148
American Arbitration Association, 19
animals, 91, 203, 292
annuity, 118, 313
annulment, 189, 190
answer of defendant, 12
antenuptial agreement, 185
appeal, 4, 9, 18, 19, 302
appellant, 18
arbitration, 19
arms, right to bear, 290
arraignment, 274, 277, 279, 280
arrest, 204, 276
arson, 273
assault, 207, 273
assent, 23
assignment, 42, 43, 81, 109, 257

assured, 104
attachment, 76, 198, 207, 340
attempt to commit crime, 274
attestation clause, 232, 234, 340
attorney, power of, 153, 354
attorney in fact, 152, 153, 340
auction, 27, 153
automobile insurance, 126
  collision, 127
  comprehensive coverage, 127, 317
  No Fault, 127

baggage, 95, 96, 99
bail, 132, 276, 280
bailment, 84, 105, 312
  for bailee's benefit 86
  for bailor's benefit, 84
  gratuitous, 84
  for hire, 89
  mutual benefit, 87
  termination, 85
bankruptcy, 43, 60, 179, 337–339, 341
bastardy proceeding, 341
battery, 208, 273
bearer paper, 135, 142, 146, 341
beneficiary, 104, 105, 106, 119, 120, 121, 230, 261
benefits, to children, 303
  disability, 302
  home care, 305, 307
  hospital, 305
  loss of, 303
  lump sum, 301
  medical, 306
  survivorship, 301
  veterans', 309
bequest, 225, 314
beyond a reasonable doubt, 14, 201, 275, 280
bigamy, 182
bill of attainder, 267
bill of exchange, 139
bill of lading, 73, 142
bill of particulars, 13

binder, 110, 111, 247
blackmail, 273
blind persons, 298
blue laws, 46
blue sky laws, 173
bona fide purchaser, 73, 74, 79, 135, 145
bond, bail, 132, 276
  corporate, 175
  and mortgage, 255
breach of contract, 21, 60, 75, 250
brief, 3, 9, 18
brokers, 45, 103, 110, 116, 153, 159, 246, 250
bulk sales, 75
bulk transfers, 75
burden of proof, 14, 16
burglar tools, 274
burglary, 11, 274
business
  bankruptcy, 337–339
  beginning a, 334, 335
  copyright, 349, 350
  corporate reorganization, 339
  debt collection, 348, 349
  individual payment plans, 339
  involuntary termination, 337
  invitee, 220
  management-labor relations, 345–348
  ownership, 161
  patents and trademarks, 350–351
  products liability, 339–341
  SBA assistance, 335, 336
  voluntary termination, 336, 337

C.F. (Cost and Freight), 73
C.I.F. (Cost, Insurance and Freight), 73
calendar, court, 12, 13
cancellation, insurance, 110, 115

capacity, to commit crime,
    269
  to contract, 24, 32
  to execute will, 228
  to marry, 181
caption, 342
carrier, common, 92, 94
cause of action, 10
caveat emptor, 71
certificate of deposit, 141,
    342
certificate of doing busi-
    ness, 163, 165
certificate of eviction, 259
certificate of incorporation,
    174
certificate of marriage, 183
certificate of partnership,
    165
certiorari, 19
certiorari proceeding (re-
    duce assessed valu-
    ation), 261
cestui que trust, 261
challenges, jury, 14
charge, of court, 16
  criminal, 275, 276, 278,
    279
charity, 233
chattel, 242
chattel mortgage, 80
check, 135
  certified, 136
  postdated, 135, 327
children, 186, 240
  adopted, 188, 240
  custody of, 194, 195, 196
  illegitimate, 188, 240
  visitation, 194
citation, 10, 237
citizenship, 41, 291
Civil Court of New York,
    11
civil law, 4
civil liberty, 284
civil rights, 182, 284
codicil, 236
coinsurance, 115
collateral, 79–80
collective bargaining, 289
collusion, 196
comity, 198
committee of incompetent,
    38
common carrier, 92
common law, 5
common-law marriage, 183,
    316
community property, 186,
    233
complainant, 267
complaint, 10, 11, 12
concealment, 106, 113
condemnation, 259, 260,
    344

condition precedent, 54, 67,
    344
condition subsequent, 55,
    67
conditional sale contract,
    78
condonation, 196
confession of judgment, 81,
    344
confrontation of witnesses,
    278, 281, 282
consanguinity, 182
consent, age of, 182
consent to contract, 23, 30,
    48, 120
consideration, contract, 24,
    30
consignment, 153
consolidation (corpora-
    tions), 179
consortium, 185
conspiracy, 196, 273
Constitution, 182, 284
consumer credit, 297, 319–
    22
consumer goods, 77
continuance, 277, 280
contract, 20, 312
  breach of, 60, 75, 250
  conditional sales, 78–79
  express, 22
  implied, 22, 23
  legality of, 44
  for personal services, 62,
    84, 101
  privity of, 70
  quasi-, 23
  real estate, 247
  sales, 65
  termination, 58, 59
  unenforcible, 45, 46, 55
  void, 22, 38, 40, 44, 46,
    48, 49, 50
  voidable, 22, 32, 34, 37
contribution, 318
conversion, 76, 212
conveyance, 345
conviction, crime, 266
convicts, 42, 267, 282
Copyright Act of 1976,
    349, 350
corporation, 12, 42, 45,
    108, 154, 171, 203,
    217
  business, 170, 172
  directors, 176
  dissolution of, 178
  foreign, 171
  formation of, 172
  membership, 171, 172
  officers of, 176, 177
  stock, 171, 174, 177
corpus delicti, 272
counsel fees, 194, 196

counterclaim, 12
courts, federal, 8
  bankruptcy, 8, 339
  of claims, 8, 9
  customs, 8
  local, 9
  patent appeals, 8
  small claims, 11
  state, 9
covenants, in deed, 254,
    318
credibility, 15
crime, 5, 201, 265
criminal court procedure,
    274
criminal law, 3
cross-examination, 15, 16,
    278, 318
curtesy, 233, 244, 296
custody, children, 346
  hiring of, 91

damages, 60, 75, 78, 201,
    214, 250
death claim actions, 221
debt collection prac-
    tices, 348, 349
decision of court, 3, 26,
    275
deeds to real estate, 249,
    253
deeds of trust, 256
defamation, 209
default, 346
defendant, 17
defenses, 12, 120, 131, 139,
    145, 149, 196, 280
demand for jury trial, 12
demurrer, 12
Department of Labor,
    Wage and Hour Divi-
    sion, 345
dependent children, 298
derivative action, 177
desertion, 184
devise, 225
diagnostic services, 306,
    307
directors of corporation,
    176
disability insurance, 301
disabled persons, 298
disaffirm contract, 32, 33,
    34, 320
discharge of contract, 58
discrimination, 297–298
dishonor, negotiable instru-
    ment, 147
dismiss complaint, 15
dispossess, 258

dissolution, of business, 164
of corporation, 178
of marriage, 190
of partnership, 168
divorce, 186, 189, 195, 196, 197
divorce decree enforcement, 196, 197, 198
double indemnity, 124, 291
double jeopardy, 267, 278, 294
dower, 232, 244
draft, 139
drawee, drawer, 135, 136, 139, 146
drug addict, 40, 189
drunkard, habitual, 39
due process of law, 284
duress, 52, 271

easement, 243
emancipated infant, 36
eminent domain, 260
employees' rights, 347
encumbrances, 249, 251
Enoch Arden decree, 191, 347
Equal Credit Opportunity Act, 341, 342
Equal Employment Opportunity Act, 343, 345
Equal Employment Opportunity Commission, 344
equipment, 79–80
equity, 5, 6, 211, 250
error of law, 4
escheat, 240
establishment of religion, 285
estates, real property, 243
of deceased person, 225, 240
estoppel, 107
eviction, 258
evidence (competent, material, relevant), 11
ex post facto, 267
examination before trial, 13
exceptions, 17, 225
execution, 19
executor (executrix), 43, 348
exhibits, 15
extended care, 305
extortion, 273

F.A.S. (Free Alongside Ship), 73

F.O.B. (Free on Board), 73
factor, 153
fair comment, 210
Fair Labor Standards Act, 345
fair preponderance of evidence, 14, 16
false arrest, 204
false imprisonment, 205
family car, 217
felony, 266, 274, 278
feme sole, 296
filiation proceedings, 341, 349, 355
financing statment, 80–81
fire arms, 291
fire insurance policy, 111
fixtures, 242, 259
foreign divorce, 196
forgery, 148, 274
former jeopardy, 263, 294, 347
fraud, 50, 74, 113, 120
and deceit, 51, 212
of creditors, 47, 74, 75, 120
frauds, statute of, 56, 65, 106, 131, 247
free exercise of religion, 285, 286
freedom of assembly, 289
of association, 289
of expression, 287
personal, 290
of the press, 289
of religion, 285
of thought, 287
Freedom of Information Act, 351
freight, 93

gambling contracts, 44
garage owner, 92
garnishee, garnishment, 81, 320–21
general denial, 12
general offer, 26
gift causa mortis, 226, 240
government agencies, privacy and, 352
grand jury, 278
guardian, 40, 203
guests, 97, 98, 99

health insurance, 125
holder in due course, 136, 142, 145
holographic will, 225
home health care, 305, 307

homestead, 260
homicide, 271
hotelkeeper, 97, 101
husband, 119, 183, 195, 203, 233

in loco parentis, 36
in transitu, 76
incompetents, 37, 108, 182, 220, 229, 270, 271
incontestability clause, 120, 121
incorporators, 350
indeterminate sentence, 281
indictment, 279
indorsements, 143
indorser, 144, 146
infant, 32, 33, 34, 35, 36, 108, 154, 181, 203, 217, 269, 270
information, 276
injury, personal, 218
injunction, 62
insane persons, 37, 108, 270
insurable interest, 105, 118, 119, 121
insurance, accident, 124
automobile, 126
burglary, 130
disability, 301
double idemnity, 124
endowment, 118
extended coverage, 116
fire, 110, 111
flood, 130
health, 125
hospital, 303
information, 312
life, 105, 117, 329
marine, 129
medical, 303, 306
No Fault, 127
pilferage, 130
public liability, 128
premiums, 111, 117, 121, 123
real estate 312
retirement 302
robbery 130
term, 117, 118
theft, 130
title, 130, 252
unemployment, 307
insurer, 108
intent, 50, 51, 209, 215, 269
interest, 44–5, 138
intestacy, 43, 225, 238
intestate's estate, distribution of, 225, 239

jewelry, 97, 99, 100
joint bank account, 241
joint tenants, 244, 324
joint will, 227

joint tort-feasors, 203
judgment, 351
  confession of, 81, 317
  enforcement of, 4, 18
  satisfaction, 19
judgment creditor, 19
judgment debtor, 19
jurisdiction, 6, 11, 197
jury, calendar, 12, 13, 17
  demand for, 12
  grand, 278
  panel, 13
  petit, 13, 14, 280
  qualifications, 13
  selection, 13

kidnaping, 273

labor, unfair practices
  against, 347
Labor-Management Re-
  lations Act, 346, 347
labor unions, 289–290
landlord, 257, 259
Landrum-Griffin Act. See
  Labor-Management
  Reporting and Dis-
  closure Act
larceny, 274
last clear chance, 216
law, 4, 5
  adjective, 5
  administrative, 5
  civil, 5
  common, 5
  criminal, 3, 4, 265
  statutory, 5
  substantive, 5
law day, 252
law merchant, 5
leases, 257, 312
legacy, 225, 227
legal process, 10, 197
legality of subject matter,
  44
legatee, 230
lessee and lessor, 257
letters of administration,
  239
letters testamentary, 238
liability insurance, 128
liability, of agents, 157
  limited, 60, 94
  for negotiable instru-
   ment, 145, 146, 149
  partner's, 166
  products, 339–341
  property owner's, 128,
   129
  restaurant's 89
  sidewalk, 128, 218
  storekeeper's, 89
libel, 209
license, 45, 103, 154
licensee, 220

lien, 75, 101
  foreclosure on, 76
lienor, 76
lis pendens, 19
livery stable, 91
loss, 78, 81, 93, 94, 104,
  110

Magnuson-Moss Federal
  Trade Commission
  Improvement Act,
  313
maker, 137, 144, 149
malice, 206, 207, 269
malicious abuse of pro-
  cess, 207
malicious prosecution, 206
malpractice, 171, 222
malum in se, 268
malum prohibitum, 268
Management-Labor Re-
  lations, 345–348
manslaughter, 272
marriage, 180
  common-law, 183
  community property, 186
  contract, 183
  dissolution of, 182, 190
  incestuous, 189
  incompatibility, 195
  prohibited, 182
  "quasi-," 198, 199
  void, 182
  voidable, 190
married women, 41, 183,
  184
Medicaid, 306
Medicare, 303
memorandum of law, see
  brief
merger, 178
metes and bounds, 247
minors, see infant
miscegenation, 182, 190
misdemeanor, 266, 276
misrepresentation, 51, 107,
  113, 120, 123
mistake, 48
monopolies, 48
mortgage, 248, 255
motion, 15
motive, 269
murder, 272

National Labor Relations
  Board, 347, 348
necessaries, 35, 40, 108, 184
negligence, 16, 84, 86, 87,
  90, 91, 100, 215
  comparative, 216
  contributory, 215
  imputed, 187, 217
negotiable instruments, 134,
  326
  alteration, 148

discharge, 149
  forgery, 148
  theft, 148
negotiation, 134, 142
non-jury cases, 12, 18
non sui juris, 187, 217
Norris-LaGuardia Act, 345,
  346
notice of claim, 202
novation, 59
nuisance, 213

oath, 15, 16
Occupational Safety and
  Health Act, 342, 343
offense, 266
offer, 24
  general, 26
  rejection of, 28, 29
  termination of, 27
opening statement to jury,
  14
options, contract, 28
  life insurance, 122

parent, 119, 186, 187, 203
parol evidence, 247
parole, 282
parties plaintiff, 11, 42
partnership, 108, 119, 154,
  165, 168
  accounting, 6, 168
  dissolution, 168
  limited, 169
passengers, 95
patents, 350, 351
pawn, 88, 89
payee, 135, 137, 139, 142
perjury 273
perpetuities, 262
personal injury, 12
personal safety, 207
plaintiff, 11, 17, 42
plea bargaining, 281
plea (criminal), 274, 277,
  280
pleadings (civil), 11, 12
pledge, 88
police power, 290, 291
policy of insurance, 104,
  105, 111
prescription, 243
presentment, 140
pre-trial, 13
  diversion program, 281
prima facie case, 10, 11
principal, 153
privacy, right of, 211
Privacy Act of 1974, 351,
  352
privilege in defamation, 210
probate proceedings, 237
probation, 277
promissory note, 137, 328
promoters, 173, 328

property owners, 218, 219, 220, 221
protest, 147, 328
proxy vote, 176, 328
public administrator, 239
public assistance, 297
public street or highway, 218
punishments, 265
putative father, 188

quasi-contract, 23, 36, 329
quasi-marriage, 198, 199
quid pro quo, 24

ratification, 32, 39, 157, 329
real property, 242, 329
  transaction 246
rebuttal, 16, 329
receiving stolen property, 274
rehabilitation services, 302
religious freedom, 285
reorganization, 179
replevin, 76, 212
reputation, 209
rescission, 320
res ipsa loquitur, 217
residuary, clause or legatee, 230
respondeat superior, 203, 205
respondent, 18
rest, 15, 16
restaurant, 89
restraint of trade, 47
restrictions, 47, 159
retirement insurance, 302
retirement security, 312–14, 330
rewards, 26
right of an accused, 293, 294
right to work laws, 290
risk, insurance, 104, 105, 106, 114, 117, 121, 124, 127, 129, 130, 301
robbery, 273

safe-deposit company, 92, 237
sale, on approval, 72
  breach of, 75
  by description, 68
  or return, 72
  by sample, 69
  "on trial," 72
sales, do-it-yourself sug-gestion, 312
sales, secured credit, 79–80
schools, private religious, 287
search and seizure, 267, 292

secured credit, 78–80
secured transaction, 78
security agreement, 79–80
seizin, 244
selection of jury, 13
self-defense, 271
self-employment
  retirement benefits, 330–31
  tax, 330
self-incrimination, 268
sentence, 277, 317
separation, 189, 192, 193
sequestration, 198
settlor, 261
sex discrimination, 297
slander, 209
Small Business Adminis-tration (SBA), 335, 336
social guest, 220
Social Security, 302, 303, 305, 327
specific performance, 6, 61, 251, 330
spell of illness, 304
squatter, 246, 330
statute of frauds, 56, 65, 102, 106, 131, 243, 247, 257, 262
statute of limitations, 57, 358
stock, corporate, 174
  common, 175
  preferred, 175
  voting, 176
stockholders, rights of, 175, 177
storekeeper, 89
sublet, 257
subpoena, 15, 301
subrogation, 127, 128, 131
suicide, 121
summary proceedings, 258, 358
summation to jury, 16. 358
summons, 9, 10, 12, 274, 358
Sunday Laws, 46, 286
supplementary proceedings, 19
surety, 131, 331
survey or real estate, 251
survivorship benefits, 301

Taft-Hartley Act. See
  Labor-Management
  Relations Act
tax
  estate, 326. 333–35
  estimated, 328
  excise, 326, 333
  gift, 326, 335–36
  income, 325, 326
  inheritance, 326, 335

property, 325
sales, 325
withholding, 331
tenant, 257, 331
  at will, 257, 260
  by the entirety, 244, 331
  in common, 244, 331
  holdover, 258, 323
  joint, 244, 324
tender, 58, 331
testamentation, 228, 331
testator (testatrix), 225, 331
testimony, 9, 15, 331
title, 65, 71, 72, 73, 90, 331
  closing, 251, 316
  marketable, 252
  search, 251
  voidable, 74
totten trust, 240
torts, 5, 178, 185, 186, 200, 312
  relief from, 214
trademark, 351
trade acceptance, 141, 332
trespass, 212, 332
trespassers, 221
trial, civil, 14
  criminal, 275
  preparation for, 12
true bill, 279, 332
trustee, 261
trusts, 261

ultra vires, 42, 177, 332
undue influence, 53
unemployment insurance, 307
unenforcible contracts, 45, 46, 55
Uniform Commercial Code, 5, 7, 21, 56, 78, 134
Uniform Consumer Credit Code, 7, 322
unions, 289
United States, Constitution, 182, 284
  Supreme Court, 182
usury, 44, 45, 138, 303

verdict, 17, 332
vesting, 313–14
veterans' benefits, 309
vocational services, 302
voir dire, 14, 332

waiver, 107, 332
warehouseman, 91, 95
warehouse receipt, 142
warrant, 204, 205, 275, 285, 293, 332

warranty, 67, 68, 69, 71,
250, 318
breach of, 68, 70, 77
of fitness for human
consumption, 70
of fitness for use, 70
of merchantability,
69
of quality, 70, 77
of title, 68, 250
wharfinger, 92
wife, 119, 183, 195, 232
wills, 224

conditional, 227
contents, of, 230
contingent, 227
execution of, 234
form of, 230
holographic, 225,
323
information, 312
joint, 227, 324
mutual, 227, 324
multiple, 227, 325
nuncupative, 226,
326

reciprocal, 227
revocation, 235, 330
sample of, 231
witness, 16, 233, 234
women's rights, 295 ff.
workmen's compensation,
308
writ of habeas corpus, 293,
323
writ of error coram nobis,
277, 295, 332

youthful offender, 281